1960s UNIVERSITY BUILDINGS

THE GOLDEN AGE OF BRITISH MODERN ARCHITECTURE

1960s UNIVERSITY BUILDINGS

JOHN BARR

LUND HUMPHRIES

First published in 2025 by Lund Humphries

Lund Humphries
Second Home Spitalfields
68-80 Hanbury Street
London
E1 5JL
UK

www.lundhumphries.com

ISBN: 978-1-84822-670-8

A Cataloguing-in-Publication record for this book is available from the British Library.

Cover: The Hilda Besse Building, St Antony's College, Oxford.

Frontispiece: Churchill College, Cambridge. Interior of the hall.

Right: St John's College, Cambridge, the Cripps Building.

Copy edited by Pamela Bertram
Designed by John Barr
Typeset by Jacqui Cornish
Proofread by Patrick Cole
Cover designed by Paul Arnot
Set in Sofia Pro and Unica77
Printed in China

This book is printed on sustainably sourced FSC® paper

MIX
Paper | Supporting responsible forestry
FSC® C008047

Contents

Introduction
The Sixties

The 1960s, or just 'the Sixties', continues to hold an almost mythical place in Western culture, particularly in Britain, which for a short time emerged as the popular-culture capital of the world. Internationally, Britain's high profile was mostly limited to the emergence of ideas in music and fashion. Within Britain, however, change was widespread and infiltrated many aspects of life. In architecture, the direction of change was hotly debated and the 1960s was the most significant period in the development of competing ideas about the role of architecture in a modern democracy and the form it should take. The opportunity to express those ideas was provided nowhere as freely as in the design of university buildings.

I came to this subject as a fan. The buildings featured in this book formed the backdrop to my architectural education. They were built in the decade immediately prior to, and some of them during, my time as a student. They were the buildings and architects that we read about, studied and tried to emulate. There were notable buildings in other spheres but somehow the university buildings of the 1960s seemed to represent the cutting edge and, in retrospect, might be described as marking a Golden Age of British modern architecture.

It was also an Age of Opportunity for British universities. There was consensus amongst the major political parties on the purpose and benefits of universities in helping create the 'good society', and agreement that university education should be extended to include more of the population.[1] Funding was readily available for the expansion of existing universities and the creation of new ones. The nature of university education was up for discussion, providing the chance to think anew about methods of organisation and teaching. The cost of university education was funded by the state in the expectation that students would benefit from broader horizons and fulfilled lives, and that society would benefit from an educated and highly skilled workforce.

The historian Eric Hobsbawm has written in more general terms of a Golden Age of 'some twenty-five or thirty years of extraordinary economic growth and social transformation, which probably changed human society more profoundly than any other period of comparable brevity' and which lasted from the end of the Second World

War until the early 1970s.[2] The wider background described by Hobsbawm must have been instrumental in the development of architecture during that period, but economic growth and social change are not, by themselves, guaranteed to produce good architecture.

As if to reinforce that point, Hobsbawm describes the 1960s as 'the most disastrous decade in modern architecture'.[3] He is not alone; there are others, including some critics and users of the buildings in this book, who are not fans. Whatever one's view, it is important to understand the causes that produced the result so that we might know how to replicate or avoid it in the future. And so, we must try to piece together the combination of circumstances and ideas that generated these buildings.

But first, a definition of the period covered by 'the Sixties'. A literal definition would be the period from 1960 to 1969 but Arthur Marwick talks of a 'long Sixties', beginning in 1958 and running through to 1974, with a 'high Sixties' from 1964 to 1968.[4] Dominic Sandbrook places the 'Swinging Sixties' between 1964 and 1970.[5] Mark Donnelly identifies a 'high Sixties' from 1964 to 1967, and Robert Hewison includes the period up until the mid-1970s in his definition.[6]

The societal changes that those authors discuss cannot always be pinned down to neat decades. There is likely to be overspill both leading into and out of the period in question, and I have included the full breadth of dates proposed by those authors (from the late 1950s to the mid-1970s) to represent the spirit of the Sixties rather than the numerically correct dates.

Once I started my research it became clear that I could not hope to include every university building from the period unless I limited coverage to a photograph and a short, general description for each building. There are excellent reference books which do that and they are noted throughout the text and in the bibliography. My task was to identify and examine ideas and themes; an encyclopaedic approach risked losing sight of the forest by trying to describe every tree. Similarly, the purpose of the plans that appear throughout the book is to illustrate elements that are discussed in the text rather than provide an exact representation in every detail. They have been redrawn from sources of variable quality. Some source material has been unclear and a degree of interpretation has been required.

Omitting some buildings meant also omitting some architects. Those I have chosen to include are amongst the most famous architects of the period. That does not mean those omitted are less worthy but, for good or ill, it is the famous who set the weather for debate and trends. It is those weather patterns that this book seeks to identify and major trends that it seeks to analyse. It has not been a straightforward process. There is sometimes overlap between categories and architects may appear in more than one category. Readers might not agree with my choice of categories, or my allocation of buildings and architects within those categories. Nevertheless, I have tried to impose some kind of structure so that lessons might be drawn from the fragmented, contentious explosion of ideas and energy that produced the university buildings of that period known as the Sixties.

Prelude
Suez, Sputnik and Socialism

In July 1956, the Egyptian president, Gamal Abdel Nasser, nationalised the Suez Canal that connects the Mediterranean Sea with the Indian Ocean via the Red Sea and provides the main route for goods and, most importantly, oil moving from the Middle and Far East to Europe. On 29 October, Israeli forces entered Egypt. Two days later they were joined by troops from France and Britain, and together they took control of the canal. The Soviet Union threatened to enter the conflict on the Egyptian side. The USA warned the Soviets to refrain from direct involvement and, to help avert that possibility, instructed the three nations to withdraw or face economic sanctions. The British and French withdrew their troops in December, the Israelis the following March, and control of the canal reverted to Egypt. It was a humiliation for the British government and provided a graphic demonstration that Britain's days as an imperial power were over.

In October 1957, the Soviet Union launched Sputnik 1, the first man-made satellite to be put into space. The first manned space flight followed on 12 April 1961, when the Soviet cosmonaut Yuri Gagarin completed an orbit of the earth in outer space. It became clear that future power would lie with those who were technologically advanced and that Britain was falling behind in the race to become so.

In October 1963, Harold Wilson, the leader of the Labour Party, addressed his party conference and declared that a new Britain must be forged in the 'white heat' of scientific revolution. In fact, Labour's message had contained references to scientific progress since the end of the Second World War and Aneurin ('Nye') Bevan addressed the Labour Party Conference in the run-up to the 1945 general election with these words:

> We cannot do in five years what needs to be done. It needs a new industrial revolution. We require that modern industrial science be applied to our heavy industry. It can only be done by men with modern minds, by men of a new age.[1]

Given the general regard for wartime leader Winston Churchill, he and his Conservative Party were expected to prevail in 1945, so it was a surprise when Labour won with a sizeable overall majority. Bevan's words proved prophetic, however. The Labour government could not overcome in five years the desperate legacy of the war: the lack of jobs for returning servicemen and servicewomen; the lack of housing; the severe poverty described in David Kynaston's *Austerity Britain*.[2] The Conservatives returned to power in 1951 and were still in power in 1963 when Wilson revisited the themes and rhetoric of science and technology, and wove them into a 'slick, resonant argument'.[3]

In April 1964, when the Conservative Prime Minister Sir Alec Douglas-Home (pronounced Hume) called for a general election to be held that October, Labour enjoyed a 20 per cent lead in opinion polls. It would not have been clear whether this was due to public enthusiasm for the Labour message or fatigue with a Conservative Party that had been in power too long. Either way, the Conservatives needed to change something. Douglas-Home's advisors urged him to follow Wilson and adopt the language of modernisation in his election campaign. To the aristocratic 14th Earl of Home (also known as Baron Home of the Hirsel of Coldstream and Lord Dunglass) the language of modernisation did not come naturally, but he took their advice and by the end of September the parties were neck and neck in the polls, suggesting that the image of a new, technological Britain that looked to the future resonated with the public. In the event, Wilson secured a narrow victory and formed the first Labour government for 14 years.[4]

The political drive for a scientific and technological revolution was combined with a more general post-war desire to create a better and more equitable society. Steven Fielding argues that in order for political parties to prosper they must successfully engage with change, and that the Labour Party in the 1960s was faced with a country that had undergone a 'cultural revolution' that questioned previous assumptions about relative roles and positions based on class, gender, age and ethnicity.[5] When the Robbins Report of 1963 promoted universities as a means of creating a 'good society', an increase in the supply of university education became a central plank of government policy – and government wanted more say in the outcomes.[6]

Since 1919 government funding to universities had been controlled by the University Grants Committee (UGC), which reported to the Treasury but had substantial freedom over how it spent its budget. After 1964 the UGC was obliged to report to the Department of Education and Science. It is generally agreed that this led to a decline in its autonomy and the increased likelihood of it being pressured into following the desires of the incumbent government.[7]

In the early 1960s both major political parties were intent on creating more university places and greater accessibility to a more socially diverse range of students.[8] Rather than consider whether this would require changes to the organisation of higher education, it was assumed that increased access would naturally lead to wider access.[9] An increase in student numbers required expansion, and when some universities proved unable or unwilling to expand fast enough, the UGC side-stepped them by declaring that it would fund the creation of seven new universities in England, followed by one each in Scotland and Northern Ireland.

That move created a new dynamic in university development. Existing universities, realising that they might miss out on available funding and might even have their positions challenged by these new institutions, redoubled their efforts to expand and increase student numbers. Meanwhile, although the initial priority had been expansion of student numbers, the UGC realised that the creation of new universities also offered an opportunity to re-examine the nature of university education.[10] The new universities were charged with developing new ways of delivering higher education, although some academics have argued that this was used as a justification for their creation rather than a reflection of serious intent; a convenient reason to increase numbers rather than a vehicle for real reform.[11]

Whether that scepticism is well-founded is not something this book will examine. What it will examine is the situation for architects designing university buildings in the 1960s: funding was available and there was an imperative to build; there were opportunities to respond to the educational and physical contexts of ancient universities, 19th-century civic universities and new universities; there was the chance, whether real or politically contrived, to examine new models for delivering education and thus new architectural solutions. Those conditions alone created intriguing and potentially exciting possibilities.

In addition to the political context, architects were working within a changing social and cultural environment. As noted in the introduction, Britain in the early 1960s became the popular-culture capital of the world and enjoyed rapid economic growth and social transformation. A significant factor in the election of the Labour government in 1964 was a desire for change: a desire to finally emerge from the grey austerity of the post-war years and to have fun, light and colour; a desire to break down a hierarchical class system and provide equality of opportunity across social boundaries; a desire amongst a younger generation to have its say.

Social analysts maintain that tensions between young and old had long existed, with the young socialising separately and finding ways to emphasise their distinctiveness. David Fowler identifies a fully formed youth culture during the inter-war years, which was expressed through its spending habits and the beginnings of a fledgling 'youth market'.[12] Nonetheless, the 1960s saw a distinct change in the attitudes and aspirations of young people. The post-war 'baby boom' meant there was a higher percentage of teenagers than there had been for several decades. At the same time, a steep rise in young workers' wages meant that those who were single and childless enjoyed relatively high disposable income. This was particularly true under the Macmillan government of 1957–63, leading to his famous claim that 'most of our people have never had it so good'.[13] That new-found affluence fuelled the development of a commercial youth market that was expressed through music, fashion, television, film and magazines – but primarily music and fashion. The young had purchasing power which, if it could be harnessed and directed, might be influential.

As Prime Minister, Harold Wilson was alert to this and 'keen to pose as the figurehead of the new swinging Britain'.[14] At the same time, and although he favoured cigars in private, he had cultivated a pipe-smoking, cardigan-wearing, man-of-the-people image that was in awkward contrast to his attempts to align himself with youth culture by courting its most famous representatives, the Beatles. The same tactic was used in 1997 when Tony Blair, as incoming Labour Prime Minister, aligned himself and his government with popular culture under the banner of 'Cool Britannia'. On neither occasion did the politicians succeed in their attempts to appear 'cool' and it is doubtful if that is a quality the public looks for in its leaders. But in both cases it demonstrated a political awareness that popular culture had become important, both commercially and as a means of influencing its consumers.

The building that best captured the combination of technology and popular culture in the 1960s was the Post Office Tower (now known as BT Tower). Designed by the Ministry of Public Buildings and Works under the direction of its chief architect, Eric Bedford, and by a team led by G.R. Yeats, it was opened by Wilson in 1965. Its height, form and aesthetic had been driven by a practical response to its purpose as a support for the most modern telecommunications equipment (fig.0.1). At the same time, its location in the centre of 'Swinging London' and the inclusion of public access to observation decks and a revolving restaurant at the top of the tower made it a popular icon (fig.0.2). The restaurant was run by Sir Billy Butlin, the king of popular leisure, who owned a string of cheap and cheerful holiday camps that offered all-inclusive holidays (accommodation, meals and entertainment for adults and children) at prices that working-class families could afford. In its popular appeal the Post Office Tower made science and technology seem not 'technical, desiccated and boring [but] inherently exciting and dynamic'.[15]

The Post Office Tower was an exception rather than a prototype. Very little British architecture in the 1960s addressed, or used, modern technology in such a direct way, and almost none of it engaged with popular culture. It had more in common with the modern jazz that was being developed by British musicians like Ronnie Scott and Tubby Hayes than the popular music of the Beatles and the Rolling Stones. Like jazz, it sat within an established modernist tradition and was an acquired taste.

Whilst a new generation of architects that emerged in the Sixties undoubtedly enjoyed the same expansion of personal freedoms as their contemporaries in wider society, along with a determination to be heard and a less deferential attitude to 'the establishment', their architecture owed more to the Labour government of 1945–51 under Clement Attlee than the Wilson government elected in 1964. Attlee had campaigned hard to introduce the Welfare State, as it became known. The origins of this idea lay in a report published by Sir William Beveridge in 1942 into 'Social Insurance and Allied Services'.[16] The Beveridge Report, as it is commonly known, formed the basis for Labour's introduction of a Welfare State that aimed to support those in need and eradicate poverty and ill health.

0.1 Post Office Tower. Shaped by technology

Attlee and Labour were swept to power in a landslide victory based, in part, on the votes of servicemen and servicewomen returning from the war and eager to create a better and fairer society. All the architects who became prominent in the Sixties had lived through the war, and many of them had served and seen combat. They were a generation who 'after the interruption of the war, entered the profession amid austerity and ruin, disciplined and clear-headed in their ambitions to rebuild and impatient to get on with it'.[17]

The Welfare State provided the opportunity to 'get on with it', designing buildings for an extensive public programme of new housing, healthcare and education facilities. It was a period that now 'seems like a golden age of a general belief in the power of architecture to change society, its architects reflecting the politics of nationalisation with a strong sense of social responsibility'.[18]

Their social aspirations were clear and agreed, and they felt the urgency for change, but unlike those involved in popular culture, who sought change through ideas that were new and revolutionary, architects sought change based on ideas that were old and revolutionary:

> . . . the ex-service students knew what they wanted. They were going to build a new Britain, both literally and metaphorically. The same overwhelming idealism which had carried the Labour Party into office in the July [1945] election, largely on the service vote, filled them with the conviction that the Modern Movement was the only way in which architecture could escape from the past and move into a new and better future.[19]

Meanwhile one of those students, James Stirling, wrote in his 'black diary':

> . . . we returned from war as students . . . The cities were bombed and devastated, from now on everything could only get better. We assumed that from here on everything would be built as modern architecture . . .[20]

The architecture that would create a better future was to be based on ideas first developed some 40 years earlier:

> By 1914 virtually everything that can take shelter under the broad and rather undefined canopy of 'modernism' was already in place . . . A large number of eminent modernists were already mature and productive or even famous in 1914 and remained powerful influences forty years later.[21]

Modernism had evolved during those 40 years and many in the new generation of post-war architects felt that British architecture had lost its way. They were unhappy about the course taken by the immediately preceding generation of British architects and looked instead to the early modernists for inspiration. Referring again to Stirling's 'black diary' we read:

> If elderly architects, men in their sixties or eighties, retain so much prestige in a world otherwise dedicated to youth, it is partly because they have carried through from the early climate of the period before World War One a strong faith in the cultural value of architecture. Dedicated, their lights still shine for the younger generation, while the sociological lights of the middle generation have now burned somewhat dim.[22]

And so, a new generation of post-war architects was committed to modernism but saw itself as starting afresh – pressing the reset button that would erase the amendments introduced in the intervening years and create a cleared platform from which to launch its own ideas. Those ideas varied, and it was not long before an opportunity arose for different approaches to be explored and displayed side by side. In response to the twin aspirations to increase university places and promote science and technology, a new college was to be built and a competition was announced inviting designs for it . . .

0.2 *Post Office Tower. A London icon*

1 Winning the Peace

Churchill College, Cambridge
Sheppard Robson (1959–68)

The necessity of possessing advanced technology had become apparent during the Second World War and it was understood that continuing development would be required if Britain was to retain a leading role in the world. Winston Churchill's private secretary, Sir John Colville, wrote that 'the Battle of Britain of the future will be fought not on the beaches but in the laboratories'.[1] In 1945, the Percy Report recommended that some technical colleges should become universities, that new institutes of technology should be created and that numbers of engineering students should be increased rapidly.[2] In 1946, the Barlow Report identified a critical shortage of scientists and recommended an 'ambitious programme of university expansion' to double the annual numbers of science graduates.[3]

When Churchill visited the Massachusetts Institute of Technology (MIT) in 1949, he became convinced that the UK must put greater emphasis on technical and scientific education and closer links between universities and industry or risk falling terminally behind the major powers. By the mid-1950s, with the Cold War at its height, he was explicitly concerned about the threat posed by the Soviet Union.[4]

After he retired as Prime Minister in 1955, he asked Colville to pursue the idea of a 'British MIT'. A similar idea was being discussed by a group of industrialists who hoped to create an institute of advanced science and engineering. Both initiatives seemed stalled until they were brought together by the Nobel Prize-winning chemist, Alexander Todd, and American industrialist, Carl Gilbert (chairman of Gillette Industries). The result was the founding of Churchill College, Cambridge in 1958 (fig.1.1).

The construction of Oxbridge (Oxford and Cambridge) colleges is not normally funded by government and so a national appeal was launched. Most of the money came from British industry but there were also contributions from international foundations and from the Transport and General Workers' Union.[5] The range of donors reflected a brief period of consensus amongst government, industry and workers (represented by trade unions) to implement an industrial strategy that promoted science and technology. As Mark Goldie writes on the Churchill College website:

> It is remarkable that the Transport and General Workers' Union made a large donation to

1.1 Churchill College, Cambridge

> establish a Cambridge college, and that the President of the Amalgamated Engineering Union sat alongside the Tory Sir Winston [Churchill] and captains of industry among its founding Trustees.[6]

The founding of Churchill College responded to the desire to increase student numbers generally and, more specifically, to the perceived necessity to create more scientists and engineers. It also attempted to address the issue of wider access to students from varying backgrounds. Oxbridge colleges had traditionally taken most of their students from fee-paying private schools and access was restricted to those who had the necessary social contacts and finances. The government's drive to widen access to university education led to the introduction, in 1962, of universal state grants to cover both tuition fees and living expenses for students. University education became effectively free, removing the financial, if not the social, barriers that had prevented many potential students from applying. Churchill was one of the first Oxbridge colleges to respond and actively seek students from a wider base: first from state Grammar schools and later from the newly established Comprehensive schools.[7]

However, the College was slower to respond to wider societal changes that emerged from the Sixties 'cultural revolution'. Despite direct lobbying to Sir Winston by the Women's Freedom League, for example, Churchill was founded as a men-only college, reflecting both the tradition of the Oxbridge colleges and prevailing assumptions about the role of women in science and the workplace. Whether in response to societal pressure, or a realisation that it was missing out on half the population as potential fee generators, the College changed its policy in 1969 and the first women students arrived in 1972. Other colleges followed and by 1986 all former male colleges at Cambridge had become mixed.[8] Oxford was slower, with the last hold-out male college voting to become mixed in 2015. The small number of women's colleges that were established at Oxbridge followed suit. At the time of writing, only two remain at Cambridge and none at Oxford.

In 1959, with the basis for the College established, a site was chosen on the outskirts of Cambridge city centre and a competition was announced for its design. The College Trustees, baulking at the potential time and expense, had not wanted a competition, while the Royal Institute of British Architects (RIBA) had pushed for one that would be open to all architects. A compromise was reached and a limited competition amongst around 20 entrants was agreed. The Trustees wanted the competitors to be split between architects working in historicist styles and modernists, but they appear to have been outmanoeuvred by Sir Leslie Martin, who drew up the list.[9]

Martin had been appointed as the first Professor of Architecture at Cambridge University in 1956 and was asked to be architectural advisor for the competition. He had previously been chief architect for the London County Council (LCC), where he had overseen the introduction of modernist designs for new housing, health centres and schools, and where he had developed a working knowledge of available architectural talent (within London at least). After his appointment at Cambridge, he became an influential figure in the choice of architects to design university buildings throughout the Sixties and was asked to recommend suitable practices by several universities. The pool of architects who designed British university buildings in the 1960s was quite small, London-centric and, amongst the newer practices at least, consisted of people who had studied or taught at the Architectural Association school or worked for Martin at the LCC, or at its later incarnation as the GLC (Greater London Council).

Twenty-one practices were invited to submit entries, all of them modernists. That decision clearly reflected Martin's preferences but may have been thought appropriate for a college that was created to produce graduates who could keep Britain at the forefront of advanced technology. It was also in line with moves towards modern architecture in the wider university sector.

In fact, modernism had come to Cambridge as early as the 1930s when Walter Gropius, having fled Nazi Germany and settled in England in 1934, was asked to design a building for Christ's College. In 'a spectacular example of architectural timidity' the College rejected Gropius's proposal and eventually settled on a predictable Neo-Georgian composition by Sir Albert Richardson.[10] By the Sixties there was a greater appetite in universities for modern architecture, which had already become the norm in other areas of the welfare state such as housing, healthcare and schools (including Impington Village College a few miles from Cambridge, designed by Gropius and completed in 1938).

The Churchill competition entrants were a mix of established names and up-and-coming practices. Amongst the former were: Casson and Conder; Maxwell Fry with Jane Drew, Lindsay Drake and Denys Lasdun; Frederick Gibberd; Ernő Goldfinger; Lyons, Israel and Ellis; Robert Matthew and Johnson-Marshall; Norman and Dawbarn; Yorke, Rosenberg and Mardall; and the eventual winners, Sheppard, Robson and Partners. Amongst the latter were: Architects' Co-Partnership; H.T. Cadbury-Brown; Chamberlin, Powell and Bon; Howell, Killick and Partridge; Alison and Peter Smithson; and Stirling and Gowan.

Of the 20 entries submitted, four were selected to go forward to a second stage. Only the winners, Sheppard, Robson and Partners, came from the more established practices. The other three (Chamberlin, Powell and Bon; Stirling and Gowan; and Howard, Killick and Partridge) were all relative newcomers. The *Architects' Journal* appears to have approved of the winning entry, describing it as 'a sober counterbalance to the more unorthodox strivings of the other three'.[11] Others saw it as a compromise and a missed opportunity, another example of 'architectural timidity'. Equally, any compromise might have been the result of the dual roles the College was expected to fulfil.

In addition to performing as an engine of modern science and technology, Churchill College was to be the national monument to its namesake, then acknowledged as the 'greatest living Englishman' and the hero who had steered the country through the war. It was known that Churchill favoured a Neoclassical design, and his private secretary, Sir John Colville, wrote to Sir John Cockcroft, Master-Elect of the new College, to explain how much Sir Winston 'hopes that the new college will be a fine Neoclassical building . . .' He went on to air his own fear that 'the architects will all produce tremendously modern designs [that] will upset Sir Winston'.[12] How much that played on the minds of the judges when they selected the least radical of the shortlisted designs is unknown.

There were five judges: two academics representing the Trustees (John Cockcroft and Noel Annan, Provost of King's College) and three architects (Sir Leslie himself, Sir William Holford and Basil Spence, who would receive his knighthood in 1960). The presence of so many knights in control of the process illustrates how much influence was wielded by a centralised establishment that revolved around royal patronage.

The decision to invite only modernists pleased the architectural press and many in the architectural community, but when the competition entries were published the critics were lukewarm at best. The consensus was that the task of creating a design that was in keeping with the pursuit of science and technology, and which would also serve as a permanent monument to a national hero, had been too much. Most competitors had taken refuge on safer ground by reflecting the traditional approach to college design in the ancient universities.

The competition brief dropped heavy hints that the Trustees would prefer a courtyard layout with student rooms accessed off stairwells (the traditional Oxbridge model), and most competitors complied with that request. As a result, most entries comprised a maximum of four-storey, walk-up student accommodation arranged in courts of some form, with other buildings like the library and dining hall expressed separately. Only a handful of entries strayed from that formula, and none of the shortlisted designs.

Sheppard Robson's winning design consisted of 20 small residential courts that enclosed three sides of an open green space described as a 'great court'. The road and main entrance were on the fourth side, from where a linear procession of administrative and communal facilities thrust towards the centre of the court. The proliferation of courtyards led the architectural critic Colin Rowe to write that the competitors appeared to think that 'a college implies a courtyard, and that the more courtyards a college possessed the more collegiate it is likely to become'.[13] This was clearly a barb aimed at the winning design in particular. It can also be interpreted as a general comment on the adoption of the courtyard typology by almost all the competitors and a near absence of anything that questioned the historical social arrangements within a college or suggested a different relationship between college and the wider population. Both the College in preparing its brief, and the competitors in answering it, emphasised the retention of a model that favoured the closed social group, within a form that had been derived from the monastery and the creation of a 'priesthood'.

As it happens, Sheppard Robson's 20 courtyards proved impractically small and during design development they were reduced to 13 more generous courtyards, of which only ten were built when funding ran out. In the process of redesign, the concept of the great court became diluted, its edges became porous, the administration and communal buildings were moved to its north-east corner, and a freestanding library and archive were placed in its centre (fig.1.2). These changes, combined with a large site and the sheer distance between buildings, mean that it is difficult to discern a court at all when actually there. The whole composition feels more like a campus in which buildings are loosely arranged within landscape. It is a pleasant environment but lacks both the enclosure and intense proximity of parts

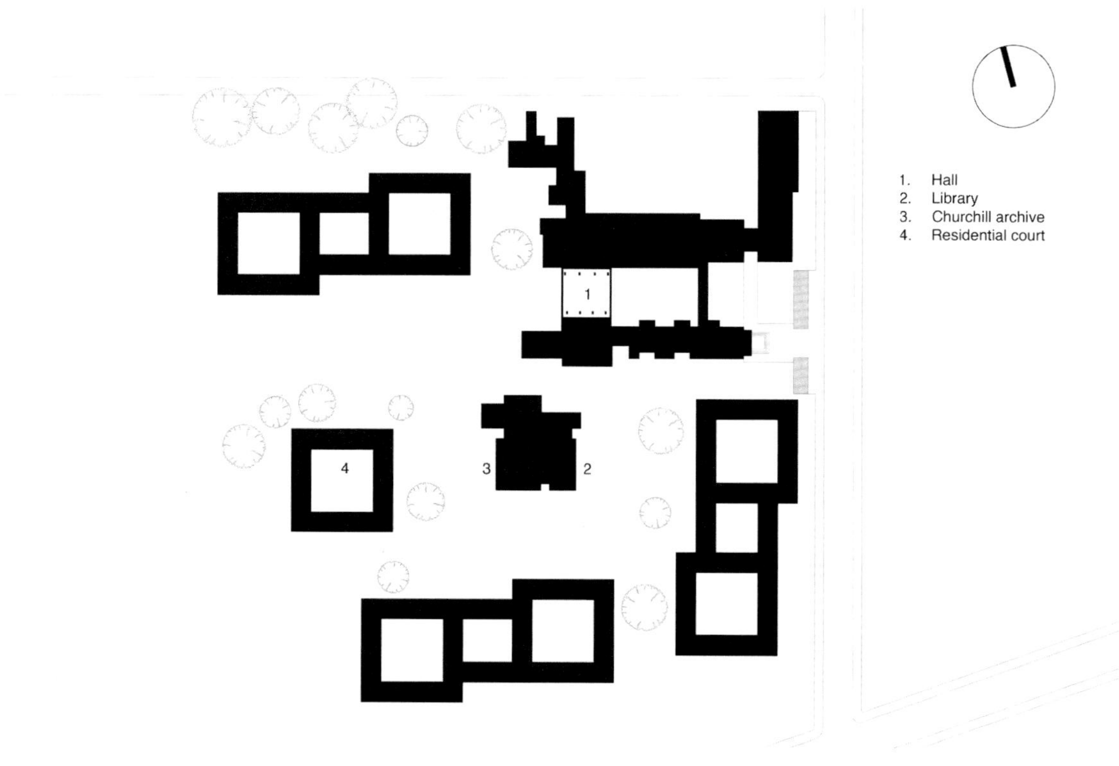

1.2 Churchill College, Cambridge. Site plan

found in a traditional courtyard college (fig.1.3). The overall effect has been described as 'an English garden party in built form'.[14]

That the Sheppard Robson design was seen as a compromise is understandable; it failed to fully resolve any of the hoped-for outcomes. The layout lacked the tightness of a traditional courtyard college and the use of rustic, hand-built materials produced an effect that was far from technological in appearance (fig.1.4). Perhaps both were inevitable. Churchill was not a traditional college, nor was it the right place to consider an architecture appropriate to the pursuit of science and technology.

Under the traditional Oxbridge model, students living in college might be taught largely through tutorials held in tutors' rooms, which were also located within the college, along with the hall, the chapel, the library and any other communal parts. It was an intense, self-contained environment where living and learning overlapped. Modern university courses, especially those engaged in science and technology, required students to use lecture theatres and specialised spaces such as laboratories and workshops located offsite. College increasingly became a place to live and socialise whilst learning elsewhere. At Churchill, the science and technology part of the equation was not located in the College.

Meanwhile the role of the College as national monument proved difficult to interpret for all the competitors. Some tried to get round the problem by including an actual monument on the site: one a massive obelisk almost twice the height of King's College Chapel, another a huge statue of Churchill the size of a four-storey building. Others included monumental buildings, in Sheppard Robson's case a pair of brick pylons of Egyptian scale that flanked the main entrance (fig.1.5) and a huge and architecturally imposing dining hall – the largest in Cambridge (fig.1.6). The latter was raised up one storey and approached via a grand staircase, past a bust of Churchill. Whether that signalled an intention that the hall should function as a monument is unclear, but it was viewed negatively by *Cambridge New Architecture* as 'something menacing – Churchillian and warlike – which is not the mood one would expect of a college hall'.[15] In hindsight, all of this was unnecessary. The later addition of the Churchill Archive housing his personal papers – which has been expanded to keep papers and mementos of many public

1.3 Churchill College, Cambridge

1.4 Churchill College, Cambridge

1.5 *Churchill College, Cambridge. View of main entrance from the road*

figures and acts as a record of 20th-century British history – proved to be a longer lasting and more meaningful memorial than any building or monument could be (fig.1.7).

The questions which the competition should have raised were not about science and technology, nor about a monument to a national hero, but concerned the appropriate architectural form for student life in the modern age. Only the proposal from Alison and Peter Smithson explored an alternative to the traditional college to a significant extent. They wrote that the 'high proportion of science and technology students suggests that the College should have a more technological character than is customary with college buildings, and that the servicing and mechanisms be comparable to a good modern hotel'.[16] Why students of science and technology should differ from other students in their domestic requirements is unclear and it seems likely that the Smithsons employed a degree of post-rationalisation to justify a position they had taken for other reasons. Nonetheless, they did recognise that the nature of university life was changing to one that separated learning and lodging, and that both would become more specialised. The Smithsons were one of the few competitors to avoid a courtyard plan, instead proposing a series of linked eight-storey glazed blocks that indeed resembled a modern, if anonymous, hotel or office building. Their entry did not advance beyond the first stage of assessment. All entries are illustrated in Mark Goldie's excellent and informative book, *Corbusier Comes to Cambridge*.

When we strip away questions about architecture that is appropriate to the study of science and technology, or the creation of a monument to a national hero, or the preservation of tradition in an ancient university, none of which was fully answered by the Churchill College competition, we are left with more abstract questions about the kind of architecture that was appropriate to the new, post-war Britain. This is where we encounter the biggest disagreements amongst competitors. They were all modernists, but could be vehement in their opposition to each other's views about the form that modernism should take. To the uninitiated, the differences might seem minor, like the

1.6 Churchill College, Cambridge. The hall looming over lower buildings in front

differences in ideology and allegiance portrayed in the Monty Python film, *Life of Brian*.[17]

> Brian: Excuse me. Are you the Judean People's Front?
> Reg: Fuck off!
> [scoffing] 'Judean People's Front'. We're the People's Front of Judea!
> [scoffing] 'Judean People's Front'.
> Francis: Wankers!
> Reg: The only people we hate more than the Romans are the fuckin' Judean People's Front.
> Francis: And the Judean Popular People's Front.

In that analogy the Romans would be the traditionalists, against whom the modernists were united. But as the traditionalists had already been ousted, they seemed irrelevant to the arguments going forward and so internal disagreements came to the fore. An editorial in *Architectural Design* magazine of December 1956 stated that: 'The time appears to be right for a reconsideration of first principles, but the first principles which looked so unassailable in the heyday of the Bauhaus are no longer acceptable without a whole string of qualifications.'[18]

Part of the problem in agreeing a direction for British modernism lay in the fact that there had never been a British modernism. Ideas had been imported, first from Germany and the Netherlands, then France, and most recently from Scandinavia. Many of the newer practices favoured the 'hard-core' modernism of the early European practitioners and were critical of the 'soft modernism' of Scandinavia that had been increasingly adopted by the previous generation. The new generation wanted change but took as their starting point the modernism of Walter Gropius, Ludwig Mies van der Rohe, the Bauhaus school and Le Corbusier. The Bauhaus had been disbanded when Hitler came to power in 1933, and Gropius and Mies moved to the USA in 1937 where they continued to develop their early ideas. Le Corbusier remained as the major influence on European modern architecture and became the benchmark against which the British modernists measured themselves, even when they did so by differentiating their work from his.

1.7 Churchill College, Cambridge. Library and archive on left and hall straight ahead

The other part of the problem was that Le Corbusier was a moving target, and his post-war work was materially different from his pre-war work. The cool, stripped-back architecture of structural frame, free walls and ribbon windows that marked his 'white villas' of the 1920s had given way to a heavy, mannered, 'Brutalist' use of in-situ concrete in projects like the Unité d'Habitation housing, the monastery at La Tourette and his projects in India, or to the sculptural, non-rational forms of the Chapelle Notre-Dame-du-Haut at Ronchamp. But amid these high-profile, high-intensity projects, it was a pair of small houses he designed in a suburb of Paris and completed in 1956 that would most occupy the thoughts of British modernists in the 1960s.

The Maisons Jaoul represented a new departure for Le Corbusier, although one that followed historical precedent. His pre-war architecture had been based on Classical principles and, just as Classicism was followed by the less refined Romanesque, so Le Corbusier moved to a technically and visually coarser style. He replaced the sophistication of columns and their proportion and spacing with the simplicity of load-bearing brick walls supporting concrete slabs and single-vault, heavy concrete roofs. He emphasised the simplicity of the construction by exposing the edges of those slabs and vaults on the elevations of the buildings.

It was an architecture that was anti-machine, anti-prefabrication, that revealed, even emphasised, the presence of the human hand. The materials and aesthetic were much adopted in Britain, although usually tidied up from the rough workmanship and robust, almost peasant-like presentation used by Le Corbusier. Colin St John Wilson's 1959 extension to the Cambridge University Department of Architecture came closest to the rawness of the original (fig.1.8). Sheppard Robson followed at Churchill College, with its rustic brickwork, exposed slab edges, heavy concrete details and vaults over the dining hall, although their neater detailing and raked brick joints owed much to Stirling and Gowan's 1958 flats at Ham Common (see Chapter 2).

Not everyone was happy with this shift in style. Traditionalists regretted any modernism, whilst the architectural historian Nikolaus Pevsner wrote:

> In the thirties and most of the fifties modern architecture was crisp, logical, of few words and easy to convince anybody, one would have thought, yet the [university building] committees shied away from it. Now architecture tends to be over-dramatic, aggressive and highly individual, and the committees lap it up . . . [19]

The modernism of the machine age that Pevsner admired had moved to the USA. It can be argued that, in comparison to the aspirations of the early modernists, European architects in the 1960s were already engaged in a kind of post-modernism, although that term would not emerge for another ten years and would describe a different architecture that might more accurately be called anti-modern.

It has been said that the work of Sheppard Robson displayed a particularly British modernism. That argument can be made on the basis that it demonstrated the British capacity for pragmatic compromise, in this case a watered-down Corbusian aesthetic combined with the humanistic, more informal approach of Scandinavian architects like Alvar Aalto.

The Churchill College competition did not offer suggestions for a different model of university education. Nor did it resolve questions as to the direction that modern architecture should take in the post-war era. It did, however, complete the route of the traditionalists and put the modernists in control of university architecture throughout the remainder of the Sixties. It also largely established the pool of architects who would dominate the sector. Add the names Powell and Moya (who were invited but did not take part due to other commitments) and Philip Dowson and his colleagues at Arup Associates to those of the competitors and judges in the Churchill College competition and you have a list of those who would design university buildings in Britain for the next decade.

1.8 Cambridge University, extension to Department of Architecture

2 The Old Knights
Sir Hugh Casson
Sir Basil Spence
Sir Leslie Martin

Sir Hugh Casson, Sir Basil Spence and Sir Leslie Martin belonged to the older generation of post-war British modernists and, as their titles suggest, had become part of the establishment and held positions of influence. Reason enough for a new generation, eager for change, to kick against the old knights, perhaps. But their criticism was also aimed at the 'soft modernism' that had been adopted by the older generation.

Sir Hugh Casson

Casson was the epitome of the establishment figure: Provost of the Royal College of Art; President of the Royal Academy; Vice-President of the Royal Institute of British Architects; Trustee of the Natural History Museum and the National Portrait Gallery; member of the editorial board of the *Architectural Review*; board member of the British Council; frequent companion of royalty; designer of interiors for Queen Elizabeth II and Prince Philip; watercolour tutor to Prince Charles (later King Charles III).[1] A consummate committee man and organiser, and by all accounts extremely affable, he was an unremarkable architect. Even his obituarists could not bring themselves to claim otherwise, one of them describing him affectionately as 'one of the sublimely second rate'. This was meant as a compliment, Casson himself having argued that second raters are nicer than first raters; more civilised, less driven.[2] Others were less sympathetic.

Casson was Director of Architecture for the 1951 Festival of Britain on London's South Bank. For many younger architects and critics, the festival epitomised the comfortable, non-challenging, middlebrow modernism of the old knights and others of their generation. Michael Frayn described it as representing 'the Britain of the radical middle class – the do-gooders; the readers of the *News Chronicle*, *The Guardian* and *The Observer*; the signers of petitions; the backbone of the BBC'.[3]

Any or all of the above might have precipitated James Stirling's explanation when asked why his design for the Cambridge History Faculty on a site adjacent to Casson Conder's Raised Faculty Building ignored both it and their masterplan for the Sidgwick site within which both buildings sat. 'To fuck Casson' was his reply.[4] Or he might have had a more specific grievance related to the cancellation of Stirling and Gowan's commission at Selwyn College. Their proposal for a series of curving linear

2.1 Queens' College, Cambridge, Erasmus Building

accommodation blocks, turned its back on the adjacent Sidgwick site to preserve the privacy of Selwyn's garden. When Casson proposed a linear building along the edge of the Sidgwick site that provided enclosure to the Selwyn garden whilst also opening a passage between the two sites, the College reassessed the design of its own site and dropped Stirling and Gowan's proposal. Stirling's opportunity for revenge came when he was commissioned to design the History Faculty within Casson's Sidgwick masterplan.[5]

Stirling was one of the younger generation seeking to become established. As noted in Chapter 1, Sir Leslie Martin had been appointed Professor of Architecture at Cambridge in 1956 and was thereafter asked by several universities to act as advisor in the choice of architects. He included Stirling and his then partner, James Gowan, in the Churchill College competition, where their design was shortlisted. He recommended them for the project at Selwyn College. When he drew up a masterplan for Leicester University he recommended them for the design of the Engineering Building – the project that made their reputation and led to commissions at Oxford and Cambridge, including the Cambridge History Faculty where, again, they were included at the behest of Martin (see Chapter 12). Younger architects like Stirling might dislike the establishment but were nonetheless reliant on its patronage for major public commissions.

The tensions over university design appropriate to the modern age that arose in the Churchill College competition had already appeared at the Sidgwick site, an area of land to the west of Cambridge city centre that had been set aside for the development of faculties of Arts, Humanities and Social Sciences. At Churchill, tensions arose from a disconnect between the desire to recreate the traditional form of a college and the way modern university education was delivered. At

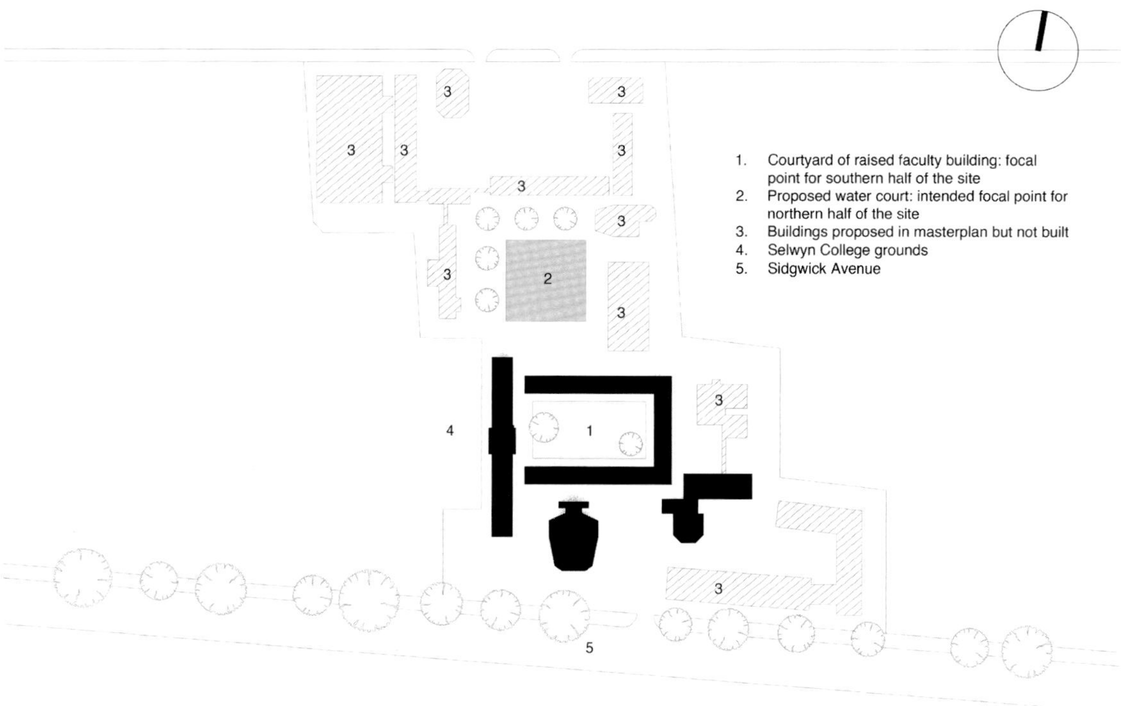

2.2 Sidgwick masterplan as intended

the Sidgwick site, tensions arose from a desire to recreate the traditional form of a college and the different natures of colleges and faculties.

The traditional model of education at Oxford and Cambridge involved most students living and learning within college. Changes to the delivery of education and increased numbers made this model inappropriate for many students, who now lived in college whilst learning in bespoke teaching spaces provided by the university faculties. The faculties were owned and run by the university; the colleges, whilst also part of the university, were financially and organisationally independent. While the colleges raised their own funding for building projects and could set their own budgets, the university was reliant on grants from the UGC and restricted by its cost limits. In addition, the university often had to negotiate with wealthy and land-rich colleges to purchase land for building. That was the case at Sidgwick and led to compromises in the planning of the site.

The masterplan prepared by Casson Conder Architects in 1952 set up a controlling framework of linear buildings arranged in a series of loose courtyards organised around two focal points.[6] At the core was the Raised Faculty Building, whose courtyard provided the focal point to the southern half of the site. It was surrounded on three sides by building raised on columns, allowing it to act as a central gathering place providing porous access to the rest of the site.

The focal point for the northern half of the site was also intended as a public open space, the Water Court (fig.2.2). However, difficulties over land purchase led to a reduced site area. The Water Court was abandoned and the History Faculty located there instead (fig.2.3).[7] If Stirling truly intended to give two fingers to Casson, he certainly achieved it by ignoring the overall loose-courtyard arrangement of the masterplan and by the spiky, aggressive angularity with which the History Faculty addressed the adjacent Raised Faculty Building. Also, by designing a stand-

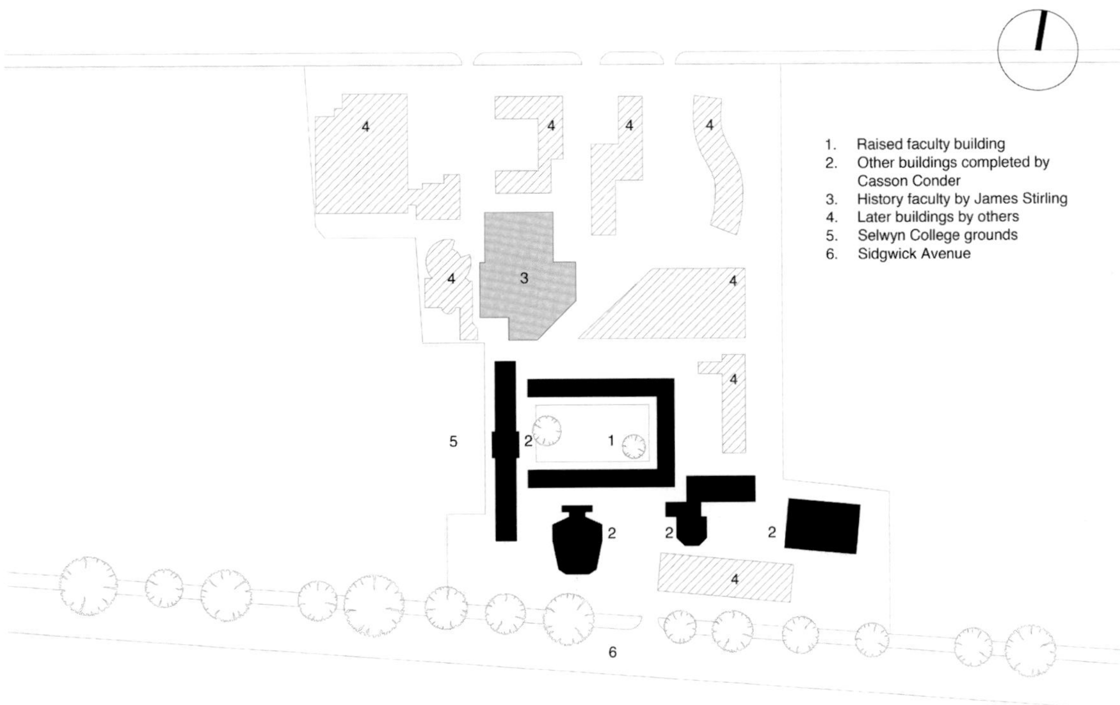

2.3 Sidgwick masterplan as realised

alone pavilion, he set a precedent for the northern half of the site, which subsequently developed as an architectural zoo of individual buildings set amongst roads and parking areas, with no common denominator to pull them together. The overall effect is rather like a business park. Comparison of figures 2.2 and 2.3 illustrates the radical change brought about by the intrusion of the History Faculty into Casson's original vision for the site.

The Sidgwick site was the first piece of comprehensive post-war university masterplanning and Casson Conder's proposal was based on two ideas. The first was the traditional Cambridge college court, which imposed informal order and scale whilst allowing freedom in the detailed design of individual buildings. The second was the picturesque 'townscape' agenda promoted since the late 1940s by the *Architectural Review* magazine with which Casson had a close relationship. Neither idea was intrinsically bad and both were realised with some success before they were abandoned in the northern half of the site. The question is whether they were appropriate.

The idea of basing the masterplan on the traditional college layout was criticised on the grounds that the intended buildings were separate university faculties, with needs and patterns of use different to those of a college. Even some who might not subscribe to the mantra that 'form follows function' felt an opportunity had been missed to consider planning principles appropriate for the changing nature of university education. The picturesque agenda was also criticised; in their comprehensive 1970 survey of new buildings in Cambridge, Nicholas Taylor and Philip Booth wrote that 'few people would deny the many successes of Casson and Conder's original plan . . . in creating a stage-set of picturesque townscape. [However] all these elegant details are only "visual aids" to an overall picture of academic life which does not carry conviction'.[8]

Casson and Conder employed a common palette of materials in their design of the buildings on the southern part of the site. Except for the Raised Faculty Building they featured brown facing brick with exposed concrete slab edges at first-floor level, forming a unifying datum around the site. Like Sheppard Robson at Churchill College, the choice of materials recalled Le Corbusier's Maisons Jaoul, which exerted a strong influence on British architects seeking an alternative to the pre-war International Style.

The brick buildings at Sidgwick were unremarkable; a tougher-minded architect would have been content to leave them so, a quiet, uniform backdrop to highlight the Raised Faculty Building as the focal point. However, Casson and Conder's attraction to the picturesque led them to introduce a variety of fussy window details that relieved the uniformity but resulted in a design that pleased neither the hard modernists nor those who still favoured more formal historicist solutions.[9]

The Raised Faculty Building was conceived as an anchor and formal foil to the looser arrangement of the rest of the site. In a move calculated to appeal to the dons, Casson described it as the 'High Table' of the design.[10] Although probably not intended so literally, the white Portland stone building rested on a 'table', a heavy concrete slab raised on chunky pairs of Le Corbusier-style columns that set the first-floor datum for the rest of the site (fig.2.4). Having established a clear basis for the design, the architects once again resorted to picturesque variety in its implementation, even when the underlying use did not require variety and would have benefited from uniformity. The result was criticised for its 'extraordinarily arbitrary and illogical fenestration', particularly in library areas, where consistency of lighting is important (fig.2.5).[11]

The soft control that was appropriate to the masterplan concept did not translate well to the design of individual buildings and the Raised Faculty Building displayed a lack of logic. References were mixed: the columns and first-floor slab recalled the post-war Brutalist architecture of Le Corbusier, in particular the Unité d'Habitation, whilst the building above was reminiscent of his pre-war architecture of structural frame and free elevation (fig.2.6). But where Le Corbusier separated the functions of

2.4 Cambridge University, Raised Faculty Building
2.5 Cambridge University, Raised Faculty Building
2.6 Cambridge University, Raised Faculty Building

structural support and external wall, in the Raised Faculty Building the external walls were load-bearing stone and shared support of the floor slabs with an internal structural frame.[12] This perceived lack of clarity, lack of adherence to strict principles, lack of toughness and willingness to compromise for the sake of picturesque effect annoyed some critics and younger architects.

> Perhaps, if Sir Hugh Casson had not been so playful [in his design of the Raised Faculty Building], James Stirling might not have been so rude [in his design of the adjacent History Faculty].[13]

Sir Basil Spence

As the Sidgwick site was being developed, just down the road at Queens' College a 'test case for modern architecture in Cambridge' was being conducted.[14] Basil Spence was appointed to design the Erasmus student residences in 1958 after a student-led campaign forced the College to abandon an historicist design by Stephen Dykes Bower. The College sought advice from Kenneth Cross, President of the RIBA, who provided a shortlist of seven architects with experience of university work, all but one of whom were modernists. Spence was the selection committee's unanimous choice.[15] Although his knighthood would not be awarded until 1960, Spence was already an establishment figure and the most famous architect in Britain. He received an OBE (Officer of the Most Excellent Order of the British Empire) in 1948 and, like Casson, served on the committees of several grand institutions. He first came to public attention through his work on the 1951 Festival of Britain, where he was appointed by Casson to design the Sea and Ships pavilion. But it was his competition-winning design that same year for a new Coventry Cathedral amongst the ruins of the bombed original that propelled him to national and international fame.

The College wanted a modern building and Spence had a history of designing modernist university buildings, but it was his ability at Coventry to design within an historic context that most appealed to the Cambridge dons. His previous university work ranged from his 1947 design for the Glasgow University Natural Philosophy Department, with its overtones of Nordic Classicism, to his designs from 1955 onwards for the Universities of Liverpool, Nottingham and Southampton, which leant towards the crisp, lightweight, steel and glass modernism that developed in the USA from the ideas taken there by Gropius and Mies when they fled Germany in the 1930s.[16] Something different was wanted at Queens'.

Throughout his career Spence collected influences from traditional and vernacular architecture, from modern architects who preceded him and from younger architects. The Erasmus Building displayed influences from all three sources. In its general aesthetic, its palette of materials and some of its detailing, it recalled Le Corbusier's Maisons Jaoul via Stirling and Gowan's flats at Ham Common. Stirling had visited Jaoul, which he found 'anti-mechanistic and un-regional', by which he meant the finish was too agricultural for Paris, the brickwork 'unintelligent'. 'If the [brick] finish had been harder . . . the appearance would have been mechanistic and I think better.'[17] Ham Common was a tidied-up version of Jaoul, with crisp concrete, clearly articulated joints between concrete and brickwork, and raked joints between bricks to give the building a much sharper 'mechanistic' appearance. The Erasmus Building was a less challenging version of Ham Common, with many of the Brutalist concrete details removed and stone facings applied to slab edges and one gable wall (fig.2.8). Like Casson and Conder's Raised Faculty Building, Erasmus was raised off the ground. However, the massive concrete columns used in the former were replaced with brick piers that aligned with the cross-wall structure of the rooms above and had arched openings driven through them to create a brick arcade inspired by Queens' 1540 Cloister Court.[18] Spence's use of stone facings and brick arches was an attempt to provide historical references to the surrounding buildings (fig.2.7).

The result was considered too picturesque by hard modernists, while it stirred up a storm of protest in the letters pages of *The Times* from those who were appalled by such an alien intrusion into one of the ancient colleges. The fact that Spence managed to upset both sides might indicate that he had struck a reasonably good balance when inserting a modern building into an historic context, or that he was hedging his bets.

Whatever criticisms might be levelled from strictly modernist or traditionalist perspectives, the Erasmus Building now looks comfortable and unremarkable in its surroundings (fig.2.1). The 'in-your-face' rawness of Le Corbusier's Maisons Jaoul had been doubly filtered out, first by Stirling and Gowan at Ham Common and then further by Spence himself. In the same way that high fashion eventually finds its way onto the high street in diluted form, the resulting aesthetic was adopted in countless blocks of suburban flats. The last point is significant; the Erasmus Building began to step away from the traditional form of college 'rooms' and provided modern standards of residential living, fulfilling the College's wish to provide 'full freedom for private study, concentration and work, for separate and individual development and social life'.[19]

Whilst this reflected a willingness to bring their accommodation into the 20th century, students at Queens' in the 1960s found other aspects of college life restrictive, paternalistic and no longer fit for the age. They demanded change, and when the College was slow to respond, unrest turned to protest.[20] They were not alone. Students were increasingly seen by the left as a group that could be radicalised and used to disrupt what it saw as the role of universities in reproducing capitalism. Many students began to demand more say in

2.7 Queens' College, Cambridge, Erasmus Building. The brick arcade

2.8 Queens' College, Cambridge, Erasmus Building

the running of their institutions. At the same time, students were joining CND (the Campaign for Nuclear Disarmament) and later the VSC (Vietnam Solidarity Campaign) which supported the Communist North Vietnamese in the war with the USA. How much of this was due to political conviction and how much, as one CND organiser put it, because it 'was the thing to do' and would 'annoy the grown-ups' is open to question. Whatever the truth, it reinforced a perception of a rebellious and radical youth culture that was, ironically, closely linked with the wholly commercial youth market in music and fashion.[21] Protest reached a peak with the anti-war demonstrations of March and October 1968, when violent clashes with police took place outside the US Embassy in Grosvenor Square. After that, large-scale student protest fell away and had mostly blown itself out by the end of the decade, suggesting that much of the activity was more about fashion than politics. Meanwhile, student demands for greater involvement in the running of universities made no difference to the way higher education was organised.

If changes to university organisation were slow, government hopes for wider access to students from different social backgrounds proved even slower to realise. When the Erasmus residences were completed in 1960 around 80 per cent of Cambridge undergraduates came from private, fee-paying schools and only 20 per cent from state schools. Twenty-five years later, students from private and state schools each made up 50 per cent, an improvement but still a huge imbalance when set against the 7 per cent of the population attending private schools.[22] The percentage of students attending Oxbridge colleges from state schools has continued to rise slowly, and in 2022 was 68 per cent at Oxford and 72.5 per cent at Cambridge, meaning that students from private schools made up around 30 per cent, still drawn from around 7 per cent of the school population.[23]

Clearly it was going to take more than the state funding of free university education to significantly change the social composition of the student population. The creation of new universities was seen as a way of widening access by developing new models of university education. Spence was appointed to design the first of these at Sussex University. The results will be examined in Chapter 3.

Sir Leslie Martin

As already noted, Leslie Martin was appointed first Professor of Architecture at Cambridge University in 1956, a position that he used to influence the choice of architects for many university buildings throughout the 1960s. In his own work, he used his academic position to pursue an approach to design based on research and the identification of building 'types'. He sought to demonstrate that optimum solutions could be developed for specific building uses: residence, library, auditorium and laboratory, for example. This can be seen as a continuation of his early career with London Midland and Scottish Railway – where he worked on a standardised building system for stations – and his pursuit of new forms of urban housing while chief architect at the LCC.[24] It also reflected a general post-war enthusiasm for systematic, quasi-scientific planning.

His greatest impact on university architecture probably came through his ability to influence the choice of architect, where he invariably promoted a relatively small number of younger modernists whose work he knew. However, he designed several buildings himself, in collaboration with younger architects that he met during his time at the LCC and Cambridge University.

When University College Leicester gained university status in 1957, Martin was commissioned to produce a masterplan for the new, expanded institution. He also designed, with Colin St John Wilson, the Physics and Astronomy Building, which formed one side of a courtyard at the core of the masterplan. The design was straightforward early modernism in the tradition of Gropius's Fagus Works: a simple brick and glass box that prioritised the efficient planning of internal functions whilst maximising daylight and natural ventilation. The result was an understated architecture that formed a quiet backdrop to the functions it contained and the activity of the social space (courtyard) that it helped enclose (fig.2.9).

At the same time, Martin and Trevor Dannatt designed College Hall women's residences for the University, but these were located away from the main campus. A loose arrangement of linear blocks forming interlocking courts, not dissimilar to Casson's masterplan for the Cambridge Sidgwick site, College Hall adopted a similar aesthetic to the Physics and Astronomy Building but with appropriately residential detailing. Blocks running north–south had rooms facing east and west, served by a central corridor. Blocks running east–west had only south-facing rooms, with service spaces on the north side of the corridor (fig.2.10). South-facing blocks were stepped back in section,

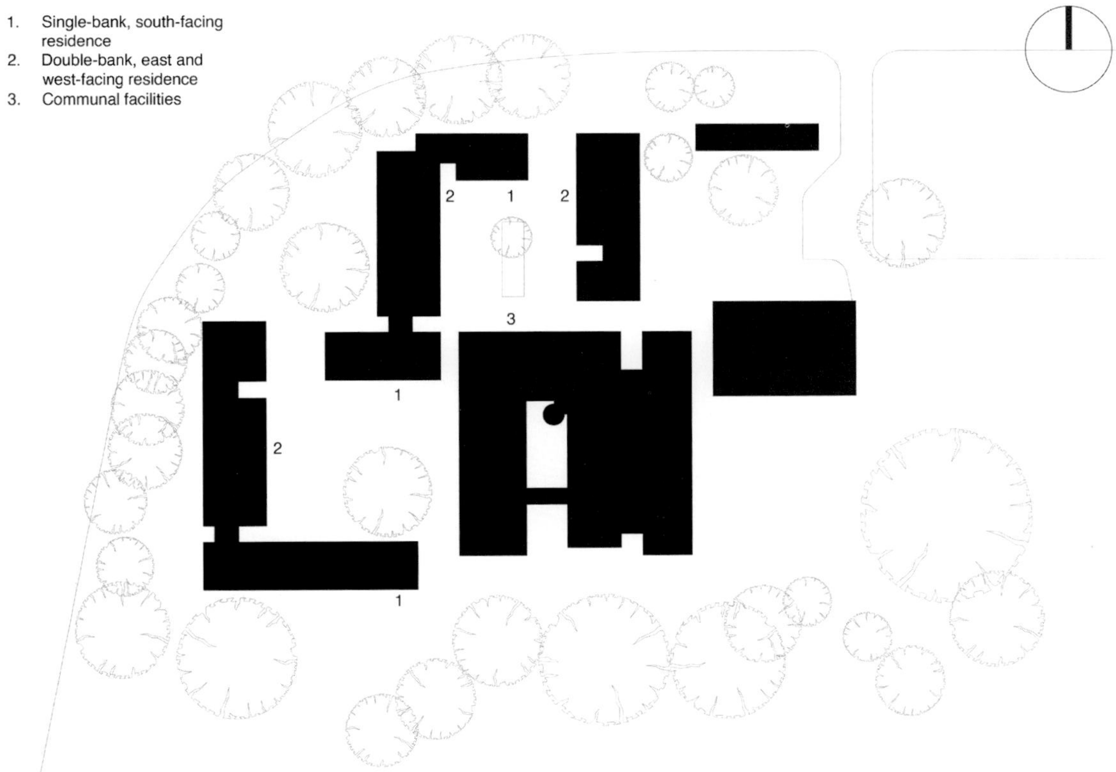

2.9 Leicester University, Physics and Astronomy Building
2.10 Leicester University, College Hall. Site plan

with individual balconies separated by projecting brick cross-walls, all features that Martin would use again when developing his residence 'type' (fig.2.11).

Martin's library type was based on a square plan with access and control at one corner, from which radiated successive L-shaped layers of reading room, bookstacks and study carrels around two sides of the perimeter. The ultimate realisation of the library type appears in a group of libraries for Oxford University that he designed with Colin St John Wilson, Patrick Hodgkinson and Douglas Lanham. The Manor Road Group was completed in 1959 and contained three libraries of different sizes for Law, English and Statistics, which were grouped around a central core of circulation, lecture theatres, seminar rooms and service spaces. Although the libraries were of different sizes and for different faculties, Martin concluded that the overriding typology of 'library' was constant, and so all of them were based on the principles outlined above (fig.2.12).

Meanwhile a project for the Zoology and Psychology Building for Oxford University, designed with Douglas Lanham and completed in 1963, gave Martin the opportunity to test ideas for the planning of science buildings. Here he sought to develop a system that would allow flexibility for specific departmental requirements. Because laboratories and workshops often require large, unobstructed spaces, the buildings were to be deep plan, with internal courtyards for light and view. Martin described them as a 'flat slab of three or four storey buildings which receive their daylight by means of courts sunk into the slab'.[25] However, when it came to the actual design, Martin set back each floor to

2.11 Leicester University, College Hall. A loose arrangement of courtyards

create wide, perimeter roof terraces at upper levels, successively reducing the amount of floor area available and therefore future flexibility to meet changing requirements.

Probably Martin's best-known university building, which one commentator judged 'Cambridge's most important post-war building',[26] is Harvey Court, a student residence for Gonville and Caius College, completed in 1962 and located in a new area developed by the University to the west of the Backs, a stretch of meadowland running along the banks of the river Cam behind some of the ancient colleges. The site was a large, mature garden that ran along the east side of the Sidgwick site, and Martin located the building at its north end (fig.2.13). Taylor and Booth argued that the design continued Martin's LCC research into low-rise, high-density, tight, urban housing.[27] Certainly Harvey Court was purely residential; on the other hand, it was not housing and was set in a leafy suburb, not a tight, urban location. The design revisited some of the themes that first appeared at College Hall, Leicester, although in a more rigid, monolithic and monumental manner, and rehashed an unbuilt design for King's College, Cambridge. The latter involved an inward-looking courtyard that, in its city-centre location, with surrounding shops and eating places and the buzz of pedestrian through traffic, could have functioned as a lively and successful public plaza located just off the main market square. That idea assumes a willingness on the part of the University to share its space with the public, something that many universities have become reluctant to do.[28] The site was later developed to a design by Architects' Co-Partnership that resembled a block

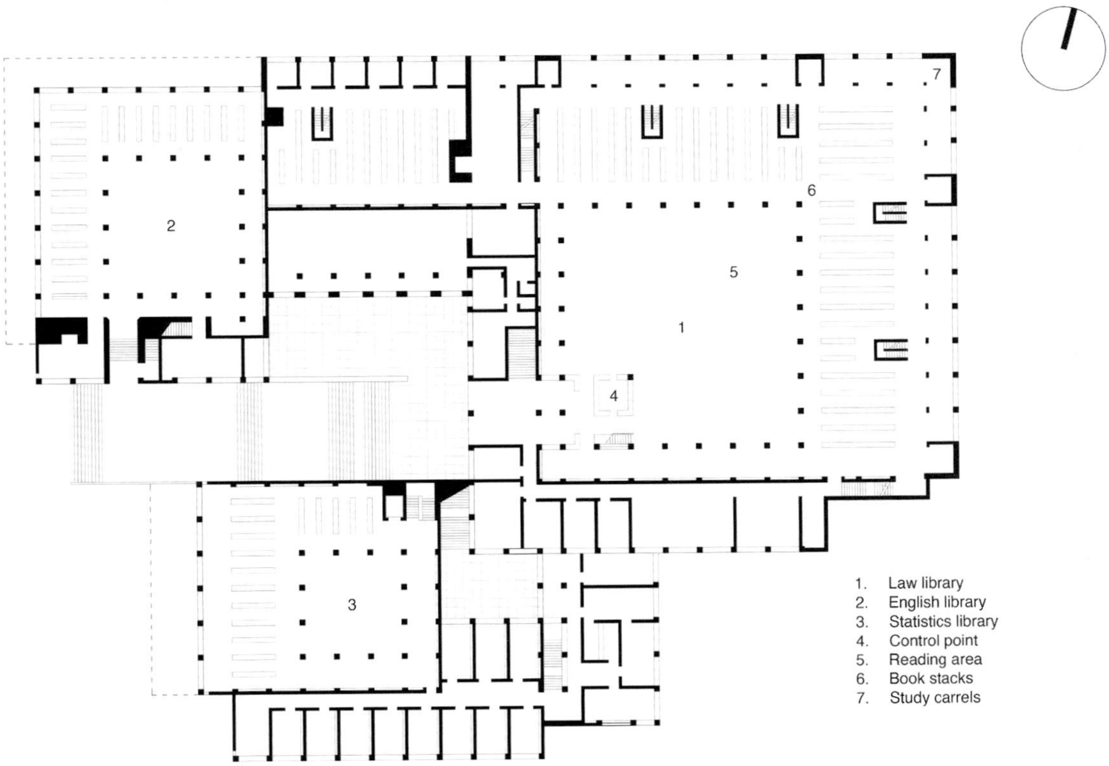

2.12 Oxford University, Manor Road Libraries. Composite plan showing main floor of each library, which are at different levels

2.13 Gonville and Caius College, Cambridge, Harvey Court. View from the garden

of urban flats over shops, with a raised back court for student use only (see Chapter 9).

Whatever Martin's intention at King's, the courtyard at Harvey Court was clearly not meant for public use; it did not even encourage use by other students. 'In refusing to be neighbourly and to suggest through routes from neighbouring [university] properties, Harvey Court has ensured that its piazza will for long remain secluded and empty, without the enriching society of strangers passing by.'[29] And yet, there was nothing in its location or function to suggest that an inward-looking courtyard was the most appropriate solution. It seems likely that these decisions were another example of a desire to perpetuate the traditional college layout and, consequently, the traditional college exclusivity. They were also the result of Martin's search for a universal 'type' that could be replicated in any situation. By refusing to engage with its surroundings, it mattered little what those surroundings were.

The design was intended as a prototype for a series of linked courtyards, each raised over a ground-floor plinth of public rooms and surrounded by residential rooms that step back in broad terraces (fig.2.14). Only one was built, a flaw in the concept being that there was not a sufficient requirement for public rooms to fill the ground floor and much of it remained empty or filled with earth.[30] The brick cross-wall construction of the perimeter rooms was expressed on the elevations. On the courtyard side they stepped back with the terraces (fig.2.15). On the perimeter elevations they remained vertical and flush with the outer wall of the top-floor rooms and were expressed as piers that became progressively deeper as

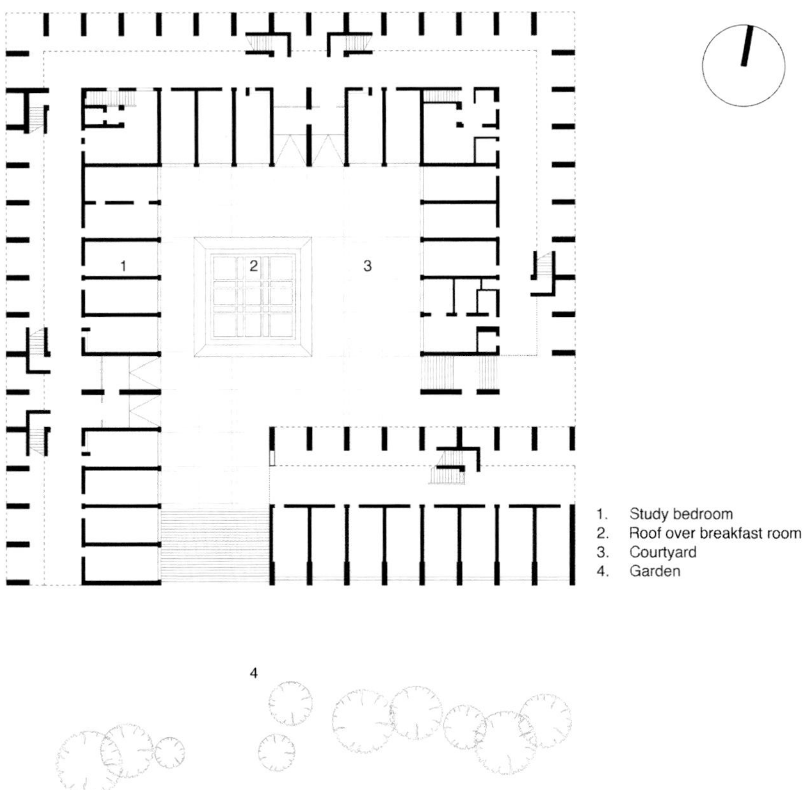

2.14 Gonville and Caius College, Cambridge, Harvey Court. Plan at courtyard level

the mid- and ground floors stepped in from the perimeter (fig.2.16). There were few openings in the perimeter walls and the overall effect was of a massive, sculpted exterior protecting a much more open, glazed interior that overlooked a central, raised courtyard. Brickwork was flush pointed to add to the massive and monolithic appearance. The diagram was appropriate if the aim was to signify a cloistered, private community insulated from the outside world.

Both the design and the use of brick owed much to Alvar Aalto's Säynätsalo Town Hall, where they were used to different effect. Aalto's plan was less rigid and more inviting – a grouping of buildings around a central space – and featured wide steps that leaked out from two corners and led visitors up, into and potentially through the central courtyard. In contrast, Harvey Court was a single, rigid building with a set of wide steps at one corner that was located away from public view and led only from the inner court down to the private gardens (fig.2.17). It might be described as Aalto without the humanity, a criticism that Geoffrey Tyack applied to much of Martin's work.[31]

Shortly after completion of Harvey Court, Martin and Wilson designed a student residence for Peterhouse College, Cambridge that was a complete departure from the 'type' they had been developing through earlier projects. The William Stone Building was set in extensive gardens to the rear of the College and, presumably to reduce the loss of garden space, they designed a point block eight storeys high (fig.2.18). Their departure from type did not signal a consequent departure from construction techniques or materials: the building was constructed of load-bearing brick. At first

2.15 Gonville and Caius College, Cambridge, Harvey Court. The courtyard with raised lantern over the breakfast room

2.16 Gonville and Caius College, Cambridge, Harvey Court. Exterior elevation

2.17 *Gonville and Caius College, Cambridge, Harvey Court. Steps linking courtyard and garden*

2.18 Peterhouse College, Cambridge, William Stone Building

glance the design seems similar to many blocks of flats that were built around that time. However, the plan form was inventive and owed much to Aalto's Neue Vahr flats in Bremen, although the execution was, again, more formal, less organic (fig.2.19). Like Spence's Erasmus Building just along the river, the William Stone Building signalled a willingness to move away from the traditional form of college rooms and provide 'civilised flats [that] suggest a new independence and freedom of student life', as opposed to the 'enforced sociability of Harvey Court'.[32]

The post-war work of the old knights displayed a restless examination of ideas and influences gleaned from a variety of sources and reflected a more general loss of conviction in the certainties of early modernism. Spence, in particular, explored a wide range of sources, and the authors of *Basil Spence: Buildings and Projects*, a comprehensive overview of his work, acknowledge that close categorisation has eluded both them and other commentators. Instead, they quote Spence's own description of the architect as 'a servant, a tailor, who cuts and measures the thin chap or the fat chap and tries to make him comfortable. He is not a reformer'.[33] In common with many of their peers in wider society, the younger generation of architects felt that reform was exactly what was needed.

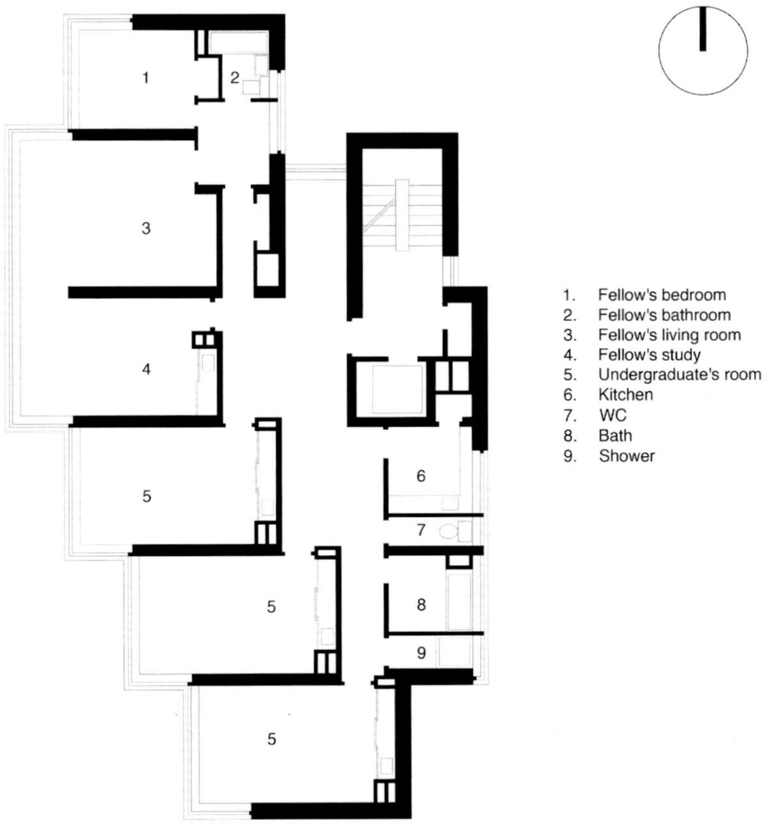

2.19 Peterhouse College, Cambridge, William Stone Building. Plan of typical upper floor

3 The New Universities

At a symposium on the planning of new universities organised by the Architectural Association with the RIBA and held at the University of Sussex in July 1964, the historian and educationalist, Asa Briggs, who was appointed Professor of History and Dean of the School of Social Studies at the University and later Vice-Chancellor, made some opening remarks:

> It is fortunate that a period of educational expansion in quantitative terms in Britain has coincided with a period of fresh thinking about the scope and content of university education in qualitative terms . . . The new universities were not only given the chance of becoming centres of educational innovation: they were each allowed to develop on their own lines . . . As a direct result of this, their policies encouraged the extension of the national debate about the scope and purposes of university education in the middle of the twentieth century . . . The new universities have the advantage of being free from vested interests and are thus able to be more radical in their approach to curriculum and organisation.[1]

All of that was surely true, but others have noted an inherent dichotomy that limited how radical the new universities could be. Funding came from government through the UGC and there would be limits to what either was prepared to sponsor. New ideas were encouraged but they could not stray too far from existing models and still be recognised as universities.[2]

Perhaps as a further check on over-zealous creativity, those charged with realising the new universities were themselves members of the educational establishment, and when a shortlist of architects was put together for the design of Sussex – the first of the new universities – candidates were drawn from the ranks of older, established (one might say establishment) architects. We have already met Casson, Martin and Spence, to which were added Sir William Holford and Richard Sheppard.[3] The first four were already knighted and Sheppard would later join them. Spence was chosen and John Fulton (later Sir John and Baron Fulton of Falmer) was appointed Vice-Chancellor.

3.1 York University

Sussex University: Sir Basil Spence, Bonnington and Collins (1959–69)

Fulton had a vision of a new type of university that followed neither the traditional Oxbridge model of collegiate life nor the civic university environment that lacked a social focus. He acknowledged that the new universities in many practical ways had an easier task than previous generations of university builders. 'There was a surging demand for university places; capital was assured; land was given.' However, these certainties made space for other, more fundamental questions: 'How big? How fast? What shall we teach?'[4] Spence's response to these unknowns was surprisingly subjective. Without any apparent analysis of alternatives, he said that:

> . . . the method of adding courtyard to courtyard seems to me to be the only logical way [of coping with unknowns] . . . I saw the university in pink brick with some arched forms peeping through the trees . . . I think we owe it to the students that they should go away with the experience that they have been at a university where there is a consistent feeling of enclosure, and a consistent feeling of having been cosseted in the architectural sense, and to be proud that they have been to their university. It should leave a lasting *visual* memory [my emphasis].[5]

Louise Campbell gave a more comprehensive account of the ideas and constraints that drove Spence's design in her essay 'Drawing a New Map of Learning' where she concluded that his approach was unashamedly driven by aesthetics.[6] Spence argued that the answer to accommodating change in a complex and rapidly evolving organisation lay not in systems or planning but in 'architecture' and 'landscape'.[7] Why the client accepted such a nebulous statement is unclear; perhaps because it had no clear idea of what it needed or because the architect's reputation discouraged critical questioning. In any event, it allowed Spence to reverse the post-war emphasis on systematic planning and reinstate the architect as lone genius with an all-encompassing vision.

The brief provided by the University Council suggested that 'while the buildings might be modern in conception the materials used should be of the kind that would age gracefully and be in tune with the surrounding countryside'.[8] That suited Spence, who was intent on creating 'noble' architecture, differentiated from the slender steel frame and lightweight cladding he had employed in some of his earlier university and school designs.[9] At the Erasmus Building (see Chapter 2), he had begun to work with load-bearing brick and concrete and to talk about creating 'chunkiness' and 'something sculptural'.[10] At Sussex, he developed these ideas into a palette of brick walls supporting massive, simple, concrete vaults, as seen at Le Corbusier's Maisons Jaoul.

However, the penalty for relying on architectural vision alone to provide the appropriate solution soon became apparent. A combination of cost overruns, insufficient local labour and the Vice-Chancellor's determination to establish the University and welcome students as quickly as possible led to the rapid adoption of a concrete frame, brick cladding panels and thin, prefabricated concrete vaults combined with arched spandrel panels that mimicked the shape of heavy vaults in elevation (fig.3.2). The result may appear 'chunky' from a distance but closer inspection reveals a construction that is far more slender and precise than the massive, earthy, Romanesque feel of the Maisons Jaoul. Whether Spence felt the result was still 'noble' is unrecorded but the compromise was criticised for lack of honesty by a group of students visiting from the Architectural Association, the school where almost all the younger architects featured in this book studied or taught.[11]

The 'method of adding courtyard to courtyard' based on 'architecture' and 'landscape' was a personal vision that did not outlive its architect. The University has expanded to accommodate new buildings, in particular a large number of student flats and residences, and in so doing has deviated from Spence's original formula. To understand his vision for the University, we must concentrate on the layout and design of the original core buildings that formed phase one of construction (fig.3.5). The first to be completed was Falmer House, which formed the social hub of the University and provided a grand entrance to the site through a huge arch and into a formal courtyard known as Falmer Court. Exiting the opposite side of the courtyard, a straight pathway led along a valley floor to the arts buildings, which provided the north end of a north–south axis with Falmer Court. To the right of the path, climbing up the valley side like a medieval hill town, were the science buildings, which looked over the valley to the library, perched on top of a mound like the Parthenon on the Acropolis hill (figs 3.3, 3.4, 3.6).

3.2 Sussex University. Main entrance and Falmer House

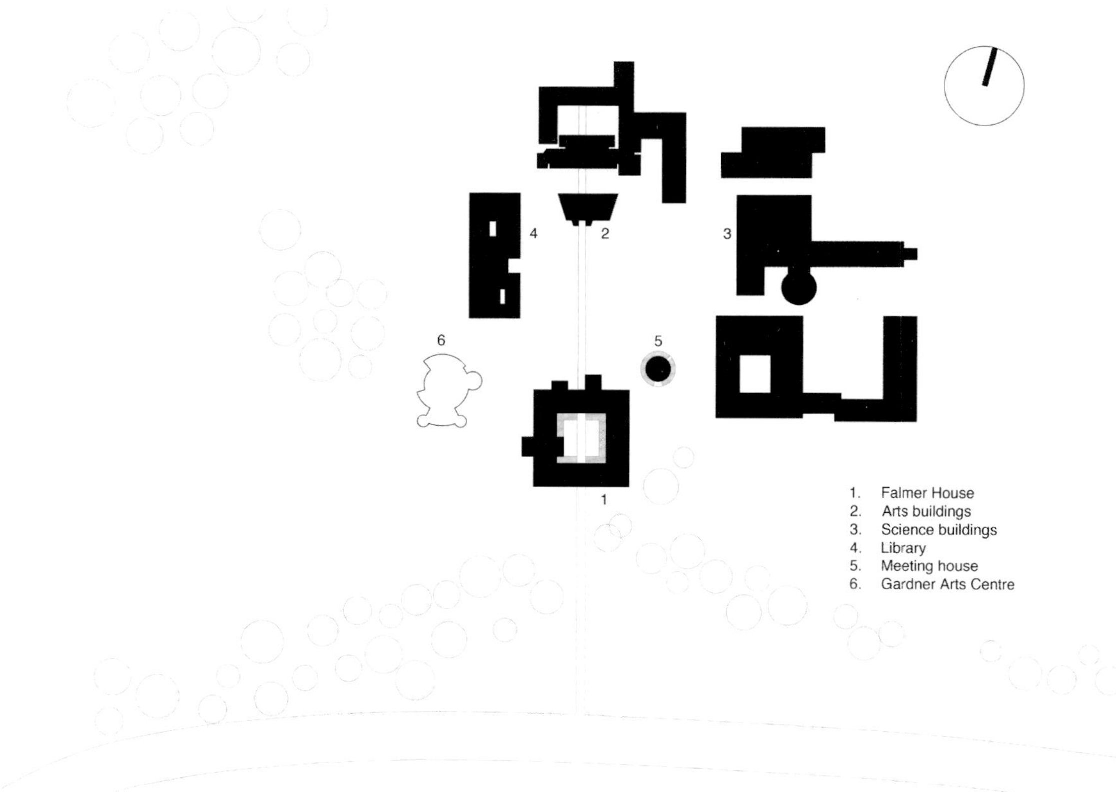

3.3 Sussex University, Science buildings

3.4 Sussex University, Science buildings

3.5 Sussex University. Masterplan, Phase 1

The historical analogies are appropriate: Maurice Howard compared the overarching idea to the Greek agora, while Spence himself cited Rome's Colosseum in its semi-ruined state with exposed vaults as the aesthetic origin of Falmer House.[12]

The area of grass and trees enclosed by these buildings was conceived as a Great Court in the Oxbridge tradition but, like the equivalent space at Churchill College (see Chapter 1), the large distances between buildings and the leaky nature of the perimeter make it feel more like an American campus. Indeed, Sussex was the first British university to describe itself as a campus.[13] And like the architects of many American universities, Spence adopted Classical references in an attempt to create an aura of history and gravitas. Further American influences can be found in the design of the Meeting House which, in its non-denominational circular plan and light-reflecting moat, owed a clear debt to Eero Saarinen's Chapel at MIT (fig.3.7). Later, the grouping of brick drums that formed the Gardner Arts Centre (now the Richard Attenborough Centre for the Creative Arts) used geometries investigated by Louis Kahn and Frank Lloyd Wright (fig.3.8).

3.6 Sussex University, Library

3.7 Sussex University, Meeting House

3.8 Sussex University, Gardner Arts Centre

Although the new universities were free to decide their organisational and teaching models individually, there were similarities in their choices. In simple terms, they opted to subsume individual departments within larger 'schools of study'. Students would join a school but might study at more than one department. The idea was to break down barriers to working across boundaries, where it was believed new and creative ideas might emerge. Sussex was the first to adopt this academic model but there was little evidence of it in the physical layout or design of the University buildings, which instead were the product of the architect's vision of architecture set in landscape. The architects of the other new universities, by comparison, made efforts to represent their academic structures in the planning of their campuses.

Essex University: Architects' Co-Partnership (1961–72)

Architects' Co-Partnership (ACP) had an approach to architecture almost diametrically divergent from that of Spence. Their ideas will be examined in more detail in Chapter 9; suffice for now to note that they adhered to the socialist-utopian principles of the 1930s and were established as a non-hierarchical co-operative of equals with 11 partners. The practice name was intended to signal a departure from 'prima donna' architecture.[14]

The Academic Planning Board for the development of Essex University was chaired by Noel Annan, the Provost of King's College Cambridge, who had also been involved in judging the competition to design Churchill College (see Chapter 1). The founding of Churchill College responded to a desire to create a British equivalent of MIT, but its very nature as social and residential accommodation, with no scientific teaching or working spaces on site, doomed that idea from the start. Annan saw Essex as a second chance. He envisaged a small number of big departments concentrating on the physical sciences and their technological applications, with an emphasis on the employability of graduates within British industry.[15] The board, chaired by Annan, appointed Albert Sloman as the first Vice-Chancellor and Kenneth Capon of ACP as the architect.[16] Annan would have seen ACP's entry for the Churchill competition, and certainly must have known them from the development plan they produced for King's College in 1961. Both these proposals included high-rise residential towers, and both were rejected as unsuitable for Cambridge. For the architects too, Essex was an opportunity to revisit ideas that had not worked out first time round.

Annan and Sloman were agreed that the science departments needed to be big because of the cost of equipment and the requirement for large research teams to produce work of international standard. However, Sloman wanted the humanities and social sciences to be equally represented to prevent the University from becoming unbalanced. As a result, they were contemplating 6,000 students rising to 10,000 or even 20,000 (other new universities were planning for 3,000 students). In 2021, Essex University recorded over 17,000 students, although these were spread over three campuses. Subjects offered appear to be overwhelmingly in the humanities and social sciences, leaving the goal of a British MIT unfulfilled.

The planning of Essex University was driven by three big ideas: size; the belief that the development of knowledge takes place in the overlaps between subjects; student freedom. There would be no Oxbridge-style colleges or civic university-style halls of residence. Students would live on site but would be housed in communal flats where they would look after themselves as independent adults.[17]

All the new universities faced a mutual dichotomy. They were envisaged as civic universities but the UGC requirement for a clear site of at least 200 acres made town centre locations impossible. They were instead located close to existing major towns, leaving university administrators and their architects to work out how to deal with that relationship. At Essex, both client and architect were keen that the University should not become a cloistered community but should be integrated with the town. Here they faced a difficulty, as the site was located two miles outside

Colchester. Their answer was to make the University itself like a small town, with some shops, restaurants and cafes forming a 'town centre' in place of the traditional students' union. They imagined that, over time, both the University and town would grow until they eventually merged and the University would become one of several social centres.[18] The town has expanded to meet the University, although the University sits very much on the edge and beyond a band of industrial estates and business parks, meaning that it remains a separate community.

The site straddled a drained river valley running east–west and the architects raised five stepped platforms on piles above the valley floor. Large, linear teaching blocks ran north–south, spanning the valley and running between the stepped platforms. These had a constant roof line and a ground line that followed the slope of the valley sides, resulting in large areas of underbuilding as they crossed the valley that were used for low-level plant rooms and deliveries (fig.3.9). A service road ran under the raised platforms, following the route of the drained riverbed. The blocks were joined at their outer ends by alternating north and south links to form a continuous snake of teaching along the valley, designed to facilitate flexibility and porous interfaces between departments. Further links spanning between teaching blocks contained social activities and together they enclosed public squares at the stepped platforms. The library was located to the east as a stand-alone building at the head of this staircase of public spaces and beyond it a lake. Fourteen-storey-high residential towers constructed of load-bearing brick radiated from the open sections of the snake loop and were to be added as necessary (fig.3.10). Six were built, four to the north and two to the south, after which the University, through loss of confidence or funding, abandoned the masterplan and resorted to low-rise housing when student numbers increased. The tower blocks provided a large amount of accommodation on a small footprint, maximising the amount of open parkland. The more recent low-rise housing takes up an area of land almost equivalent to the University teaching and social buildings. Like many of the new universities, later additions have ignored the original masterplan and diluted its clarity.

Capon wanted the layout to resemble a town centre, with shops, cafes and other commercial premises surrounding the public squares: 'I should like to see neon lights there; I should even like to see a certain amount of controlled vulgarity . . .'[19] The public spaces were similar in many ways to post-war town centres like that for Coventry (fig.3.11). It is interesting that Capon was in favour of 'controlled vulgarity' which probably meant the kind of vulgarity that he found aesthetically appealing. The students were to be treated as independent adults in the privacy of their flats, but not in public. The purity of the architecture could be sullied but only within limits.

The architectural precedent for Essex lay in Le Corbusier's convent at La Tourette, another enclosed community (fig.3.12). The design has been criticised for imposing a harsh, concrete environment on users and landscape. It has been described as not really lying *in* the valley but

3.9 Essex University

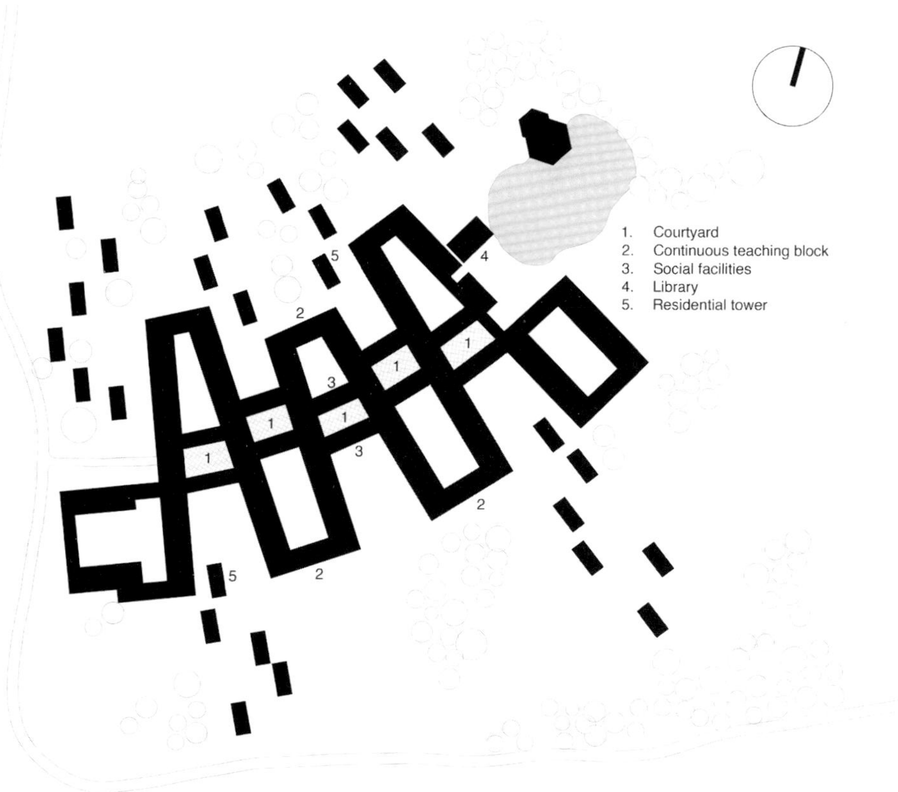

obliterating it, and for failing to connect with users at a human level.[20] That is one view; another is that it answered the brief by creating a continuous and closely integrated environment that encouraged both academic and social communication whilst allowing students independence in their residential arrangements and preserving as much open parkland as possible. In short, it tried to realise a new form of university that accommodated new ideas about higher education. In seeking to reflect the principles behind the academic strategy it was in stark contrast to the aesthetic approach adopted by Spence at Sussex.

Both Sussex and Essex illustrated the dichotomy faced by the new universities when attempting to create a civic university within a rural setting. At Sussex, Spence attempted to create a sense of community through imagery borrowed from the Greek *polis* and Roman *civitas*, while the University tried to link itself with Brighton by deliberately omitting student residences so that students would commute from town. As student numbers grew Brighton could no longer contain them and the University was forced to build residences on site. The original strategy may have created links with Brighton but had resulted in a campus that was deserted at evenings and weekends.[21] Determined to avoid that situation at Essex, client and architect tried to create a small, self-contained town. The problem is that the University could never include the range of facilities to be found in a town. The variety, vibrancy and delight to be found in towns is something that grows organically and incrementally from the ideas, needs and competing interests of many individuals. It is difficult to recreate that in a single-authored plan,

3.10 Essex University. Masterplan

3.11 Essex University. One of the public squares

3.12 Essex University, Continuous teaching block

and that was probably in Capon's mind when he encouraged the introduction of 'controlled vulgarity'.

Lancaster University: Shepheard and Epstein (1963–8)

Lancaster also tried to create a self-contained 'town' but there the architects took a less prescriptive approach. Shepheard and Epstein were appointed to produce a masterplan for the new University where individual buildings would be designed by them and five other practices. The basis of the masterplan was a pedestrian spine that ran the length of the campus, weaving through one major and several minor public squares and between residential, social and teaching buildings (fig.3.13).

> The Spine is to be continuously flanked from end to end with public rooms, lively and inviting places lit up at night, which the students will go there to mix [*sic*]. These rooms will be more like the lively high street of a small town than part of a secluded campus . . . the first aim is to prevent the emergence of a 'nine to five' university.[22]

Having established the central spine, Shepheard and Epstein set up a grid for the development of ribs that ran off both sides of the spine at right angles. The grid consisted of building zones 35ft (10.7m) wide and public spaces 100ft (30.5m) wide.[23] Within the controlling grid, the University could grow away from the central spine in a natural and incremental fashion (fig.3.15). Like Essex, there was no students' union; the pedestrian street provided for social life. Unlike Essex, students were housed in colleges, which followed the traditional Oxbridge courtyard layout and were interspersed with teaching buildings and social facilities along the length of the street in a way that, of all the new universities, most resembled a town, albeit a new, planned town (fig.3.14). A consequence of this approach is than Lancaster has dealt with expansion more gracefully that some of the other new universities when it needed to add large

3.13 Lancaster University. South end of spine looking North
3.14 Lancaster University. The spine

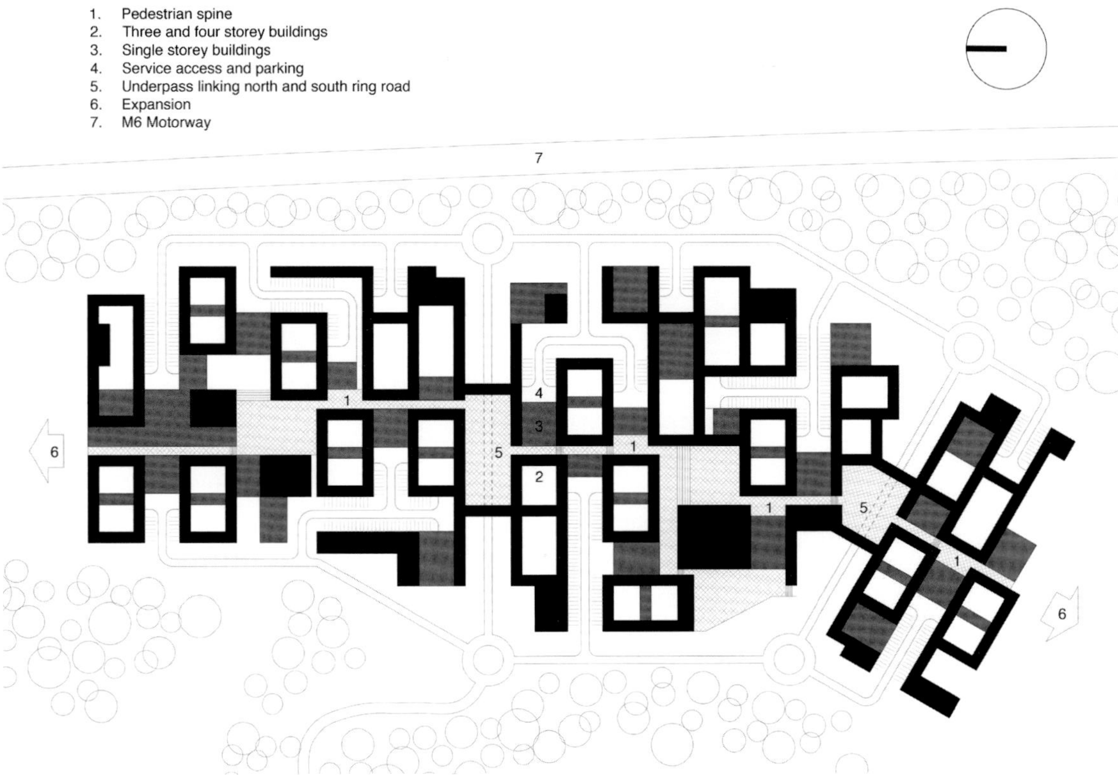

numbers of student residences that broke away from the original concept. At Lancaster, these have grown naturally on the periphery, like housing on the edge of town. Those universities conceived as powerful architectural statements have suffered when expansion has strayed from the masterplan, the original part of the campus looking like a marooned relic of the Sixties or, one could argue, like an island of purpose and rationality surrounded by a sea of expediency and mediocrity.

The aesthetic adopted at Lancaster was that of brick and exposed concrete slab edges handed down from Le Corbusier's Maisons Jaoul through Stirling and Gowan's Ham Common to Spence's Erasmus Building and many other buildings of that period (fig.3.16). At Lancaster, it was used to create a horizontal composition, three storeys high, above which Shepheard and Epstein introduced, and encouraged other architects working on the site to introduce, set-back extrusions in 'unusual shapes' and coloured white to contrast with the brickwork below.[24] These housed lift towers, water tanks, plant rooms and other ancillary accommodations and were intended to create a more interesting skyline, perhaps in an attempt to recall the spires of the ancient universities (fig.3.17).

3.15 Lancaster University. Masterplan

University of East Anglia: Denys Lasdun (1962–8)

The University of East Anglia (UEA) was the first of the new universities to attempt an 'urban' solution, followed by Essex, Lancaster and Warwick. The architect was Denys Lasdun, who was appointed when Sir Leslie Martin declined.[25] The educational model was the same as the other new universities where subjects were grouped in broad schools of study to encourage cross-fertilisation of ideas across disciplines. The organisational model was a mixture of the 'federal' – which meant the traditional Oxbridge system where educational, social and cultural activities were grouped together in colleges – and the 'unitary', where halls of residence

3.16 Lancaster University, Alexandra Square. The main square located at the midpoint of the spine

were separate components used primarily for sleeping.[26] The schools were to foster a social as well as academic community, a kind of non-residential college, the focus for many student activities and a sense of belonging.[27]

The site sat in a bend of the River Yare, which was used to form a lake along its southern edge. Extending north from the lake was flat meadowland which rose gently before levelling out again. Lasdun's masterplan ran an access road along the contour at the top of the slope. Immediately to the south of the road he placed two, 1500ft (460 m)-long teaching blocks running parallel to each other with a gap between them and cranked to follow the contour lines. At five storeys high, these formed what Lasdun called

3.17 Lancaster University. A typical courtyard set off to the side of the spine

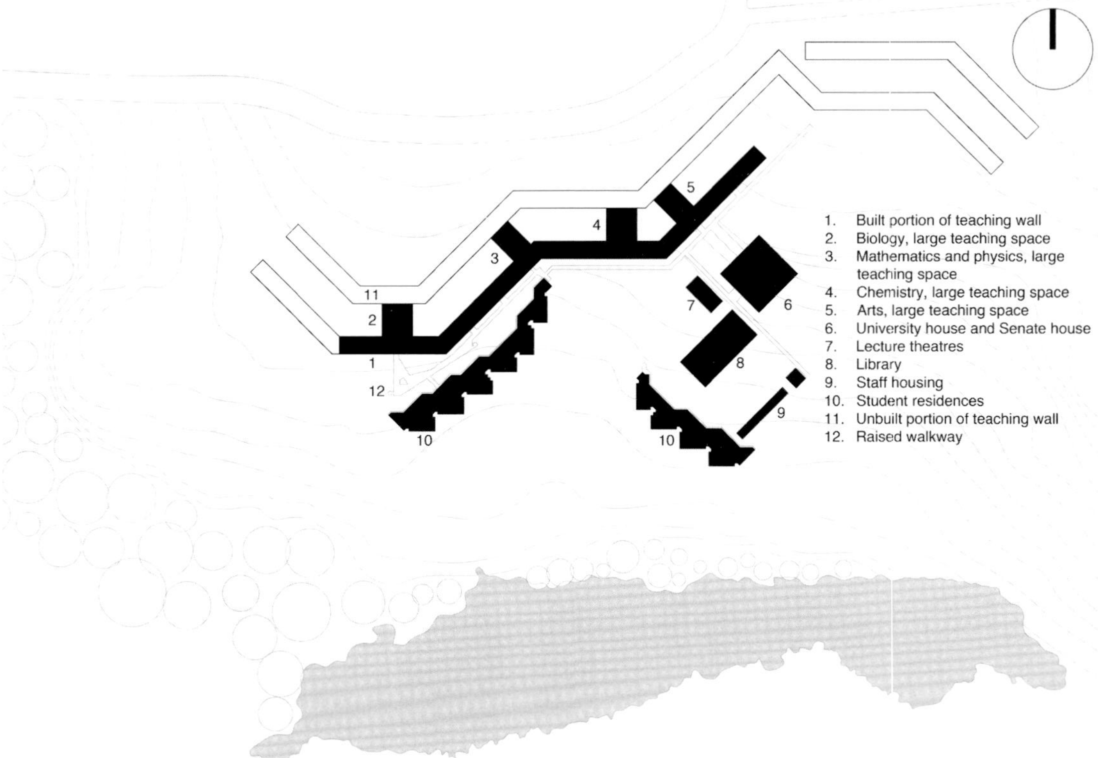

a 'teaching wall' along the northern edge of the site. Each block allowed flexible provision of small and medium-sized rooms for general-purpose teaching by any of the schools of study. Larger spaces, like lecture theatres or laboratories, were to span the gap between the two blocks and could be specific to individual schools. To the south of the teaching blocks he ran a freestanding, high-level walkway that connected to the southern block via intermittent bridges leading to entry points at mid-level (fig.3.18).

On its south side, the walkway fed the rear of a series of residential blocks, strung along its length like beads on a necklace and stepped down the slope in V-shaped ziggurat formations (fig.3.19). These had seven levels of accommodation and the walkway connected at level six, from where long, straight stairs cascaded down through the levels, which stepped in concert with the slope of the land. Below the raised walkway, a service road fed the rear of the residences at level three. The residences could be accessed from either the walkway or the road, negating the need for lifts, as students had only to walk up or down a couple of flights to reach their rooms. Although student accommodation did not follow the Oxbridge college model, it did borrow the idea of the staircase as a social group. Rooms were placed in groups of 12 around a common staircase, sharing washrooms and a kitchen/breakfast room. Other eating and social facilities were provided in one centralised building serving the entire University.[28] The walkway was to act as a 'main street' connecting teaching and living spaces and the 'town centre', a collection of communal buildings at the east end of the masterplan that included the library, main lecture theatre and the social and dining hub. All of this was envisaged as a compact

3.18 University of East Anglia. Masterplan

continuum of teaching, living and social spaces forming an urban landscape that would emerge, like a rocky escarpment, from the rolling green natural landscape.

The raised walkway was a logical solution that provided a common and clearly identifiable means of moving around the site, emphasising a feeling of community, encouraging chance encounters (both social and academic), separating pedestrians from vehicles and reducing the need for lifts within buildings . . . but it was not a street. It did not provide continuous access to the buildings that lined it; in other words, it lacked a multitude of front doors outside which chance encounters might take place and where people might linger. There were no social facilities along its length and so there was no street life (fig.3.20). It was a means of getting to a destination, not a destination in itself. Other new universities that wished to create an urban community took note, most notably at Lancaster.

Those shortcomings should be set against the fact that Lasdun was attempting to create a new type of university with its own architectural language. For the plan, he promoted ideas of compactness and connectivity. For the form, he investigated ideas of architecture as urban landscape. For the aesthetic, he relied heavily on the use of concrete:

> The infinite variety of colour in the valley landscape makes the choice of external materials and colour of particular importance. Of all the suitable materials available today concrete in its natural grey state appears to enhance the colours of the landscape to greatest advantage. It is important, therefore, that there should be a predominance of this

3.19 University of East Anglia. Residences

> material with its range of neutral colours depending on whether it is precast, in situ or in the form of concrete blocks.[29]

Lasdun used all three types to varying effect: areas of concrete block were utilitarian; in-situ concrete was massive and monolithic and provided a counterpoint to the crisp, white, crystalline delicacy of the precast units used in the ziggurat residences. The Smithsons described the latter as 'possibly the only successful large-scale, post-war, industrialised, precast, reinforced concrete building complex yet built' (fig.3.21).[30]

The planning concept illustrated a clarity of thought and purpose that is still powerfully visible today. However, the plan was never completed. The northern block of the teaching wall was never built, leaving the exposed rear of the southern block, its stair towers and service spaces as the public face of the University when approached from the main access road. More teaching accommodation has been added and appears to take up roughly the same area as the northern teaching block would have done but comprises an ad hoc collection of buildings strung along both sides of the access road. Similarly, the masterplan allowed for more ziggurats to the south as student numbers increased, but instead student accommodation has been augmented by the addition of a variety of flat blocks to the east that bear the signs of having been designed under a succession of PFI (Private Finance Initiative) design-build contracts.

The Lasdun design proved expensive to build and the abandonment of the masterplan was largely due to funding issues, but it was also a result of overambition. The brief was for a university of 3,000 students, but the plan envisaged 6,000 rising to 15,000. When the anticipated growth failed to materialise, funding dried up and Lasdun left the project in 1968 with only half the plan built. Bernard Feilden, who had been associated with the project since 1962 and would later become a prominent and respected conservation architect, took over the completion of the social and dining buildings.[31] Student numbers would eventually rise to over 15,000 and, as noted above, new teaching buildings and residences were added, but too late to be included in the original vision of a unified architectural landscape that sat in counterpoint to the surrounding natural landscape. Too late because the entire conversation about higher education, its purpose and how it should be funded had changed since those optimistic and exhilarating times in the Sixties (see Chapter 5).

3.20 University of East Anglia. Raised walkway with teaching wall on left

3.21 University of East Anglia. Residences

University of Kent: Sir William Holford (1962–6)

The approach to planning adopted at the University of Kent was the opposite of that used at UEA. Where UEA was the product of a tightly controlled masterplan, Dr Geoffrey Templeman, the Vice-Chancellor at Kent, refused to have a masterplan because he believed that before it could be completed, changing circumstances would have rendered it redundant.[32] His point would seem to be borne out by the experiences of UEA and others, where circumstances led to abandonment of masterplans before they could be fully realised. Nevertheless, to start developing a large site with no organising principles seems foolhardy – and surprising for an architect like Holford, who was best known and recognised for his planning work rather than his architecture.

Holford was another of the Old Knights: knighted in 1953, he was made a life peer in 1965; Professor of Civic Design at Liverpool University, then Professor of Town Planning at University College London; President of the Royal Town Planning Institute, then President of the RIBA; member of the Royal Fine Art Commission and a Royal Academician. He was closely involved in post-war British town planning and largely responsible for drafting the Town and Country Planning Act 1947.

One result of the no-masterplan approach was to focus minds on immediate requirements. A college system was chosen, with first one college being built as a self-sufficient entity, then two, etc. In that respect, the approach was similar to that adopted at Lancaster, but Lancaster had the benefit of the 'street' as an organising armature around which the University would grow. At Kent, the colleges were scattered across the site. In the absence of a masterplan to generate the character of the University, Holford, rather like Spence at Sussex, relied on the architecture to create an atmosphere. And, like Spence, he chose a romantic vision of the past. The initial colleges sat like massive fortifications on a hilltop, reminiscent of a medieval town or castle, an impression that would have been heightened if a proposal to link them with a wall had been realised.

Holford resigned from the project in 1966, with five major buildings completed. It had always been intended that a number of architects would work on individual buildings and William Henderson of Farmer and Dark chose to infill some areas between existing buildings, creating a denser plan and closing off panoramic views in favour of more intermittent, framed views of the surrounding countryside and nearby Canterbury with its cathedral.[33] Like other new universities, a combination of rapidly increasing student numbers and funding restrictions led to the construction of low-rise, low-cost student housing on the site, frustrating the initial concept of expansion through the addition of self-contained college communities. In the end, 'refusing to have a masterplan is not much of a consolation when the squeeze comes'.[34]

York University: Robert Matthew, Johnson-Marshall and Partners (1962–5)

> Among the products of the academic boom of the 1960s, York has proved one of the happiest . . . nowhere else did concentrated thought about what a university ought to be like in a modern democracy come so close to finding integrated physical expression.[35]

Sir Robert Matthew's career followed a similar trajectory to that of Holford and Martin: Chief Architect and Planning Officer at the Department of Health for Scotland, then Chief Architect and Planning Officer at the LCC (where he was succeeded by Martin); President of the RIBA, the Commonwealth Association of Architects and the International Union of Architects; he was awarded an OBE in 1952 and knighted in 1962. Like Martin, he left the public sector to take up an academic post as Professor of Architecture at Edinburgh University, a role that he combined with private practice. But Matthew was not directly involved in the planning or design of York University; it was his partner, Stirrat Johnson-Marshall, who took the lead.

Johnson-Marshall had also come from a career in public service, most notably at Hertfordshire County Council and later the Ministry of Education.

In both roles he was instrumental in developing the successful post-war schools-building programme in England. He favoured a collaborative approach to design, research and development that conceived of buildings 'not as individual, sufficient entities but as items in a concerted programme of production [rather than] the intellectual and artistic property of individual architects working in isolation'.[36] In 1956, Johnson-Marshall left the Ministry of Education to join Matthew in forming Robert Matthew Johnson-Marshall (later RMJMP), with the intention of developing the work begun in the public sector 'in directions which local authority offices were too preoccupied and cumbersome to consider'.[37] The practice went on to design four new universities: York, Bath, Stirling and Ulster.

The site at York was marshland, and it was Johnson-Marshall who suggested flooding part of it to create a lake that would unify the layout. Several architects were under consideration, but that remark, made to John West-Taylor of the University Promotion Committee during a visit to view the site, was described as clinching the job for RMJMP.[38] The fact that Johnson-Marshall was a long-standing friend of West-Taylor may also have helped.

RMJMP was originally required to produce only a development plan for the first ten years of the new University, but not to design it (see Chapter 6). Johnson-Marshall asked Andrew Derbyshire to join him from the Sheffield City Architect's Department to work on the plan. The two already knew each other through Derbyshire's work at the Building Research Station and on local authority housing and schools.

York was the first of the new universities to be based on the Oxbridge collegiate model: communities of just under 400 male and female undergraduates, graduates and staff that represented a cross-section of the University. The figure of 400 was arrived at by a combination of practical and social constraints, being the most economic size for kitchen provision and also the greatest number of people that can comfortably get to know one another in the space of a year or two.[39] All students and staff belonged to a college, even those living off-campus. Colleges consisted of blocks of study-bedrooms and tutorial rooms for all subjects except those that required major laboratories or workshops.[40] Unlike the Oxbridge model, however, colleges were not financially or organisationally autonomous and the layout and architecture were quite different, illustrating that a college does not necessarily imply a courtyard (see Colin Rowe's criticism of Churchill College in Chapter 1). Buildings were placed in a carefully designed landscape, creating a pleasant and relaxing campus (fig.3.1).

Based on everything he had done in the Hertfordshire County Council schools programme and at the Department of Education, Johnson-Marshall was convinced of the advantages of prefabricated construction systems and proposed this approach at York. He had to convince others, including his colleague Derbyshire, but in the end a combination of labour shortages, poor ground conditions and a need for speed led to the adoption of the CLASP system initially developed by a consortium of local authorities for school buildings. The acronym stands for Consortium of Local Authorities' Special Programme, and it epitomises the research-based, collaborative working methods that Johnson-Marshall championed his whole career. CLASP was used for the colleges and many of the smaller buildings (fig.3.22), but not for major stand-alone buildings like the library and hall (fig.3.23). As in the schools building programme, prefabrication was not promoted as being cheaper *per se*; rather the architects argued that it offered better value through greater predictability, speed, and better and more flexible accommodation for a given sum of money.

The time spent on creating a rigorous development plan, combined with a rational approach to design and budgeting, was vindicated and no building in the first ten years suffered a cost or programme overrun, whilst other new universities were beset by both these problems.[41]

Of all the university buildings of the Sixties, those constructed at York using the CLASP system perhaps came closest to the modernist aspiration to create an ego-free, rational, democratic architecture that utilised industrial means

3.22 York University, James College

3.23 York University, Central Hall

of production. The overall effect is of quietly considered buildings of human scale sitting in a pleasant, man-made landscape.

Stirling University: Robert Matthew, Johnson-Marshall and Partners (1968–74)

If York can be described as quiet buildings sitting in a pleasant, man-made landscape, Stirling University consists of quiet buildings set against a backdrop of magnificent natural landscape (fig.3.25). However, where York grew out of the application of a set of principles and research developed over a long period of time, Stirling appears to have relied more on the inspiration of precedents, and the precedents are very clear. First is Lasdun's plan at UEA. Like it, Stirling is focused on a lake, has a continuous 'teaching wall' consisting of two, parallel, cranked blocks with links running between them, a high-level walkway that connects the teaching blocks to a core of communal buildings and separate student residences (fig.3.24). Those residences, in the way they cascade down the slope and in their plan form, owe something to James Stirling's residences at St Andrews University (see Chapter 11).

The similarities with Lasdun's design at UEA are so striking that it is worth examining the differences. Probably the most significant difference lay in the two parallel teaching blocks being built simultaneously and at a rate that matched demand. Both would grow in length as the need arose. By contrast, at UEA the southern teaching block was built first in order to provide enough length to link the residences and the communal buildings in one continuous, urban form. When demand did not grow as quickly as anticipated

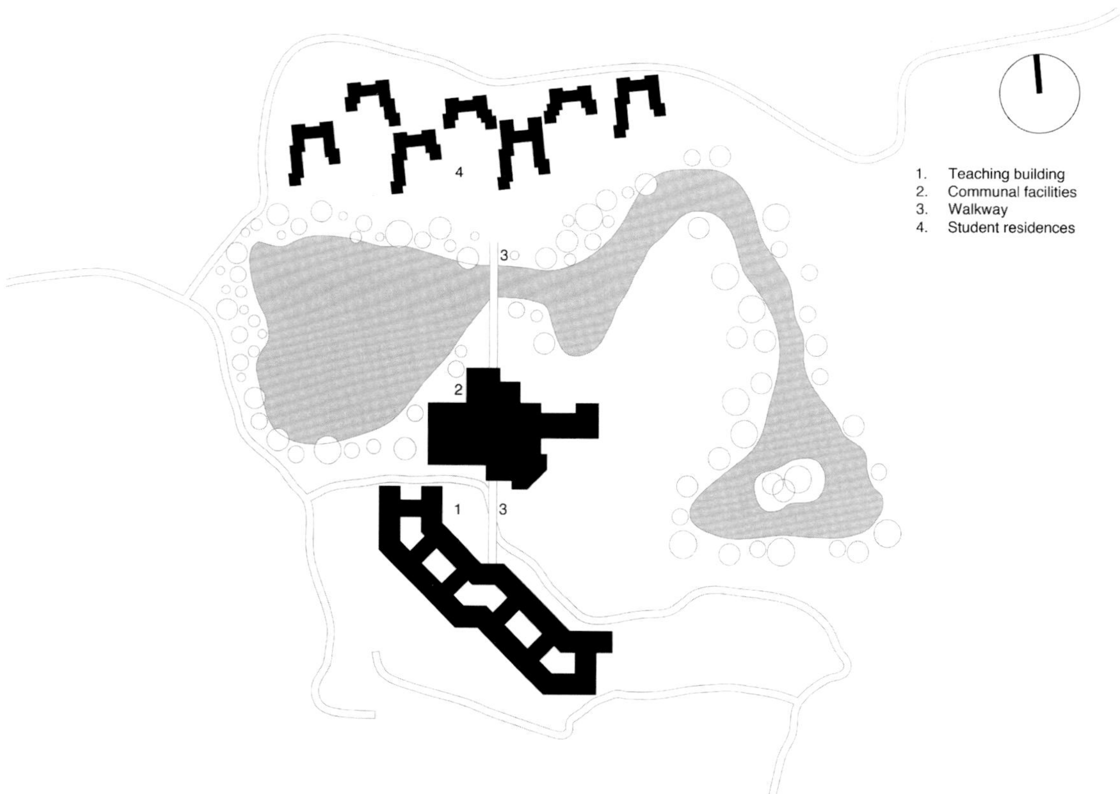

3.24 Stirling University. Masterplan

and funding dried up, the northern block was never constructed, leaving the concept only half realised.

The second major difference is related to the first. Where Lasdun was intent on achieving a compact, continuous, urban massing that would sit in contrast to the rural landscape, RMJMP were content to disperse the different elements of their design and allow them to sit into the landscape. Paradoxically, whilst a major design driver for Lasdun was the creation of strata (see Chapter 7), RMJMP's more relaxed approach has resulted in a clear, if different, definition of strata that precisely reflects the experience of visiting Stirling University: water, building, hills.

3.25 Stirling University. Water, building, hills

Warwick University: Yorke, Rosenberg and Mardall (1963–70)

Warwick University had an untidy start. An initial masterplan prepared by the Chief Architect to Coventry City Council, Arthur Ling, in association with Alan Goodman, was abandoned for being overambitious and requiring too large a share of available government funding. The UGC recommendation was to plan for 3,000 students in the first ten years. Warwick was not the only new university to think bigger, but it overshot spectacularly with plans for a university town of 20,000. In some ways the plan prepared by Goodman and Ling was similar to that at Essex University, a compact urban form in which study, living and socialising were interwoven in a multi-level complex that vertically separated pedestrians and vehicles.[42] A new plan was prepared by Yorke, Rosenberg and Mardall (YRM). It also envisaged a future student population of 20,000 but could be achieved in a more incremental fashion.[43] Like other new universities, Warwick eventually reached those numbers (in 2023 it claimed over 29,000 students) but long after the masterplan had been abandoned and the funding system and assumed role of universities had been transformed.

F.R.S. Yorke had been a prominent modernist in Britain in the 1930s, Eugene Rosenberg was born in what is now Slovakia and came to Britain in 1939 via a stint working for Le Corbusier, and Cyril Mardall was born in Finland. The three met through their membership of the Modern Architectural Research group (MARS) and formed a partnership in 1944. MARS was formed as a British offshoot of CIAM (the Congrès Internationaux d'Architecture Moderne) which attracted all the leading international modernists. It was openly elitist and exclusive; those not considered modern enough or eminent enough by the executive committee were excluded.[44]

It is clear from their backgrounds that YRM were modernists of the old school. Their masterplan consisted of grids within grids: a rectilinear grid of wide roads containing rectangular buildings where an expressed structural grid was infilled with glazing and clad in a grid of white tiles emphasised by the use of black joints (fig.3.26). Within the road grid, buildings were zoned by function: teaching, living, administration, leisure. Both the organisation and the architecture were the antitheses of York University, where self-sufficient college communities were informally distributed amongst naturalistic landscape and where mechanised production techniques were harnessed to create a humane environment. It is one of the paradoxes of early modernism that buildings which looked 'machine-like', or as if they were the product of a logical, mechanical process, were built using traditional, labour-intensive techniques – at Warwick, the use of in-situ reinforced concrete and hand-applied tiles.

YRM resigned from the project in 1970 with only one of the intended roads in place, a broad avenue that runs between a long block of science and engineering departments on one side and the university library on the other (fig.3.27). Other buildings completed by YRM were a humanities block and two halls of residence that between them housed over 1,000 students.[45] With only a fragment of the masterplan realised, it fell to other architects to design the campus as student numbers increased, including Shepheard and Epstein, who designed Lancaster University. The result is piecemeal, as it is at other new universities where an ambitious masterplan could not be realised within the time and funding available before the situation for higher education in Britain changed.

Almost like a light dessert after the heavy main course of modernism served up by YRM at the main campus, there came a separate group of small houses clustered round a village green designed by Howard Killick Partridge and Amis (HKPA).

In keeping with the ethos of the new universities, Warwick was organised in broad schools of study and ten professors were given the freedom to determine the academic structure of the University and to commission their own buildings. The mathematician Christopher Zeeman was invited to build a research-focused maths department. Previous institutions where Zeeman had worked had provided on-campus housing for researchers, and he was convinced of the success of this model. In 1966, he commissioned HKPA to design housing for visiting mathematicians and their families.[46] The architects proposed a 'think village', a group of small, detached, brick houses set in a circle around a 'village green' and sitting behind a screen wall (fig.3.28). Like rooms opening off a hall, the front doors to the houses pierced the screen, linking each family to the communal green whilst retaining their privacy (fig.3.29). Each house had a study in a linked but discrete annexe. The studies were top-lit and designed with curved corners to enable a continuous blackboard to run round the interior without the interruption that right-angled corners would have caused (fig.3.30). The curved-corner motif was extended to the main house and was a stylistic choice that HKPA had employed on other projects.

The stark, mechanical, black and white graph paper of YRM and the rustic, hand-made curves of HKPA mark the opposites in the range of solutions that architects brought to the questions raised by the new universities. Asa Briggs said that the new universities were given the freedom to develop on their own lines. In fact, the academics chose similar routes; it was their architects who took the opportunity to explore divergent lines of enquiry into what modern architecture meant in post-war Britain.

3.26 Warwick University

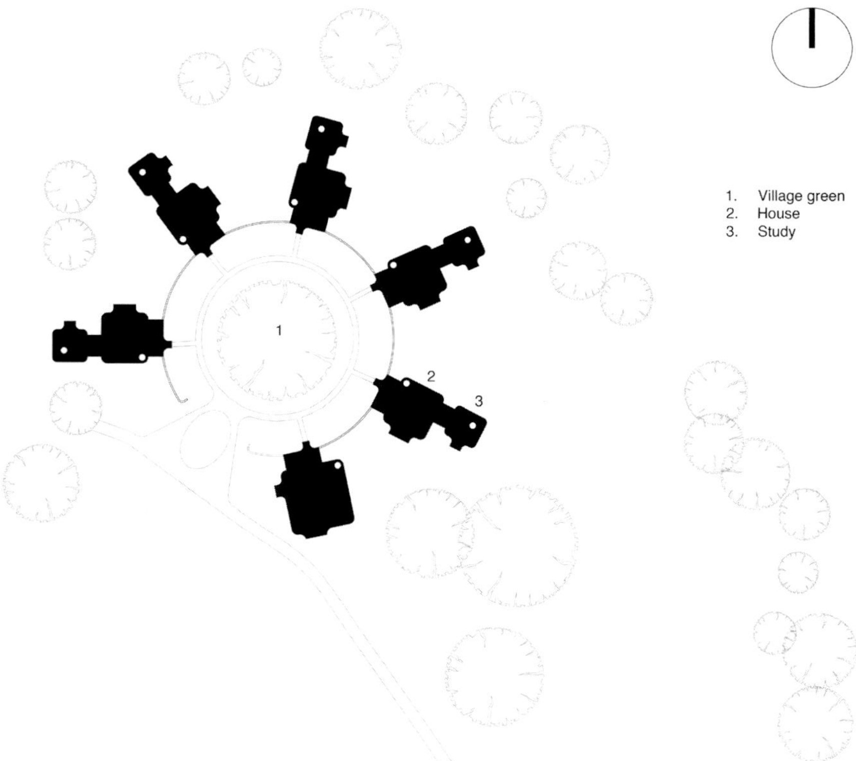

3.27 Warwick University, Library

3.28 Warwick University, Mathematics Research Centre (MRC) houses. Site plan

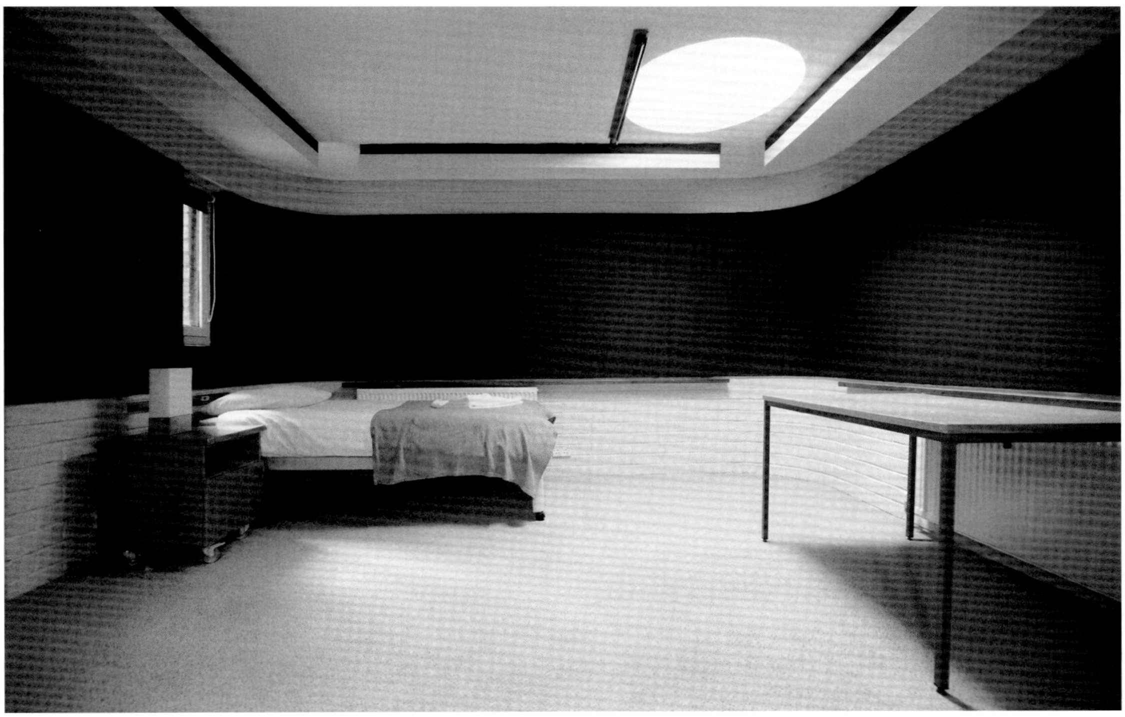

3.29 Warwick University, MRC houses

3.30 Warwick University, MRC houses. Interior of study (here used as a guest bedroom)

4 The New Colleges

The design of Churchill College, Cambridge carried the burden of expectations for both the creation of a British MIT and a monument to a national hero. It also offered an opportunity for competitors to display their ideas about the directions that modern architecture in Britain might take. These circumstances coloured its ability to address fundamental questions regarding the appropriate form for a university college in post-war Britain. However, Churchill was closely followed by other new colleges which were not so encumbered and were thus freer to consider those primary issues.

Fitzwilliam College, Cambridge: Denys Lasdun (1961–3 and 1966–7)

Fitzwilliam College occupies a site just to the north of Churchill College. The design featured a courtyard layout where residential accommodation surrounded a core of social and communal buildings such as the hall and library. Lasdun referred to these two elements as 'buildings that enclose space' and 'buildings that stand in space'.[1] This arrangement differed from the traditional Oxbridge model where, for the most part, residential and communal buildings sat side by side to enclose a central court. They were all 'buildings that enclose space' and their architects were not driven by any aspiration to express function through form.

Like Casson and Conder at the Sidgwick site (see Chapter 2), Lasdun was working to UGC space standards and cost limits. He adopted a similar palette of exposed concrete floor slabs forming horizontal bands between panels of brown facing brick. Where Casson used detailing to deliver a picturesque result, Lasdun's elevations were resolutely primeval in their Stonehenge-like arrangement of vertical brick panels supporting horizontal concrete slabs (fig.4.2). Openings were simply the spaces left between panels. In its expression of basic, load-bearing elements, simply assembled, it followed Le Corbusier's lead at the Maisons Jaoul, but as if to emphasise the elemental nature of the construction, Lasdun offset the brick panels on each floor so that they do not align vertically. He also varied the width of brick panels and the openings that separate them in the kind of 'barcode' pattern that became popular in the early 21st century. The logic behind this last move is questionable, except that it heightened

4.1 St Catherine's College, Oxford

an impression of naturally formed cave dwellings that Lasdun called a 'three storey inhabited wall', echoing his idea of a 'teaching wall' at the University of East Anglia (see Chapter 3). The result was not universally liked, being described in one review as 'a worrying design, tossed off in a perverse moment by an architect who, at his best and with a big budget, is equal to any of the world's grand masters'.[2] That view is reinforced by the fact that Lasdun produced an identical solution in his contemporaneous design for Stamford Hall student residences at Leicester University: shown an elevation of each, removed from its context, one would be hard pressed to tell the difference. Equally similar is RMJMP's design for the Local Examinations Board in Cambridge, produced at the same time (fig.4.3). It is an aesthetic that seems to have been adopted by several architects at that time, although Lasdun's examples are probably the strongest architecturally.

When a new phase of student accommodation was designed by MacCormac Jamieson Prichard (MJP) in 1985, the architects retreated to the kind of picturesque handling of windows and detailing employed by Casson and Conder at Sidgwick some 30 years earlier, an indication of a general move away from modernism to 'post-modernism' that had begun in the 1970s and came to full flower in the Thatcherite, free-market 1980s.

A further deviation was in MJP's handling of the masterplan. Lasdun's original plan had envisaged a theoretically infinite expansion of residences in a square spiral reminiscent of Le Corbusier's concept for a Museum of Unlimited Growth (fig.4.4). The idea was more abstract than realistic as there was no land available for unlimited expansion, so MJP's decision to revert to a more traditional courtyard plan made little practical difference.

The focal point of Lasdun's design was the hall which, curiously, he buried in the middle of a group of other communal buildings that shared the same architectural vocabulary as the residences. Lacking external walls, the hall needed to be top-lit and it announced its presence through a storey-high lantern that rose above the surrounding buildings

4.2 Fitzwilliam College, Cambridge. Student residences
4.3 Local Examinations Board, Cambridge

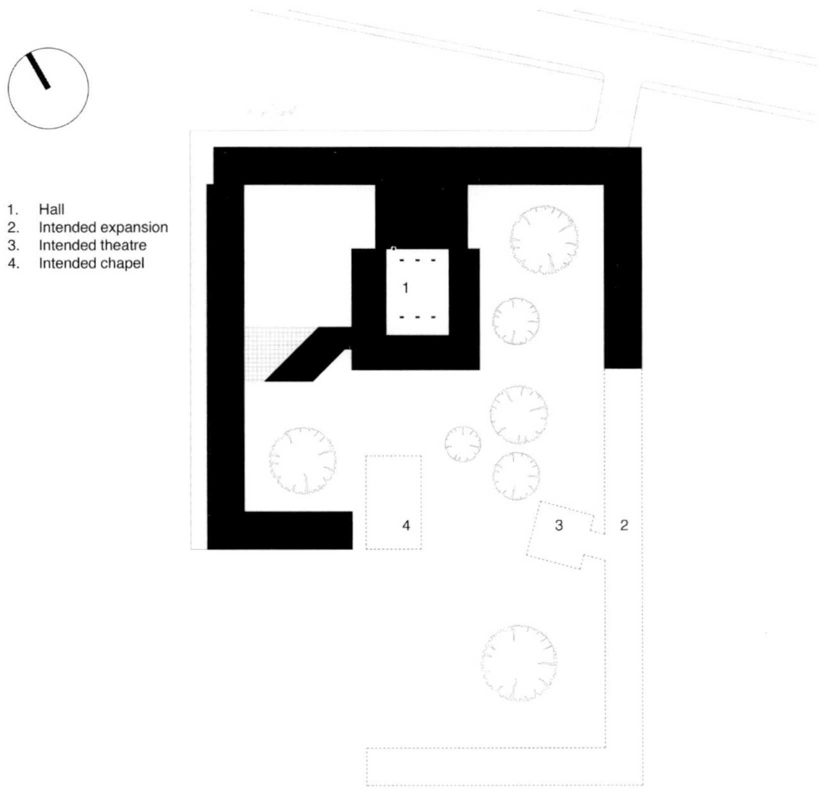

and was expressed as a series of Gothic-style vaults that were only facade deep (fig.4.5). The roof behind them was flat and supported on a diagonal lattice of concrete beams (fig.4.6). Had the full height of the hall been visible and the Gothic arches continued to the ground, it would have sat like a jewel in the centre of an otherwise restrained composition, its fine, sophisticated structure in contrast to the robust simplicity of the surrounding residences. As it is, it looks a bit like a wedding cake perched on top of a brick base, a piece of 'sheer pastry-cookery'.[3] Nonetheless, the interior of the hall is a genuinely impressive and uplifting space, partly due to its height and partly due to the ecclesiastical overtones of the glazed, Gothic arches that flood it with light, a further reference to the monastic origins of the ancient universities, perhaps (fig.4.7).

4.4 Fitzwilliam College, Cambridge. Masterplan

4.5 Fitzwilliam College, Cambridge. The lantern of the hall rising above its surrounding buildings

4.6 Fitzwilliam College, Cambridge. The roof of the hall

Lasdun talked of the Modern Movement, not as a style but as a process that demanded reason and research in order to produce sane and purposeful architecture.[4] It is difficult to reconcile that with some of his choices at Fitzwilliam College, which seem to have been driven by another of his beliefs, that 'it is no use hoping that architecture can be made into a wholly intellectual pursuit, the essence will always escape the intellect'.[5] However we interpret his motivation, Lasdun's preoccupations at Fitzwilliam appear to have been intellectually and stylistically architectural, with little thought given to changing the social arrangements of the traditional college model.

New Hall, Cambridge: Chamberlin, Powell and Bon (1958–66)

New Hall (now Murray Edwards College) was first proposed as a women's college in 1948 and formally recognised in 1952. It was part of an initiative to improve the ratio of female students at Cambridge (1:11 compared with 1:6 at Oxford and 1:4 nationally).[6] A site was secured immediately to the east of Fitzwilliam College and Chamberlin, Powell and Bon (CPB) were appointed as architects in 1958.

Peter Chamberlin, Geoffry Powell and Christoph Bon were around six years younger than Lasdun but essentially of the same generation that sat between the old knights and the younger post-war architects. They were committed modernists but, like Spence, had been on a journey from a lightweight architecture in the early 1950s towards something more monumental and, like Casson, were influenced by Gordon Cullen's ideas on townscape. The combination of influences meant they were infused with 'a romantic enthusiasm for the cities of Italy and the colleges of Oxford and Cambridge'.[7] They were not members of any organisations like CIAM, which had been formed by leading early European modernists, or its British arm MARS, nor of the breakaway Team 10 that had been formed by younger architects who saw the ideas of CIAM as no longer valid in a post-war context.

4.7 Fitzwilliam College, Cambridge. Interior of the hall

CPB's entry to the Churchill College competition proposed that Churchill, Fitzwilliam and New Hall be linked to create a new urban precinct to the west of the River Cam. When they failed to win the competition but were appointed to design New Hall, they resurrected the idea. Once again it was rejected and the three colleges developed as separate and unconnected entities. Having failed in their bid to create an urban district connecting the colleges, they sought to design an urban space within New Hall.

A first design was rejected as too simple and unglamorous for 'new women'.[8] The revised design followed the Oxbridge courtyard model: two adjacent courts slid past one another, a large court for residential accommodation and a smaller one for communal facilities. Where they touched, they shared a cloistered spine that started at the porters' lodge and ran through the centre of the College (fig.4.8). The larger court was a straightforward arrangement of student rooms surrounding a landscaped garden (fig.4.9). The smaller court was a sunken space with the library at one end facing the hall at the other in a formal arrangement whose inspiration could have come from an Italian piazza or a Moorish garden. Dominating the composition was a large, segmented dome over the hall, which might evoke either church or mosque. However, the four stair towers that surrounded it, whilst probably informed by Le Corbusier's Chapelle Notre-Dame-du-Haut at Ronchamp, lent it a distinctly Islamic appearance, which was reinforced by the reflecting water pools within the courtyard (fig.4.10). Several commentators perceived an Eastern influence in the 'snow-white dome and attendant minarets . . .'[9] Others felt that the monumentality

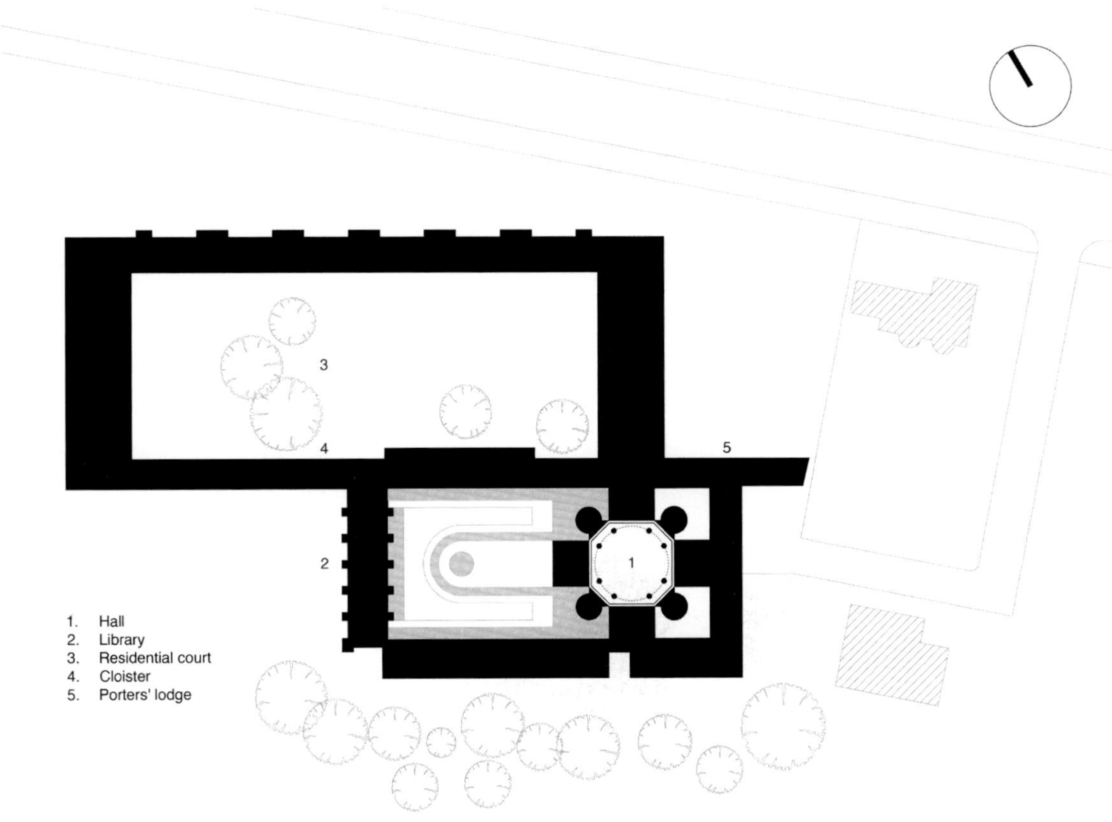

4.8 New Hall, Cambridge. Site plan

4.9 New Hall, Cambridge. Residences and garden
4.10 New Hall, Cambridge. Communal courtyard with hall at the far end

of the design was inappropriate, a criticism that Elain Harwood suggested 'combined presumptions about femininity with concerns that such an impecunious foundation was acting irresponsibly in commissioning so imperious a building'. The writer P.D. James likened the arched formality of the library interior and the petal-like dome of the dining hall to a harem (fig.4.11).[10] Meanwhile the locals christened the dome 'the Great Tit'.

Whether criticising the architecture for not being 'feminine' enough or for imposing a male view on what a building housing women should look like, or engaging in sexist nicknaming, it is apparent that the idea of a women's college that taught more than secretarial or nursing skills was still a puzzling concept, even in 1966, at the height of the alleged social revolution. Those attitudes would not be surprising to social historians who argue that the arrival of a more open and equal society in the 1960s was largely a political construction that came from the top down, rather than growing by popular consent.[11] A survey of 1,000 adults published in *New Society* in 1969, asking people what changes they most disliked, revealed a pattern of opposition to easier laws for homosexuality, divorce, abortion and immigration for 'coloured people'.[12] The legalisation of abortion and the introduction of the pill, whilst marking important new freedoms for women, suggest a view of women's rights that focused on matters concerning reproduction rather than career opportunities.

Leaving aside questions of the appropriateness of New Hall's design as a women's college, it was an attempt to convey an impression of substance through symmetry, monumentality, historical forms and material choices. The architects wanted a monolithic appearance and had originally proposed concrete throughout. However, like Lasdun at Fitzwilliam, they were constrained by UGC budgets, although supplemented by grants from the Wolfson and Nuffield Foundations. They substituted a combination of exposed concrete frame, facing-brick infill and brick cross-wall construction. To maintain a monolithic appearance, they chose white Sevenoaks brick to blend as closely as possible with the concrete frame. The segmented dome over the hall was cast in thin, lightweight ferro-cement sections, employing techniques developed by Pier Luigi Nervi in Italy and previously adopted by Spence at Sussex (see Chapter 3). Like Spence, the intention was to suggest a more massive, load-bearing form.[13]

The roots of modern architecture lay in a rational analysis of function and an efficient use of material: lightweight structures and finishes that enclosed the greatest volume of space using the least amount of mass. Those principles had migrated to North America, where they were still applied, and pushed to their limits by architect-engineers like Buckminster Fuller and Matthew Nowicki. In Europe, Le Corbusier had moved to a more massive architecture that concentrated

4.11 New Hall, Cambridge. Interior of library

on form, and many British architects followed. In university design, some architects used mass, or the appearance of mass, to signify substance and combined it with Classical forms and symmetry to signify importance, suggesting that those things could not be achieved by modern architecture as it had previously been understood. Those convinced by early modernism were not in favour, Pevsner writing that 'Historic allusions are in the mid C20 always a sign of weakness, if they are not even a sign of faltering conviction.'[14]

St Catherine's College, Oxford: Arne Jacobsen (1960–64)

St Catherine's College was the first new college to be built in Oxford in the modern era. It was completed four years earlier than Churchill College, Cambridge but was not subjected to the same levels of anticipation, expectation and scrutiny. This was partly because the process started later, after all eyes were already focused on Churchill, but was also due to the nature of the process. Churchill was a competition amongst 20 leading British modern architects, all vying not only to win the competition to design the College but also to win the competition of ideas about the future direction of modern architecture in Britain.

While British architects were self-consciously trying to find a voice, St Catherine's simply chose a Dane. Arne Jacobsen was its choice, albeit after an extensive selection process based on visits to existing buildings that saw it consider 37 British architects and nine Danish.[15] Having been chosen in this way, and enjoying the full support of the client, Jacobsen did not need to compete in either of the senses mentioned above, and his relaxed confidence is evident in the result. He was appointed in 1960, the College was opened in 1962 and completed in 1964.

Jacobsen's work was in many ways typical of the Nordic modernism of the time. Little moved by Le Corbusier, his designs owed more to Mies and Gropius and exhibited a preference for understatement and integration with landscape. Where the landscape was neutral, he extended the building's organising principles out into its surroundings in order to manufacture a relationship between the two. Michael Sheridan argued that Jacobsen developed a unique synthesis of abstraction and naturalism in his 1960 design for the SAS Royal Hotel in Copenhagen, which served as a foundation for his later work, including St Catherine's College.[16]

Other qualities attributed to Danish architecture were moderation and balance, a consistently high standard of workmanship and a tradition of standardised sizes and spacing that was carried forward from timber construction into modern building techniques and materials.[17] While some British architects sought to make modern architecture more approachable by referencing recognisable Classical forms, their Nordic counterparts pursued the same goal by building on their vernacular traditions. Other Jacobsen projects from that time, such as the Gertie Wandel House of 1961, exhibited a simple, unpretentious use of brick walls and flat roofs that can be found in his design of St Catherine's (fig.4.12).

4.12 St Catherine's College, Oxford. Lecture theatre (Bernard Sunley Building)

The layout consisted of two parallel, three-storey residential blocks that ran almost the entire length of the site, defining its east and west edges. Individual communal buildings were placed on an axis running up the centre of the area between the residences in such a way as to create a series of interlinked spaces that can be read as courts without following the traditional college layout. A building housing kitchens and common rooms was set along the north edge of the site to close it off from the approach road. The entire composition was relentlessly horizontal and its symmetry was broken only by two vertical elements: a bell tower in the minor court between the auditorium and library, and a large tree in the major court between the library and dining hall (fig.4.13). The placing of the bell tower off centre followed Classical precedent, which Jacobsen balanced with the placement of the tree.

The entire site layout was controlled by a 3-metre grid, including landscaping, where a series of external 'rooms' were defined by hedges, brick walls and covered walks that continued the strong lines of the buildings (fig.4.1).[18] Meanwhile the buildings formed a refined, quiet backdrop to the human activity in those external rooms, with simple, modest material choices: concrete, brick and metal-faced panels that weathered to an attractive but unassertive, mottled, dark grey-green and copper-brown.

The plan is formal, symmetrical and strictly controlled, but the experience is relaxed and informal. This is achieved primarily by Jacobsen's choice of materials and use of landscape, but is also inherent in his planning. The intended entrance to the site, for example, is not on the main north–south axis as one would expect but sneaks in under the western residential block about one third along its length. Informal but logical, it lies on the east–west axis of the courtyard garden that sits between the dining hall and library and forms

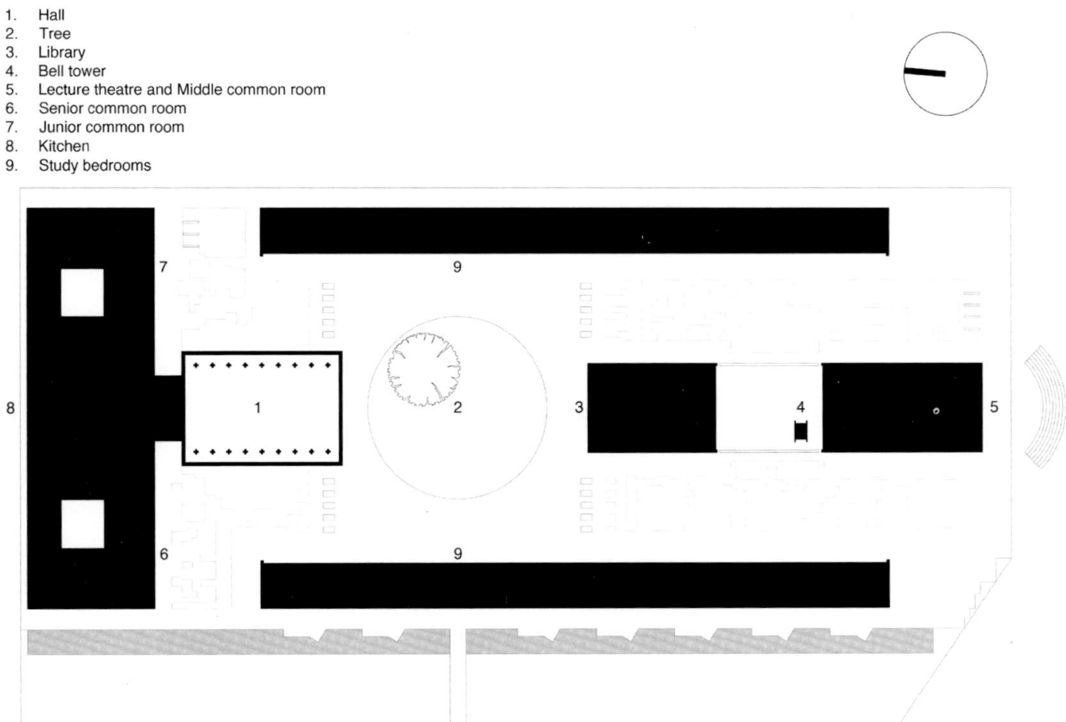

4.13 St Catherine's College, Oxford. Site plan

the focal point of the composition (fig.4.14). The site is so porous, however, that it can be accessed at several points in a democratically non-hierarchical fashion. Rational, symmetrical, controlled but also informal, non-hierarchical and democratic could describe Jacobsen's achievement here.

Geoffrey Tyack considered it the Oxford building that gave the strongest sense of a modern, secular and utilitarian university, whilst Reed and Opher declared that 'Oxford is fortunate to have such an immaculate example of classical modern architecture'.[19]

4.14 St Catherine's College, Oxford. Courtyard garden between dining hall and library, looking towards library with bell tower behind and large tree on the circular lawn

Wolfson College, Oxford: Powell and Moya (1967–74)

Originally founded in 1965 as Iffley College to provide a home for fellows without a college, Wolfson College was expanded by its first president, Isaiah Berlin, who secured funding from the Wolfson Foundation and the Ford Foundation that enabled a site to be purchased and a new college to be constructed. Like the other post-war colleges, Wolfson consisted almost entirely of residential and social facilities, in this case for graduate students and researchers as well as fellows and staff. Its function in housing older students, combined with Berlin's determination to create a modern, egalitarian college, led to a more socially enlightened policy where not only male and female students but also married students were catered for by including family housing and facilities such as a nursery.

The site lies north of the city centre, away from the urban setting of the established colleges, on the west bank of the River Cherwell, in an area that is otherwise residential and suburban. Given its situation, there was nothing to suggest that it need follow the traditional college layout, other than a particular view of how college life should be organised.

Powell and Moya's masterplan consisted of three courtyards: the Berlin Quad named after the first president (fig.4.15); the Tree Quad constructed around existing trees (fig.4.16); and the open-ended River Quad that contained a meadow running down to the river and a man-made punt basin that was formed by bringing the river into the site (fig.4.18). The original porters' lodge and entrance were located on the north side of Berlin Quad, a rectangular court that included the hall on its south side and the library on its west side, integrated in the style of a traditional Oxbridge college. From the northeast and southeast corners of Berlin Quad, two arms stretched eastward towards the river, the north arm straight, the south arm curving outwards slightly. Between them they embraced a meadow that ran down to the punt basin and the river. The north arm also formed the south side of Tree Quad, an irregular shaped courtyard that housed some communal activities and backed onto terraces of family accommodation

4.15 Wolfson College, Oxford. Berlin Quad with roof of hall ahead and library on right

to its north, where they were screened from the rest of the College (fig.4.17). Whilst the use of courtyards recalled the traditional Oxbridge model, the presence of family housing and student rooms accessed by corridors or external decks, rather than grouped in stairwells, introduced contemporary thinking about the nature of student life that was closer to life outside the University.

Powell and Moya had developed and refined an architectural language on Oxford projects stretching back as far as 1957 and their design for residences at Brasenose College (see Chapter 8). It was modern architecture constructed using a blend of contemporary materials like concrete and glass and traditional materials like stone and lead in a modern interpretation of traditional craft. Those previous projects had all been located within existing, ancient colleges. Wolfson offered an essentially greenfield site and the architects

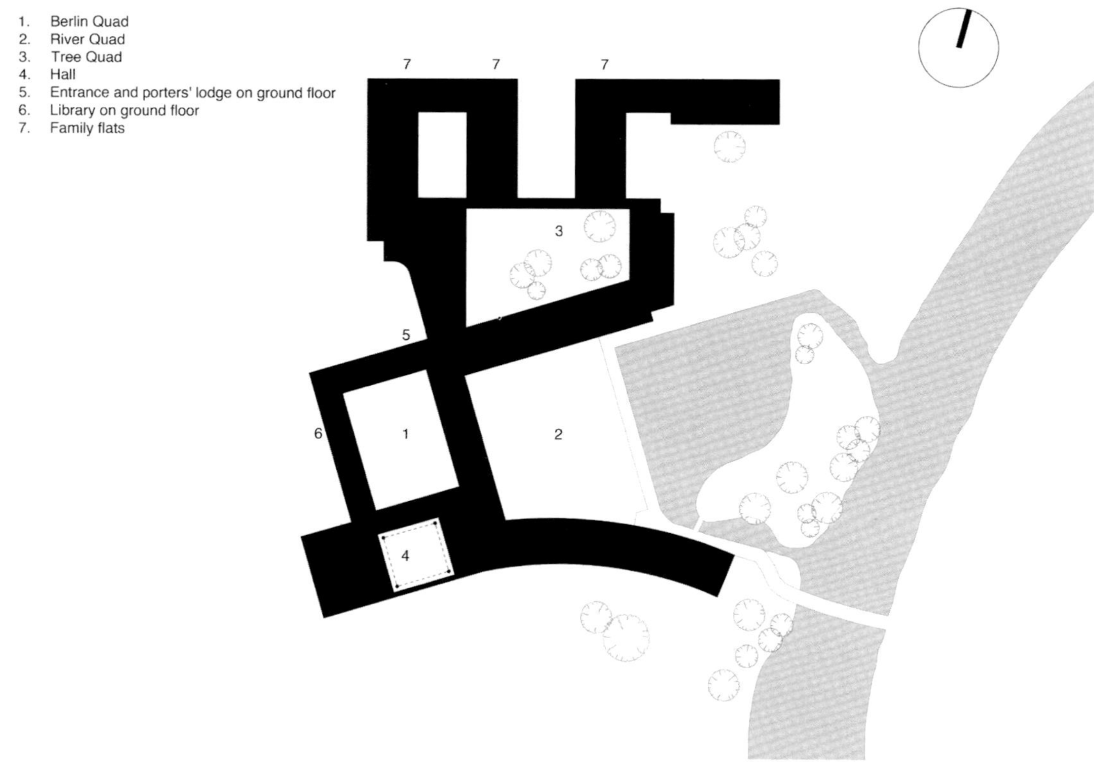

4.16 Wolfson College, Oxford. Tree Quad
4.17 Wolfson College, Oxford. Masterplan

4.18 Wolfson College, Oxford. Punt basin at the end of River Quad, looking across to curving south arm of residences

chose a more clearly modernist aesthetic of white concrete raised on circular columns – similar to Le Corbusier's white villas – sitting in a green landscape. They had used the same aesthetic on other greenfield sites for different building types, such as hospitals, suggesting that their choice of materials was influenced more by the site's immediate surroundings than the function of the building.

Darwin College, Cambridge: Howard Killick Partridge and Amis (1966–70)

Darwin College was established in 1964 by Caius, St John's, and Trinity Colleges as the first all-graduate foundation at Cambridge. It sits on the corner of Silver Street and Newnham Road and took over a group of 18th and 19th-century houses that occupied those two streets. One of the houses on Silver Street, Newnham Grange, was home to Charles Darwin for a time.[20] HKPA adapted the existing houses and stitched them together by inserting a student residence on Silver Street and a dining hall on Newnham Road to create a continuous, L-shape of accommodation that enclosed a garden to the rear (fig.4.19).

The design of the student residence, whilst modern, was unassuming and calculated to fit into the street. Its eaves height matched that of the adjacent Newnham Grange and its dark grey/brown brick, whilst not the same colour, harmonised with the brick of the existing houses (fig.4.20). A decision to lay the bricks on edge is puzzling and resulted in the height of a brick course being considerably greater than that seen on the existing buildings, a feature that was emphasised by the use of recessed joints between bricks.

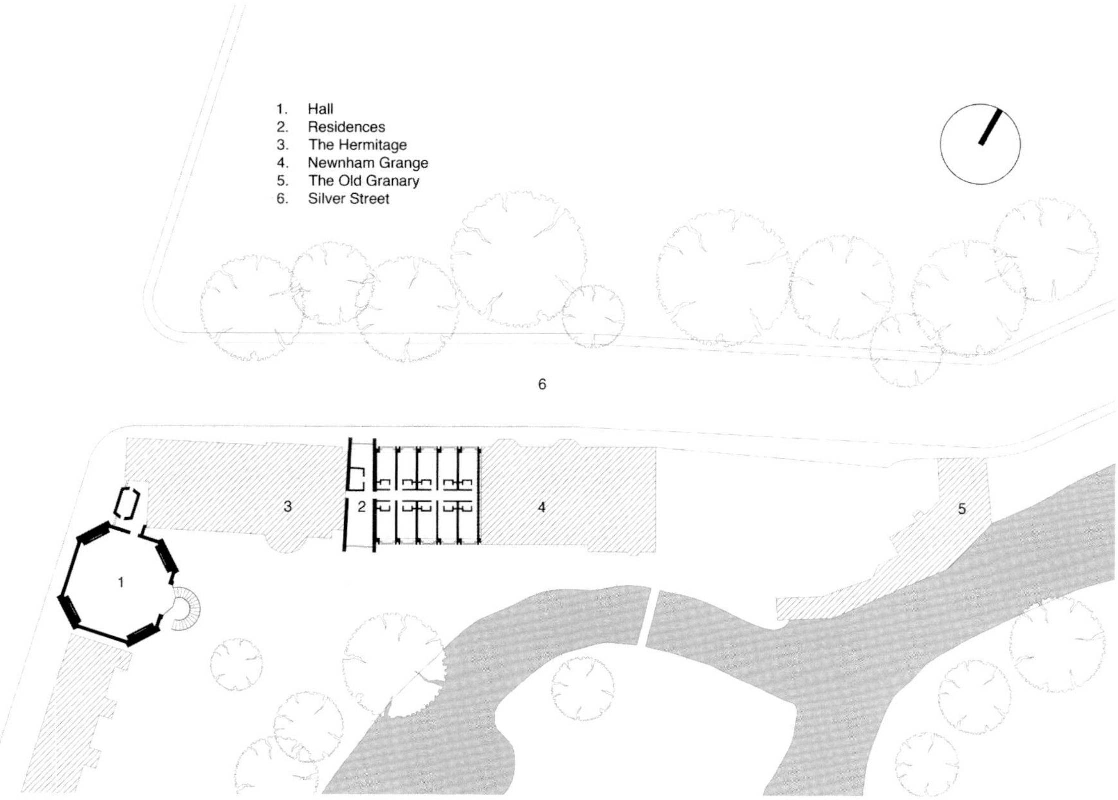

4.19 Darwin College, Cambridge. Site plan

4.20 *Darwin College, Cambridge. Silver Street with Newnham Grange in foreground*

Perhaps the architects wished to indicate that they had not attempted to match the existing brickwork but rather to complement it, just as their overall design was not intended to copy but to complement the existing buildings.

The elevations were composed of a series of inverted brick bays that ran the height of the building to form a series of alcoves that contained protruding, lead-clad, box windows at each floor (fig.4.21). The detail seems overcomplicated, as if the architects were tired of being reticent and wanted to show off a bit. Protruding window surrounds, normally of precast concrete, were a common feature of HKPA buildings and had become something of a trademark for them (see Chapters 10 and 11). Here, they were achieved with traditional materials that blended with their surroundings. They first developed a similar detail at Blundell Court, a student residence they had recently designed for Sidney Sussex College, Cambridge. Unlike Darwin, however, Blundell Court was a poor piece of urban design that did not relate well to the street, and it became an unfortunate piece of architecture with the addition of a mismatched storey in 2005 by Pleasance Hookham and Nix. Projecting brick piers that demarcate window zones can also be found at Warwick University's housing for visiting mathematicians that was designed at the same time (see Chapter 3). Meanwhile, back at Darwin College, the motif was also used to create a larger and taller entrance bay where the projecting piers recalled the twin towers that mark the Great Gate to Trinity College, Cambridge – Tudor-era imagery that was enhanced by the presence of a small, lead-panelled entrance door.

The showing off continued round the corner, where the dining hall was constructed of the same

4.21 Darwin College, Cambridge. Garden

quiet brick but with a more assertive, exposed concrete structure and an exuberant form (fig.4.22). An octagon, raised off the ground on four massive concrete legs and with a pyramid roof, it was suggestive of a 1950s image of a flying saucer. The octagon was a common feature of HKPA designs, leading to the suspicion that it was not chosen specifically to suit the circumstances of this site.

Science-fiction imagery and trademark motifs notwithstanding, HKPA's work at Darwin was a successful piece of urban infill that achieved the holy grail of differentiating new from old (through its use of form) whilst blending with its surroundings (through its use of materials and scale). It was modest without being invisible and, together with the informal gardens to the rear, created probably the most home-like environment of any Oxbridge college (fig.4.23). Whether that is something that students value is an open question – and not one that any of the other new colleges or their architects seem to have asked.

Clare Hall, Cambridge: Ralph Erskine (1966–9)

The idea of student accommodation that was closer to mainstream housing had been explored by several architects, but an entire setting that was closer to life outside university was explored nowhere as closely as at Clare Hall, Cambridge, another small graduate college founded in the mid-1960s. Its architect, Ralph Erskine, seems to have been intent on dispensing with all the elements that defined the traditional model of a college and promoting his Scandinavian-acquired ideas of community. It is difficult to differentiate the result from his designs for social housing, raising questions about the differences between university life and everyday life, and whether they should be encouraged or resisted (fig.5.1).

4.22 Darwin College, Cambridge. Interior of hall

4.23 Darwin College, Cambridge. The garden with the hall at the far end

5 Interlude

Education . . . a Nubile Cinderella

'Education in Britain is a nubile Cinderella, sparsely clad and much interfered with.'[1]

At the beginning of the 1960s, there was a consensus in Britain on the purpose and benefits of university education. The introduction of student grants in 1962 meant that the state paid for it and, in return, society benefitted from the presence of educated and highly skilled graduates. There was also a consensus that more graduates were needed and a belief that resources should be made available to fund initiatives for the public good.[2] Following the Robbins Report of 1963, the number of students attending university doubled, from around 108,000 in 1960 to around 228,000 in 1970.[3] Previously, most students had come from middle-class backgrounds and it was thought that an increase in student numbers would lead to a widening of opportunity for all sectors of society.

The political preoccupation was to make higher education available to more students rather than to change its nature or the purpose it served.[4] However, from 1964, the University Grants Committee (UGC), which had previously acted autonomously in deciding how and where to allocate its budget, was obliged to report to the Department of Education, giving government the potential to influence the direction of funding. As we have seen in earlier chapters, the initial government emphasis was on maintaining the UK's position as a leading military and industrial power. As economic stagnation took hold in the 1970s, the emphasis shifted to universities becoming more directly engaged in securing the economic wellbeing of the nation.[5] Under the Educational Reform Act introduced by the Conservative government of Margaret Thatcher in 1988, the UGC was disbanded and the funding councils that replaced it were given the job of implementing government policy.[6]

The Thatcher government had already made sharp cuts to the higher education budget in 1981 and introduced a research-driven model to determine the distribution of funding to individual universities. Targeted research rather than student numbers became the motivation for funding and led to priority being given to a limited number of research-rich universities.[7] For some others, receiving a lesser share of a smaller budget led to reductions in staff and student numbers, which

5.1 Clare Hall, Cambridge

the government expected to be taken up by polytechnics, whose funding was not cut.[8]

At the same time, a government that stressed consumerism and deregulation, and looked to competition and the market to drive academic activity, considered ending student grants and introducing tuition fees.[9] The idea was initially applied only to overseas students but was later extended to home-grown students by the Labour government under Tony Blair and further reinforced by the Conservative/Liberal Democrat coalition government of David Cameron.[10]

As a result, many institutions that did not have their own financial resources or private benefactors came to rely on student tuition fees to survive. By 2015, the average amount of public funding for universities was 15 per cent, whilst tuition fees accounted for 48 per cent and research grants around 18 per cent, with the rest coming from other income sources or endowments.[11] Universities became businesses vying to attract customers (students). Student numbers increased, driven by the financial imperative to secure as much fee income as possible. Fees for home-grown students were capped by government which, following the law of unintended consequences, led to universities prioritising the recruitment of overseas students, whose fees were not capped.

Where does all this leave the post-war consensus that saw university education as a publicly funded benefit to society? It has moved from the Robbins Report's objective of enhancing the 'good society', through periods as state-directed tool to maintain the UK's global standing or boost the economy by prioritising training and research for specific industries, to a purely economic transaction between university and individual student. The student pays the university a fee and, in return, receives a degree that is promoted as a passport to higher earnings.

And where does it leave the ambition to create greater access for students from disadvantaged backgrounds? The initial increase in student places that was achieved in the 1960s made little difference to the ratio of students from working-class or disadvantaged backgrounds. The bulk of students still came from middle-class homes – there were just more of them than before. That situation was unlikely to be improved by the removal of student grants and the imposition of fees. Vicki Boliver has noted that 'socioeconomic differences in relative rates of progression to higher education have so far shown no sign of equalising', and the most prestigious higher education programmes continue to be dominated by students from the most privileged family backgrounds. The current contract between student and university, whereby a university degree is seen as a gateway to a well-paid job, is also socially skewed. Degrees in more prestigious subjects from more prestigious institutions are more marketable than those from less regarded disciplines or institutions. The former are largely secured by middle-class students from affluent backgrounds; the latter by students from working-class backgrounds, who can struggle to secure graduate-level jobs, or any job.[12]

This situation might have been averted if the concept of the New Universities had been followed through successfully and they had developed alternative approaches to higher education that came to be seen as different from, but equal to, those of the elite universities. That goal was never fully realised and some academics have argued that the emphasis was always on increasing student numbers rather than creating alternative models. Those institutions that did develop alternative models largely abandoned them after the funding cuts of 1981 and the imposition of research-driven government funding. The two new universities with the best research records (York and Warwick) pulled out of the group formed by the new universities to join the Russell Group of elite research institutions, reflecting the perceived hierarchy of merit.

In fact, the priority of the Labour governments of the 1960s was to tackle the problems of inequality in education upstream, in the secondary schools. The 1964 Labour Party manifesto had promised a 'revolution in our educational system'.[13] There was a plan to increase university places, but the task of increasing access to students from working-class and disadvantaged backgrounds was to be tackled by reforming secondary education through implementation of unified Comprehensive schools in place of the previously segregated Grammar and Secondary Modern school system. There was no governmental intention to reform universities as such. However, although pupils of all social classes attended the same school under the Comprehensive system, they were streamed for academic ability, meaning that children were still taught in separate groups that were often affected by economic or cultural background.[14] As a result, although the number of university students increased, diversity was not radically improved. The initiative was also undermined by local authorities who refused to change to Comprehensive schooling and continued to maintain Grammar schools and a two-tier system. When Harold Wilson called a general election in 1970, legislation was on its way to force local authorities to adopt Comprehensive schooling, but Labour lost the election and the legislation was abandoned.[15]

The later removal of grants and the imposition of tuition fees made it even more difficult for those who could not rely on financial support from home to attend university. In my own discipline of architecture, I have taught students who combined study with working shifts in care homes or similar jobs. Even in those situations, able students will turn in work of a standard that allows them to progress and graduate, but they have little chance to enjoy the benefits of university life or to indulge in broader study or consideration of ideas that would allow them to expand their horizons in ways that might benefit both themselves and wider society. Less able students in the same situation may find it all too hard and drop out, whilst students attending some courses often find it difficult to get a job even when they graduate.

Small wonder that many working-class teenagers see their way to a successful career through celebrity: in sport, in music or, increasingly, on social media. It is clear how this financially benefits those individuals who succeed; it is unclear how it benefits the country or society in general. If there is now any consensus on the purpose and benefit of university education in the UK, it is far removed from the one that existed in the 1960s.

6 The Planners
Chamberlin, Powell and Bon
RMJMP

Planning of social, industrial and economic activity was intrinsic to modernism's ideas about creating a fairer society, and from the 1920s onwards intellectual and political opinion in Britain swung behind it. Urban planning in particular was seen as the path to eradicating inner-city slums and controlling the spread of suburbia. Sir William Beveridge, author of the Beveridge Report that led to the establishment of the Welfare State, declared: 'We shall need to have planning on a national scale, boldly overstepping the traditional boundaries of urban council, rural council, County Council.'[1] Eradication of the slums was recognised as a social necessity, whilst proliferation of the suburbs was opposed primarily on intellectual – some might say elitist – grounds, although there was also a case made that it was an inefficient use of land. The planning consultant, Thomas Sharp, condemned suburbia for its 'social sterility, aesthetic emptiness and economic wastefulness', whilst the architect, Sir Clough Williams-Ellis, found it full of 'mean and perky little houses that surely none but mean and perky little souls should inhabit with satisfaction'.[2] Not that Williams-Ellis promoted the urban environment: he is best known for his design of Portmeirion, a mixture of theme park and Italian fishing village in rural North Wales, which was developed as a commercial enterprise and tourist attraction.

The Town and Country Planning Act of 1944 gave far-reaching powers to local authorities to instruct reconstruction and redevelopment, but the Labour government elected in 1945 went further, with a commitment to introduce centralist planning to all policy areas. Herbert Morrison, the minister responsible for coordinating planning, declared it to be 'something new and constructively revolutionary which will be regarded in times to come as a contribution to civilisation as vital and distinctly British as parliamentary democracy under the rule of law'.[3]

That government was too short-lived to put much of its policy into action, but in the early 1960s there was still an appetite for centralised planning amongst Labour politicians. They, along with some journalists and academics, argued that it represented the best chance of modernising Britain's economy and encouraging higher productivity.[4] However, when the Labour government came to power in 1964 it

6.1 Leeds University. Lecture theatres

inherited previously undisclosed levels of debt that compromised its whole term in office and prevented it from enacting much of its economic and industrial programme.[5]

In the meantime, those involved specifically in urban planning had formed two distinct groups. Both subscribed to the notion that the answer lay in planning but, where one group embraced modernism and believed that the future lay in big cities, the other supported the ideas of Ebenezer Howard and the development of Garden Cities and later New Towns. The former group was influenced by Le Corbusier's proposals to sweep away the old city and replace it with a planned city of high and medium-rise housing blocks, zoning by activity and separation of cars and pedestrians.

A third way had been promoted by Elizabeth Denby in the 1930s. Denby was a housing consultant with a background in housing management, where she witnessed the consequences of planning theory in practice. She worked with Maxwell Fry on the 1937 design of the Kensal House Flats in London, a tenant-focused project that provided social and communal facilities, including a workshop and nursery school. Denby called the scheme an 'urban village' and claimed that the residents had enthusiastically embraced the concept and its opportunities for gardening and self-maintenance. Along with other activists, many of them women, she helped produce a series of exhibitions between 1931 and 1938 under the heading *New Homes for Old* which considered the form that new housing should take. She concluded that the solution lay beyond the 'two impractical and unnecessary extremes' of Garden Cities or Le Corbusier's Ville Radieuse.[6] She proposed housing that merged invisibly into the urban fabric through a mixture of rehabilitation and new-build infill and an end to extreme zoning. Clean and quiet industries would be readmitted to 'encourage a welcome return to street architecture . . .'[7]

Denby's ideas were overtaken by the wholesale destruction of housing areas during the war and the imperative to rebuild quickly. Even in those circumstances, the basis of her proposals might have been given more consideration when it came to the choice of housing type or the planning of mixed-use neighbourhoods. Her ideas may have been overlooked because she was not an architect, a planner or a man, and almost certainly because they did not fit with the big planning that was fashionable. Interestingly, it was another woman who proposed an alternative to mainstream planning policies in the 1960s when Jane Jacobs published her seminal book, *The Death and Life of Great American Cities.*

The above overview is brief and oversimplified but is enough to illustrate that most planning theory in the post-war period revolved around the need to provide mass housing. Few architects carried the discussion of planning ideas into other sectors.

Chamberlin, Powell and Bon

As it happens, Chamberlin, Powell and Bon's most notable planning achievements were in housing: the Golden Lane Housing Estate, designed and built between 1951 and 1963, and the Barbican complex, designed between 1955 and 1958, with construction from 1963 to 1983. The sites sat next to one another, just north of St Paul's Cathedral and the City of London. They were typical of a post-war landscape of destruction and dereliction. Both designs proposed high-density mixed developments of high and medium-rise housing with commercial, entertainment and social facilities, and in the case of the Barbican, a major arts venue. Golden Lane was the result of the first major design competition for housing since the Churchill Gardens competition won by Powell and Moya. That win had allowed Powell and Moya to launch their practice, and Golden Lane allowed CPB to formalise a working relationship they had already established.

Golden Lane was a social housing development and the initial blocks featured facades of lightweight, colourful cladding panels. However, when the site was extended, later blocks were more subdued and the curving terrace facing Goswell Road introduced a more explicit use of heavy, in-situ concrete and vaults that were reminiscent of Le Corbusier's Maisons Jaoul.[8]

The origins of the Barbican were quite different. The site was originally earmarked for commercial development and it was only through the sustained campaigning of pressure groups like the New Barbican Committee that consideration was given to accommodating large numbers of residential units. Rival schemes were put forward, including some by the LCC under Leslie Martin, before the CPB design was finally accepted. Its financial viability, however, relied on exceptionally high densities and a target population of middle and high-income residents.[9] Whether it was a desire to give the intended middle-class occupants more substantial homes or the architects' own progress along the route already intimated by the later parts of Golden Lane is unclear, but the architecture of the Barbican was heavier, with much use of massive, exposed concrete, barrel vaults and Le Corbusian references. Whatever the architectural drivers, the scale and ambition of the project was 'witness to an order of civic valour of which this country seems no longer capable'.[10]

That idea of 'civic valour' is something that CPB increasingly tried to include in their work. It was present in their design for New Hall, Cambridge and it became a regular feature of their university projects, whether or not required by the brief. We have already seen how CPB tried to expand their remit in both the Churchill College competition and at New Hall to propose a new urban quarter to the west of the River Cam (see Chapter 4). Other wide-ranging proposals that the practice made for re-planning Cambridge included the demolition of the row of buildings dating from the 16th to 19th centuries that face King's College across King's Parade, to be replaced with five-storey residences. The College asked for the planning report to be withdrawn following uproar over these suggestions.

At Oxford University, CPB grew their brief for the expansion of the Radcliffe Science Library and the Zoology Department to include the remodelling of a whole area of the University, and at Birmingham University, when asked to design residences for 200 students, they produced a scheme for 600. Neither proposal was accepted and, as Elain Harwood has noted, CPB's increasing propensity to expand the brief was matched by the rate of unbuilt projects.[11] Their most successful attempt to design a university based on urban planning principles was at Leeds University.

Leeds was unique amongst established universities that were expanded in the 1960s, in that its new buildings were conceived as part of a coordinated plan and construction programme. It was built in three main phases, each the work of a single architect, each of whom was initially welcomed by the University, only for relationships to later cool. CPB was the last of the three, appointed in 1959.

They prepared a report and masterplan based on extensive research of how existing departments operated and interacted. In his foreword to the report, the Vice-Chancellor, Sir Charles Morris, discussed the difficulty of anticipating student numbers in the longer term. The University had been anticipating student numbers reaching around 5,500 by 1964, but with the first wave of baby boomers due to reach university age that same year, the Vice-Chancellor thought as many as 7,000 places might be required by the end of the decade.[12] The architects concluded that no definite end to the development programme could be foreseen and, if no exact limits to the issues involved could be predicted, no finite, rigid layout for the Development Plan was appropriate. What was needed, they concluded, was a coherent pattern of development which would continue to be viable when circumstances changed. They suggested that not only the physical plan, but also the report should be open-ended and capable of revision through supplementary reports that accommodated changes in circumstances within an overall agreed pattern of development.[13]

The initial phase of development was based on the concept of a communal block of shared lecture theatres with departments arranged around it (fig.6.2). Teaching accommodation was organised in long spines of a width that ensured daylight penetration to the centre of the block (fig.6.3). Structure and plan were set out on the kind of tartan grid employed by Louis Kahn at the Richards Medical Research Laboratories in Philadelphia and by Arup Associates at the Department of Mining and Metallurgy Laboratories at Birmingham University (see Chapter 10). The continuous teaching buildings reflected contemporaneous educational thinking, where departments were placed together to encourage interdisciplinary working, an idea developed by the new universities at East Anglia and Essex (see Chapter 3).[14]

When it came to designing individual buildings, CPB were pressured to work with other architects. They resisted, causing some friction with the University, and in the end retained the commission to design all the central core buildings, with outlying buildings designed by others.[15]

6.2 Leeds University. Communal block of shared lecture theatres with teaching block behind

In a lecture given by Chamberlin to the RIBA in 1969 he avoided discussing style, but instead talked about the urban landscape that is common to many cities: a backdrop of anonymous blocks that forms the ground against which important buildings are inserted as highlights. That was the pattern that CPB established at Leeds University, where the repetitive teaching blocks formed a background to the landmark lecture theatres (fig.6.1).[16]

Robert Matthew Johnson-Marshall and Partners

The strategy of unassuming background buildings and highlighted important buildings was adopted by RMJMP in their design for York University,

6.3 Leeds University. Typical teaching block

although with quite different results. In some respects, the design at York conforms to the urban pattern of standardised residences forming an unobtrusive backdrop that further emphasises the importance of communal buildings, in this case the hall, library and lecture theatres (fig.6.4). In other respects it is not urban, with colleges, other student accommodation and teaching buildings set amongst landscape to create a tranquil campus, with 'cells' formed around nuclei of communal buildings (figs 6.5, 6.7).

The important aspect of the planning work carried out by RMJMP at York and CPB at Leeds, was that it entailed extensive research and analysis of needs and conditions before any specific design work was attempted. This

6.4 York University. Central hall

is particularly apparent in the diagrammatic presentation of relationships, organisation and growth patterns prepared by RMJMP, with no hint of an architectural solution (fig.6.6). It is perhaps no coincidence that the resulting diagrams resembled those representing chemical organisms. Like the latter, they illustrated the organising principles rather than the physical form, which was allowed to grow in accordance with needs and the natural features of the site (fig.6.8). Other architects designing whole universities or colleges produced masterplans, but with Spence at Sussex, for example, the plan came after the architectural vision of what the University should look like; or with Lasdun at UEA and Architects' Co-Partnership at Essex, there was

6.5 York University. Typical student housing

a determination to carry the diagram literally into the physical form. At UEA, the form exceeded the growth rate of needs and was abandoned before the needs caught up. At Essex, some thought the form obliterated the natural features of the site (see Chapter 3). The approach at York was both more rigorous in the conceptual planning stage and more relaxed in the architectural realisation.

The York plan and report were prepared by Stirrat Johnson-Marshall and Andrew Derbyshire. Both men were convinced of the benefits of rigorous research and insisted on a six-month period to work on the report. Nothing like this had been attempted before; the nearest equivalent was the CPB report for Leeds, but that was for the expansion of an existing university where the educational and organisational philosophy was already in place. York needed a document that it could use to fund-raise, to describe its philosophy to potential academic applicants, and to function as a design guide if RMJMP were not retained for the design phase. Derbyshire said: 'Nobody had talked about the architectural implications of academic and social ideas, and nobody had produced theoretical relationships and developed them into a plan with a time-dimension in it.'[17] In the event, RMJMP were retained to design the University, which has been described as 'more deeply pondered and clearly conceived than any of its potential rivals'.[18]

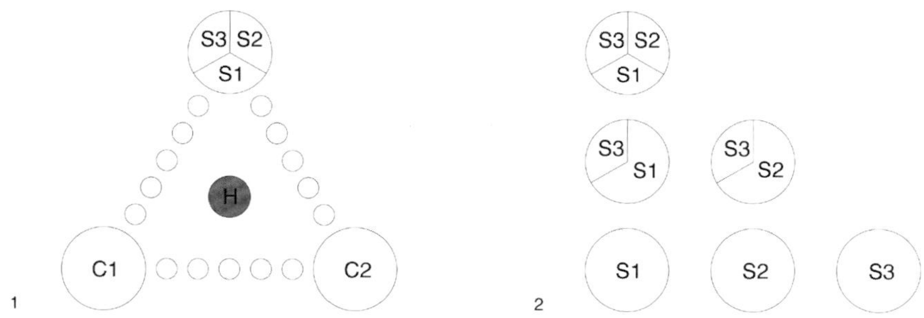

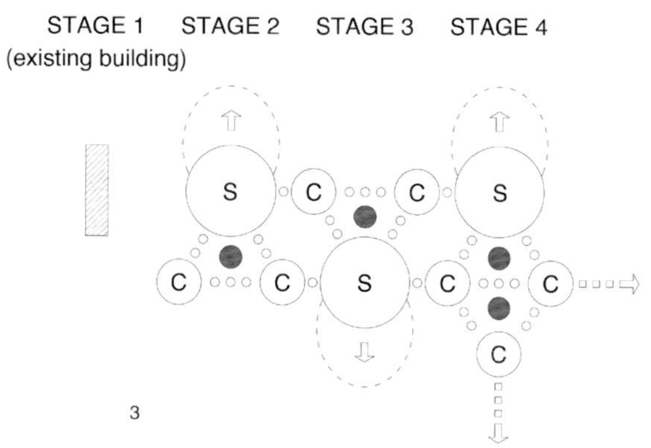

1. The basic unit of university growth (the cell within the organism): two colleges with associated housing are paired with a science building and all are linked by non-science teaching buildings. At the core of each cell is a hub building (concert hall, library, sports building, etc), giving each unit a distinct identity.
2. Stages of development for science buildings: three subjects (physics, chemistry and biology) are accommodated at every stage, with each eventually having its own building.
3. Diagram of growth: each new cell contains a science building, which has room for expansion without being isolated.

6.6 York University. Diagram of structure for expansion

6.7 York University. Typical teaching building
6.8 York University. Masterplan

7 The Urbanists

Denys Lasdun
Sheppard Robson

Architects practising planning as an activity in its own right, setting the ground rules within which an open-ended and as yet undetermined architecture could evolve, were rare. However, there were a number of architects who took urban-planning principles into their architectural designs.

Denys Lasdun

Lasdun's interest in urban forms dates to at least the late 1950s and his design for the Royal College of Physicians in Regent's Park, London (fig.7.2). Although the form was recognisably that of a modernist building, he wanted to move from the idea of 'organisation' to that of an 'organism' that represented a 'microcosm of the city'.[1] In the projects that followed, he became intent on creating architecture as urban landscape, where a series of horizontal platforms that he referred to as 'strata' were stacked up like the contour lines of a hillside and interspersed with towers carrying vertical circulation and services (fig.7.1).[2] Although he wrote of modern architecture as a process that demanded research in order to produce sane and purposeful architecture, he does not appear to have meant research in the sense that CPB employed it at Leeds or RMJMP at York (see Chapter 6).[3] Lasdun sought to create an architectural language that transcended 'the particulars of each site, programme and set of clients' aims'.[4] He thought that the Modern Movement had concentrated on function at the expense of context but, having subordinated site, programme and the client's aims, it appears that the context he valued most was his quest to set a new direction for modern architecture. In that pursuit, he specifically ruled out social context as having any relevance to architectural quality and wrote that 'It is vitally important to . . . release architects so that they can give people the only thing that they really require from the profession – an elevation of spirit and an environment which assists the good life.'[5] He had not always felt that way. After the break-up of the Tecton Group, where he had worked with early modernists like Berthold Lubetkin, he designed housing in Bethnal Green where he attempted to address the social needs of a newly formed community. It was deemed 'a social failure though a sculptural triumph', a verdict that may have helped determine the direction of his later work.[6]

7.1 The National Theatre, London

The outcome of his thinking on such matters was the development of a common architectural language that he employed on a range of projects with different briefs. An unbuilt design for the Royal Institution of Chartered Surveyors in London's Parliament Square looked like a dry run for his National Theatre design on the South Bank. The same patterns emerged in his European Investment Bank headquarters on a sloping, wooded site in Luxembourg. He used the same language at a smaller, domestic scale in the design of student residences at UEA and Christ's College, Cambridge (fig.7.3). He explained the former as architectural hills and valleys that related to the site's natural landscape (see Chapter 3). The latter is more difficult to place in a site context; it related neither

7.2 Royal College of Physicians, London. Interior of lobby

to the existing College buildings nor to the town. Its stepped terraces backed onto a narrow street and loomed over it like the back end of a football stand that has been dropped into the middle of a village. Its lack of sympathy for scale or context made it an easy target for those who disliked modern architecture. In recent years it has been disguised behind a frontage of shops with flats above that are decidedly post-modern in their treatment. To paraphrase Pevsner: Perhaps if Lasdun had been less rude, others might not have been so playful (see Chapter 2).

At the University of London, Lasdun was working to a masterplan produced by Leslie Martin and within the London tradition of strong street lines and public gardens. His design for the Institutes of

7.3 Christ's College, Cambridge. New Court residences

Education and Law was a long slab with horizontal bands of glazing and bronzed cladding that ran the entire length of Bedford Way and appeared to be supported on five massive concrete brackets formed by service cores that rose at the rear of the building and outcrops that projected in front of it (fig.7.4). To the rear of each service core and running perpendicular to the street block, wings stepped down in Lasdun's trademark terraces to Woburn Square and a new School of Oriental and African Studies, also designed by Lasdun (figs 7.5, 7.7). Only one wing was built: a growing conservationist movement won protection for existing Georgian buildings that prevented the other wings from going ahead. The linear block maintained the line and scale of the street while

7.4 London University, Institutes of Education and Law. View from Bedford Way

providing visual and acoustic protection to quiet gardens and a pedestrian precinct behind that linked existing gardens at Russell, Woburn and Gordon Squares (fig.7.6). Other recognisable urban elements included a vertical street elevation, repetition of uniform structure and windows, and the creation of a constant rhythm. On this occasion, Lasdun appears to have taken more notice of the physical context and provided a convincing addition to the urban grain. At the same time, the teaching block revisits his 'teaching wall' at UEA, and that was not the first time Lasdun had explored the form. Although of a completely different scale and use, his plan for Hallfield Primary School (1951–5) is remarkably similar to the cranked teaching wall and echelon residences at UEA,

7.5 London University, Institutes of Education and Law. Service tower and stepped-down wing to rear (tower obscured by scaffold)

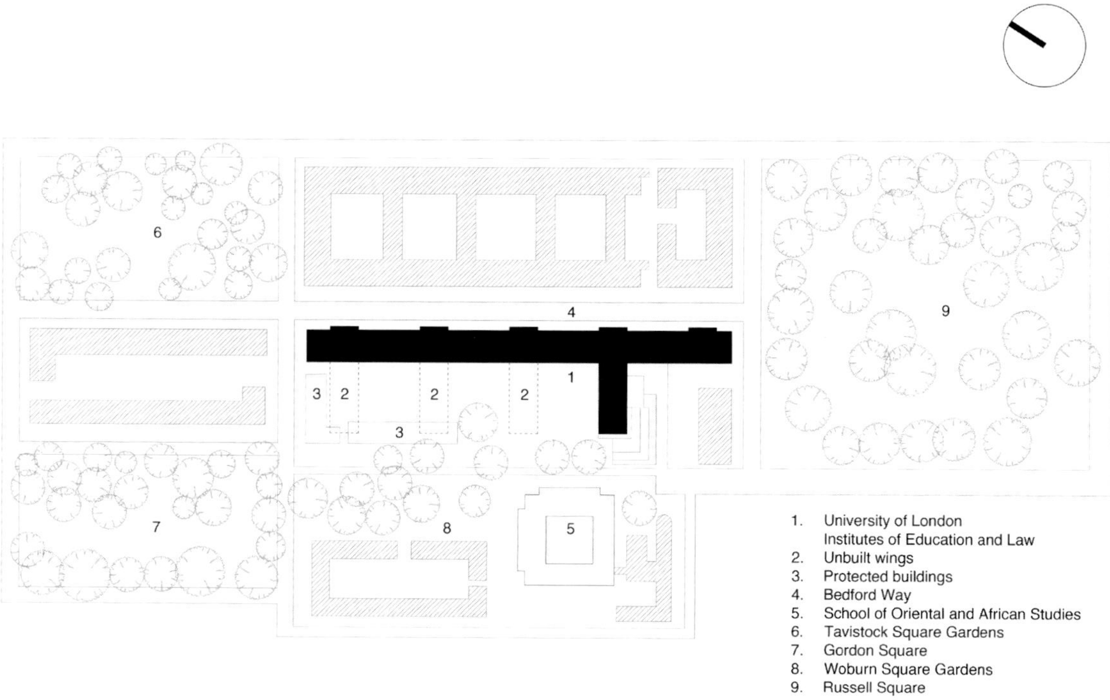

another example of Lasdun applying similar design principles to projects of different use, scale and location (fig.7.8).

Sheppard Robson

Sheppard Robson faced a similar central London site at the bomb-damaged Prince's Gardens, where they were asked to prepare designs for residences for the Imperial College of Science and Technology. The College dated from 1907 and was an amalgamation of three earlier institutions. A plan to double the number of students was developed in 1953 and Sheppard Robson was appointed to design student residences around three sides of the square, which sits just off Exhibition Road.

At that time the College already produced more engineers than any other British institution, prompting a question as to why it was not chosen as the appropriate location for a 'British MIT', rather than the proposed new Churchill College in Cambridge. It appears that the Ministry of Education and those funding the idea of a British MIT insisted on an Oxbridge location and Winston Churchill, after whom the new College would be named, would not countenance Oxford.[7] Sheppard Robson won the competition to design Churchill College, but the very nature of the brief ensured that it would never operate like the Massachusetts model (see Chapter 1).

For the expansion of the Imperial College of Science and Technology, they proposed 13, eight-storey halls of residence which, although separate social units, were linked in a continuous building form.[8] The design was unashamedly modernist, with references to Le Corbusier's Unité d'Habitation in the visually differentiated gallery floor inserted halfway up the block between layers

7.6 London University, Institutes of Education and Law. Masterplan

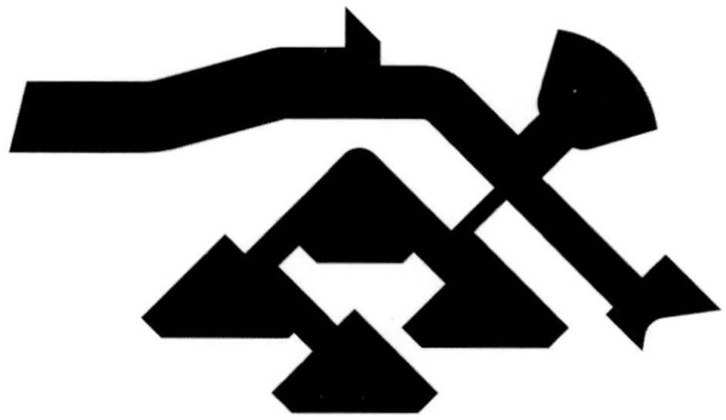

of residential accommodation. Due to funding shortfalls only the south side of the square and the isolated Weeks Hall just off the northeast corner of the square were built in their entirety. The massive building constructed on the south side provided an indication of the scale of ambition, but a programme of replacement begun around 2005 means that nothing remains of the original design except Weeks Hall (fig.7.9).

Both the construction of Churchill College and the expansion of Imperial College were part of the drive to produce more graduates in science and technology. The same initiative saw the creation of ten Colleges of Advanced Technology (CAT) around the country, which were upgraded to universities in 1966. One of these was Brunel College, which moved to a new site in Uxbridge, to the west of London, and was renamed Brunel University.

Brunel offered a sandwich course in which students spent half their time gaining practical experience outside the University. The client requested a design that focused activity and attention on the University, rather than on individual colleges or faculties, to promote a feeling of attachment to the institution. In that respect it was like the new universities featured in Chapter 3, and the architects followed a similar path to many of those designs in creating a self-contained 'town' with a distinct social centre. The masterplan was based on a grid, where residential and specialist teaching blocks were arranged around a central core of communal buildings that contained eating places and common rooms for all staff and students, and was located adjacent to the library, theatre, shops and a building for lecture theatres and classrooms (fig.7.10).[9]

7.7 London University, School of Oriental and African Studies

7.8 Hallfield Primary School. Outline plan

7.9 Imperial College of Science and Technology, London, Weeks Hall

In their design of Churchill College, Sheppard Robson adopted the materials of Le Corbusier's Maisons Jaoul and used them to create a relaxed and humanistic design that displayed Scandinavian influences. At Brunel, they took the same materials and created a standardised kit of parts to produce buildings that spoke to an older, rational modernism. They deconstructed elements of Jaoul and reassembled them in a controlled, regular arrangement of exposed concrete frame, brick infill panels and glazing, often arranged in continuous bands (fig.7.11). An exception was the lecture theatre block, which appeared as an institution of the State apparatus in Stanley Kubrick's dystopian film, *A Clockwork Orange*. Here, they adopted the mannered and heavy use of in-situ concrete from Le Corbusier's post-war work but stepped further back in time for their architectural references, which clearly sprang from Konstantin Melnikov's Rusakov Workers' Club (1928) in Moscow (fig.7.12).

Sheppard Robson's diverse and distant stylistic sources and Lasdun's application of similar solutions to dissimilar situations illustrate two approaches to architecture that sought context in the broad principles of urban design rather than the specific nature of immediate surroundings. The next chapter will look at architects who took a more localised view of context.

7.10 Brunel University. Masterplan

7.11 Brunel University. Typical teaching block

7.12 Brunel University. Lecture theatres

8 The Contextualists

Stirrat Johnson-Marshall
Powell and Moya
Arup Associates

Every building has context: geographic, economic, political, cultural. Early modernist buildings were political and social statements that sought to break away from localised constraints and forge something new, liberated and universal. By the 1960s, some architects who would describe themselves as modernists nonetheless felt the pendulum had swung too far and a movement that promoted equality and democracy had, paradoxically, become the preserve of an elite. They wanted to make architecture more accessible by tying it back to a recognisable tradition. For them, context meant the physical environment and historical and cultural influences that surrounded a project. The results were widely admired, although there were critics who felt that, without a political and social agenda, they represented nothing more than 'technically competent sentimentality'.[1]

Stirrat Johnson-Marshall

One of the most literal interpretations of context was a small building inserted in a corner of the main courtyard of Selwyn College, Cambridge. The College was mostly designed in the late 19th and early 20th centuries in a Victorian, Neo-Tudor style of red brick with stone detailing around windows and doors. In 1960, Stirrat Johnson-Marshall of RMJMP was asked to design new Junior and Senior Combination Rooms (the Cambridge University term for common rooms). Johnson-Marshall had built his reputation in the public sector, where he was instrumental in developing a schools' programme based on the development of standardised prefabricated systems, first at Hertfordshire County Council and later the Ministry of Education. In both positions he had acted as an organiser and enabler of a collaborative approach to design (see Chapter 3). This was a rare example of a building personally designed by him. His instructions were to be 'as modern as he liked, provided he harmonised with the existing Court'.[2]

Johnson-Marshall responded with a polite brick box, finished in the same brick as the existing buildings. The features that marked it as modern were a low-pitched 'butterfly' roof, some continuous ribbon windows to the rear and the exposed edges of the concrete floor slabs, although these were faced in stone (fig.8.2). These features were borrowed from Le Corbusier but, as with Spence at Queens' College, were rendered in a

8.1 St John's College, Cambridge, Cripps Building. View from undercroft, across the River Cam to the library at Third Court

much more courteous manner than the original (see Chapter 2) and were only visible from outside the perimeter of the College. The new building's only interaction with the Court occurred where it pushed through a narrow gap between existing buildings with a concrete and stone bay. This formed the entrance at ground level and a feature window at upper level and was plainly modelled on a projecting stone bay on the nearby Hall (fig.8.3). It was a pragmatic but uncommitted approach that tried to keep a foot in both modernist and traditionalist camps and was unlikely to satisfy either. Pevsner was relaxed about the 'little brick box with two opposite monopitch roofs' but felt that 'the bay window to the court is a pity'.[3] Such close referencing was uncommon in the university buildings of the 1960s. Most of their architects were less direct in their quotations.

Powell and Moya

The architectural critic, Reyner Banham, characterised Powell and Moya's work as 'nice, modern and British'.[4] It is the word 'nice' that is so damning. Banham was a promoter of the 'New Brutalism' and favoured the resolutely un-picturesque, unsentimental work of architects like Alison and Peter Smithson. What some described as 'picturesque', others would call 'situational' or 'contextual' and was precisely the quality that drew admirers to Powell and Moya's work. Alan Powers described it as 'a middle way between the simplification of high modernism and the reactionaries opposed to it'.[5]

That middle way saw Powell and Moya secure a string of prestigious projects, and it has been suggested that commissions like the British Pavilion at the 1970 Osaka Expo and the Queen Elizabeth II Conference Centre in Westminster positioned them as potential successors to Basil Spence as the establishment's favoured architects.[6] Powell was more comfortable than Moya in that role. He had a family background in public school, Oxbridge and the Church. He was appointed to the Royal Fine Art Commission, made a Royal Academician and knighted in 1975, going on to become the first architect to be made a Companion of Honour in

8.2 Selwyn College, Cambridge, Junior and Senior Combination Rooms. Viewed from outside the College

8.3 Selwyn College, Cambridge, Junior and Senior Combination Rooms. Viewed from inside the Court

1984.[7] Those were some of the rewards of success, the origins of which lay in the socialist agenda of the immediate post-war years.

The Labour government elected in 1945 was intent on building a Welfare State through investment in housing, education and healthcare. Freshly graduated from the Architectural Association (AA) in 1946, Philip Powell and Hidalgo Moya set up practice together after winning the competition to design social housing for around 6,000 residents at Churchill Gardens in Pimlico. Their proposal was a brick and glass, Gropius-like design of mostly nine-storey slab blocks. The project would take 15 years to complete, by which time they had designed the most enduring symbol of the Festival of Britain (the Skylon), become heavily involved in education and healthcare buildings, and were busy enough to decline an invitation to enter the Churchill College competition. Their involvement in education began in the mid 1950s with the design of Mayfield School in Putney, and in the late 1950s they began what would become a long involvement in the design of university buildings.

Brasenose College, Oxford, Staircases 16 and 17, 1957–61

Powell and Moya's first university building was at Brasenose College, Oxford and involved a modest provision of student rooms in what was known as Staircases 16 and 17. Talks regarding the project had begun as early as 1954, although construction was not completed until 1961. Preliminary sketches prepared in 1956 showed a sharp, lightweight facade, similar to the refined, industrial look developed in their earlier design for Mayfield School. The final design exhibited a heavier use of load-bearing stone walls coupled with lead sheet and large, single-pane windows. It was a formula they would develop and refine in Oxbridge buildings that followed. The move to heavier, more traditional materials was clearly designed to place the project in the physical and historical setting of Oxford, even though the buildings were shoe-horned into a tight, irregularly shaped backyard and were nowhere visible from the street (fig.8.4). The project quickly acquired a reputation as a highly innovative intervention in an historic context, and *New Oxford* judged it 'one of the most important post-war contributions to Oxford's architectural heritage'.[8]

The brief was to fit as many rooms as possible on a tightly restricted and awkwardly shaped site. Views out were limited, but some pleasant views were available to the north. To take advantage of these, a four-storey block of study bedrooms with two tutor rooms above was placed at the widest part of the site. Rooms and windows were arranged to take maximum advantage of available views, resulting in an irregularly shaped plan. Rooms at ground level were separated by paths, creating a porous external space. Two single-storey groups of three and four rooms respectively, with each group

8.4 Brasenose College, Oxford. View over roofs of single-storey rooms towards four-storey block

sharing a small garden, were strung in a line along the edge of the narrow passage that ran north from the four-storey building (fig.8.5).[9]

The palette consisted of Portland stone wall panels with bush-hammered concrete cills and transoms spanning between them and lead cladding below windows. It was a modern interpretation of traditional craft techniques and the construction led to problems. By 1965, lead cladding had become detached from walls and water had penetrated flat roofs. The problems were resolved, but not before the architects agreed to pay £1,000 towards the cost of repairs (equivalent to around £30,000 in 2024).[10] Meanwhile, the building was a critical success and marked a change of direction from their earlier International Style to buildings that were more attuned to local context. Banham, in the same article quoted above, conceded that 'they have an uncanny and seemingly uncontrived ability to sense the mood of place and time – and client'.

Cripps Building, St John's College, Cambridge, 1962–6

The architectural historian, Nikolaus Pevsner, declared Powell and Moya's next university project, the Cripps Building at St John's College, Cambridge, to be 'a masterpiece by one of the best architectural partnerships in the country'.[11] Pevsner had been on a similar journey to those architects who wished to inject more local context into their buildings. In the 1930s he wrote that 'what had been achieved in 1914 was the style of the century [and] it seemed folly to think that anyone would wish to abandon it'.[12] 'It was a style of service, neutral, rational, functional, sensible'.[13] Later he would become an admirer of buildings that, whilst modern, were designed to fit their surroundings by employing variety and using materials that would weather and melt into their setting.[14] He became an advocate of 18th-century English Picturesque theory as key to developing an English modernism. That theory promoted an informal and emotional – as opposed to a formal and rational – approach to design. Pevsner favoured the approach, not the direct imitation of past styles.

Powell and Moya were selected to design the Cripps Building after a wide-ranging search of British, European, Scandinavian and American architects. In the end, the selection came down to a choice between them and Denys Lasdun. The funder, Humphrey Cripps, wanted a building that would last 500 years and was prepared to pay for high-quality materials. This allowed the architects

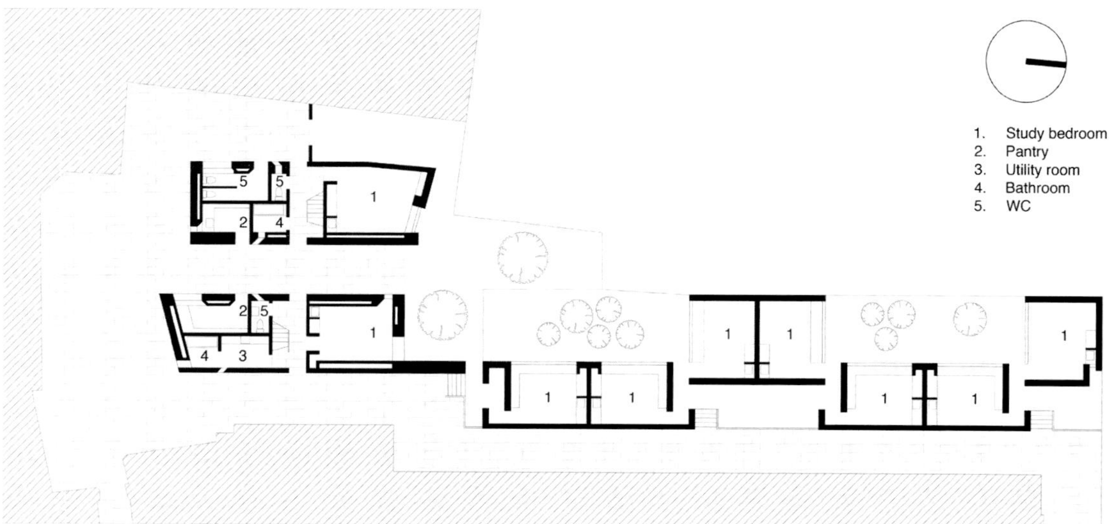

8.5 Brasenose College, Oxford. Site plan

to repeat the palette of stone and lead that they had used successfully at Brasenose College, Oxford (fig.8.6). However, the College wanted flexibility and so the load-bearing stone walls of Brasenose were replaced by a concrete frame with stone cladding.[15]

Like Brasenose, the Cripps Building was praised for its sensitivity to context. A long, stretched-out and cranked string of a building, it was ingeniously threaded between and around existing buildings in such a way that it created courtyards (or spaces that gave the feeling of courtyards) in the relationships it formed with those other buildings (fig.8.7). As Philip Powell explained: 'whilst never containing courtyards itself, it gives the effect of courtyards by its confrontations with other buildings or with other parts of itself, continuing the collegiate pattern of court following court established by older parts of the college'.[16]

Rooms were planned around stairwells in the traditional Oxbridge fashion (fig.8.8). The architects were inventive in providing a variety of room plans, which resulted in the charge that they had employed variety for its own sake and not based on an understanding of student needs or the way in which the rooms would be used.[17] The implication of that view was that Powell and Moya had indulged in variety merely to create picturesque modulation in the built form (fig.8.9).

A similar criticism was levelled at the expression of structure. The building is raised to create a series of covered cloisters at ground level and appears to be supported on massive stone columns (fig.8.1). In reality it is supported on slender, L-shaped concrete columns, boxed out in stone cladding to form rectangular ducts. In the rooms above, the stone boxing-out is replaced by storage cupboards or recessed baths or basins. The ducts were to cause future maintenance problems, as were leaking flat roofs.[18] At the time, what many saw as inventive, its critics found disturbing because it did not provide an honest expression of structure.[19]

These criticisms bring into sharp focus the areas of disagreement between those who believed in an architecture driven by universal values of logic, rationalism and truth as the route to a more just and free society, and those who thought it important to acknowledge local custom and maintain links with tradition in order to build a new society that fitted its citizens. What some saw as an illogical manipulation and complication of building design solely for visual effect, the Contextualists saw as providing a deeper layering of meaning and cultural response – a recognition that one size does not fit all.

8.6 St John's College, Cambridge, Cripps Building

Christ Church College, Oxford, Blue Boar Quad and Picture Gallery, 1964–8

On the back of the Brasenose College project, Powell and Moya were awarded a larger commission to design residences for Oxford's Christ Church College, and the two buildings share a similar palette of materials. The site is long and narrow, running along the curving edge of Blue Boar Street. An existing stone wall was retained along the street frontage and the buildings pushed up against it, in some parts overhanging it, to leave as much open space as possible within the site (fig.8.10). To reduce the apparent bulk of the building and bring it closer in height to the older buildings on the street, the site was excavated behind the street wall so that the buildings appear one storey lower when viewed from the street (fig.8.11). Windows were located between apparently massive stone piers that, like those of the Cripps Building at St John's College in Cambridge, were hollow.[20] Stone-clad staircases containing toilets and pantries at half-landings were arranged at intervals along the edge, like a line of towers rising above the street wall. The effect has been described as almost medieval, an approach that was admired by some and regretted by others.[21] Pevsner, who had so admired the Cripps Building at St John's, whilst praising the design generally, found it a trifle self-indulgent, implying that it had gone too far in trying to fit into its context.[22]

Like Brasenose, the building had technical problems. The failure of mechanical services and persistent problems with leaking roofs led the College to consider demolition. That option was removed when the building was protected by a Grade II listing, so instead a major repair and refurbishment was completed by Purcell Miller Tritton in 2008.[23]

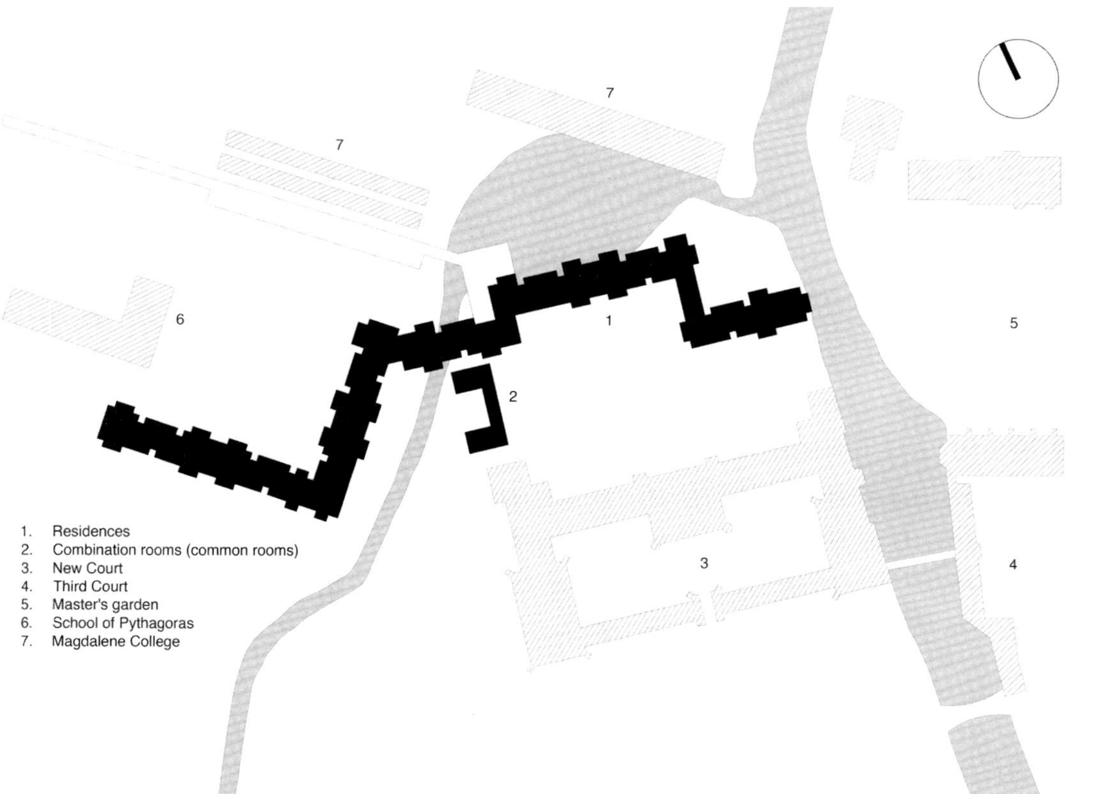

8.7 St John's College, Cambridge, Cripps Building. Site plan

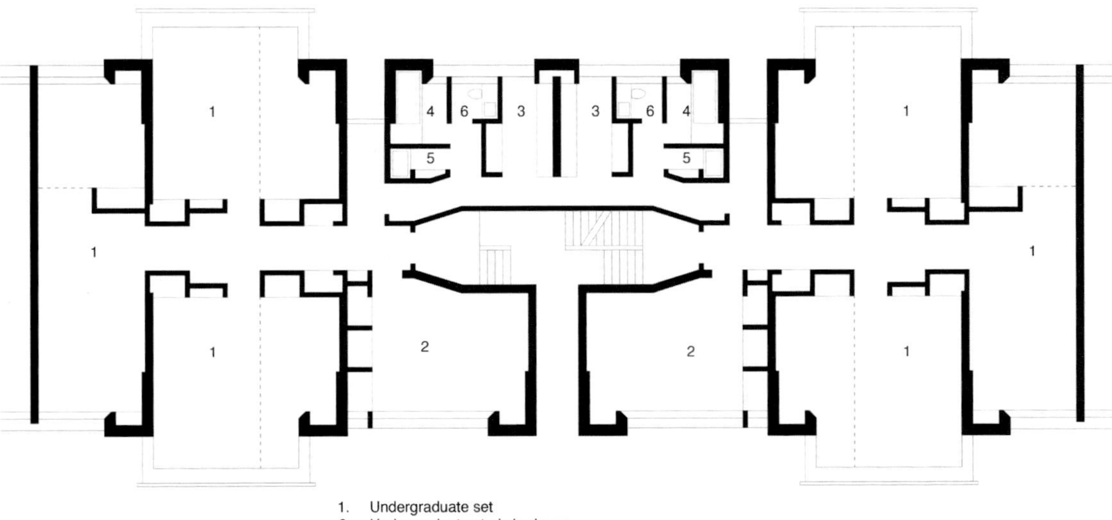

1. Undergraduate set
2. Undergraduate study bedroom
3. Gyp-room
4. Bathroom
5. Shower
6. WC

8.8 St John's College, Cambridge, Cripps Building. Rooms are grouped around individual stairwells
8.9 St John's College, Cambridge, Cripps Building. Plan of a typical grouping of rooms

8.10 Christ's Church College, Oxford, Blue Boar Quad. View from Blue Boar Street

8.11 *Christ's Church College, Oxford, Blue Boar Quad. View from the quad*

8.12 Christ's Church College, Oxford, Blue Boar Quad. Contextual use of materials

Powell and Moya were also asked to design a picture gallery for the College to house its major collection of paintings and drawings. The collection had previously been housed in the library, and when space for more books and readers was needed the College decided to commission a purpose-built gallery on a restricted site that raised similar problems to those encountered at Brasenose. The site chosen was the Deanery Garden, and in order to preserve outlook and amenity for the surrounding college buildings the architects housed the paintings at basement level and the drawings at ground level, with a grassed roof that formed a raised extension to the garden.[24] They connected the two galleries by a wide ramp with a parallel roof that emerged from the garden and wound around its edge to create an outdoor ramp that gave access to the grassed roof above the drawings collection. The glazed side wall of the ramp as it rose through and around the garden provided light and view to the journey between the two galleries.

The building was designed to disturb the existing context as little as possible and is self-effacing almost to the point of invisibility. Inasmuch as it is noticeable, it consists of the concrete, stone and glass combination that the architects had used elsewhere in Oxford. It was described by one critic as 'an example of immaculate if rather sterile good taste', which seems like an unnecessarily backhanded compliment for a design that solved a difficult set of problems whilst leaving very few fingerprints to show that the architects had ever been there.[25]

Corpus Christi College, Oxford, Magpie Lane Annexe, 1964–8

This three-storey residential building is located on a tight urban site at the corner of two narrow streets. The plan was a simple rectangle, with rooms to front and back served by a central corridor, and the building was entered from a small courtyard to the rear. The ground floor was raised above street level so that window cills were above the eye level of passers-by.

Rooms to the street side were grouped together to form large projecting bays on either side of a service zone – one, three rooms wide and the other, two rooms wide. Within each bay, floor slab and cross-wall edges were expressed in elevation as a concrete grid containing individual windows that ran the full width of each room with lead spandrel panels below (now replaced by grey metal cladding panels). The central service bay and gable walls were faced with random Oxford stone to match the existing buildings on the street and separated into horizontal bands by exposed concrete slab edges.

This was an understated design that tried to blend with the surrounding context by maintaining the street edge, using the same materials as the existing buildings and incorporating traditional elements like bay windows. However, the sheer bulk of the building compared to its domestic neighbours, along with different expectations for a modern lifestyle – expressed in large areas of glass, for example – illustrate the limitations of blending modern buildings into an historic context.

Wolfson College, Oxford, 1967–74

Wolfson College was set in a greenfield site in a suburban, residential part of the city, quite different to the tight, urban sites of Powell and Moya's other Oxford projects. Where the other designs had been site-specific, here the architects abstracted elements developed at other greenfield sites – most notably from ten years of hospital work – and refined them into a kit of parts that they employed repetitively across the site. The result was described as 'monotonous' by Geoffrey Tyack but can also be seen as cleaving closer to the modernist goal of creating rational, functional buildings as a sedate backdrop to a series of well-designed and landscaped external spaces (see Chapter 4).[26]

Cripps Court, Queens' College, Cambridge, 1971–82

Following the success of the Cripps Building at St John's College, the funder, Humphrey Cripps, asked Powell and Moya to design a building at Queens' College. In this instance, the College had no choice of architects, who came with the funding.[27] In contrast to the subtle, meandering design at St John's, with its modulated facades and use of traditional materials, the Queens' design was much sharper, rational and rigid, creating a square court surrounded by the slender, crisp, white, exposed concrete structure of the buildings (fig.8.13). Three sides of the court were taken up by student rooms and the fourth by the dining hall which, with its enormous, hipped roof and lantern, was a modern interpretation of the great halls at the ancient Oxbridge colleges (fig.8.14).

The design received mixed reviews, depending on the disposition of the reviewer. Stephen Gardiner, architectural correspondent for *The Observer* and a fan of Powell and Moya, called it 'easily the best piece of modern architecture by a British architect anywhere'.[28] In Tom Sharpe's novel, *Porterhouse Blue*, the fictional Cornelius Carrington, a popular television presenter whose programmes were marked by a 'discriminating nostalgia' and a 'denunciation of the present', visited Cambridge, where he had been a student. He 'pottered on through St Catherine's and Queens', over the wooden bridge and shuddered at the desecration of concrete that had been erected over the river . . . In the afternoon he continued his pilgrimage through Trinity and John's and fulminated at the huge new building there'.[29] The wooden bridge refers to the Mathematical Bridge that links Cripps Court with the ancient part of Queens', whilst the 'huge new building' at St John's refers to the Cripps Building described earlier. Meanwhile, Tim Rawle suggested that the building at Queens' related badly to its site and that a similar approach to that taken by the same architects at St John's would have been more appropriate.[30]

In some ways the design at Queens' is the opposite of that at St John's, which clad an imaginative and unconventional interpretation of the traditional college layout in traditional materials. At Queens', the architects enclosed a conventional college courtyard with entirely modern buildings built of modern materials. These differences might be explained by differences in the

8.13 Queens' College, Cambridge, Cripps Court. The top floor is a later addition by Bland, Brown and Cole

8.14 Queens' College, Cambridge, Cripps Court. The hall to the left and the Mathematical Bridge to the right, linking the new additions to the ancient college on the other bank of the river

two sites. At St John's, the architects were working in and around existing buildings which they played against to create a series of interlinked spaces. The new building at Queens', although part of an ancient college, sat on the other side of the river from the existing buildings, on what was essentially a greenfield site. The only adjacent building was the Fisher Building, designed by George Drinkwater and completed in 1936, that was widely criticised for its pastiche historical style. Powell and Moya clearly chose not to engage with it and instead created their own enclosed community. Their choice of modern materials expressed in a modernist design was consistent with their work on other greenfield sites such as Wolfson College, Oxford and their hospital projects (see Chapter 4).

Arup Associates

Arup Associates grew out of the Building Group within the engineering practice of Ove Arup and Partners when it recruited architects Philip Dowson and Francis Pym fresh from the AA in 1953 and paired them with engineer Derek Sugden to form the nucleus of what would become Arup Associates in 1963.[31] It was the result of Ove Arup's quest to produce integrated 'total' design through a multi-disciplinary team where all members 'want to help produce good architecture, architecture in depth so to speak – not just artificially imposed formalism or applied make-up – as well as efficient function and economy . . .'[32]

Given those roots, it is unsurprising that Arup Associates' work revolved around a sound analysis of structure and services, and their integration within the overall design of the building. Services were generally unseen, but structure was often expressed and for a variety of objectives. In this chapter I examine the use of structure as a tool for relating to context.

Gothic architecture was the predominant style for Oxbridge colleges until the arrival of Christopher Wren in the 17th century, who brought a theoretical, as opposed to practical, approach to architecture. Wren completed a handful of Classical designs at Oxford and Cambridge and is seen by some commentators as 'the precursor of the star architects of the modern age . . . those critically acclaimed designers of headline-grabbing, prestige-generating structures hankered after by present-day university presidents and vice-chancellors'.[33]

Arup Associates' use of expressed structure in their designs, in particular their use of thin, finely crafted structural elements and exoskeleton, was a return to a Gothic sensibility; a return to the language of ribbed vaults and flying buttresses expressed in modern terms.

Somerville College, Oxford, Fry, Vaughan and Wolfson Buildings, 1958–67

Founded in 1879, Somerville was established as the second Oxford institution for women but only received college status in 1960. Margaret Fry House and Vaughan House formed a grouping of student rooms, raised on a plinth that accommodated shops to the street frontage and parking behind (fig.8.15). Arup Associates' inclusion of shops at street level, set back behind a generous arcade, was replicated by adjacent developments and helped revitalise the street as a busy fringe shopping area with an interesting variety of independent shops.[34]

Fry was completed in 1964 and Vaughan in 1966. Both adopted the language of fine concrete exoskeleton frame with a mostly glazed facade behind. The architect Tim Sturgis, who assisted Philip Dowson on the project, said that inspiration had come from Gothic stone buildings, 'with their single material for all elements, and their slim window mullions, grooved for glazing, moulded to catch the light . . . '[35] The architects also maintained that the use of an exoskeleton prevented rain-washed dirt from windows marking the concrete and avoided glare and excessive heat gain within rooms by projecting floor slabs beyond the window line to provide shading.[36]

The Fry and Vaughan buildings were followed by the Wolfson Building, completed in 1967. Arup Associates again employed an expressed concrete exoskeleton but, instead of the facade sheltering behind it, completely glazed bay windows burst

8.15 *Somerville College, Oxford, Margaret Fry House*

through and projected beyond the structure, appearing to negate the advantages claimed above (fig.8.16). Dowson stated that his aim in this instance was to allow for variety and personal expression, and to plan against loneliness through the creation of 'aedicules' where people could make their own human-sized spaces (fig.8.17). In contrast to Powell and Moya's forced variety at St John's College, Cambridge, Arup sought to provide scope for the individual occupant to create their own place within a standardised structure.

Corpus Christi College, Cambridge, George Thomson Building, 1961–4

The George Thomson Building was constructed in the grounds of the Victorian Leckhampton House to

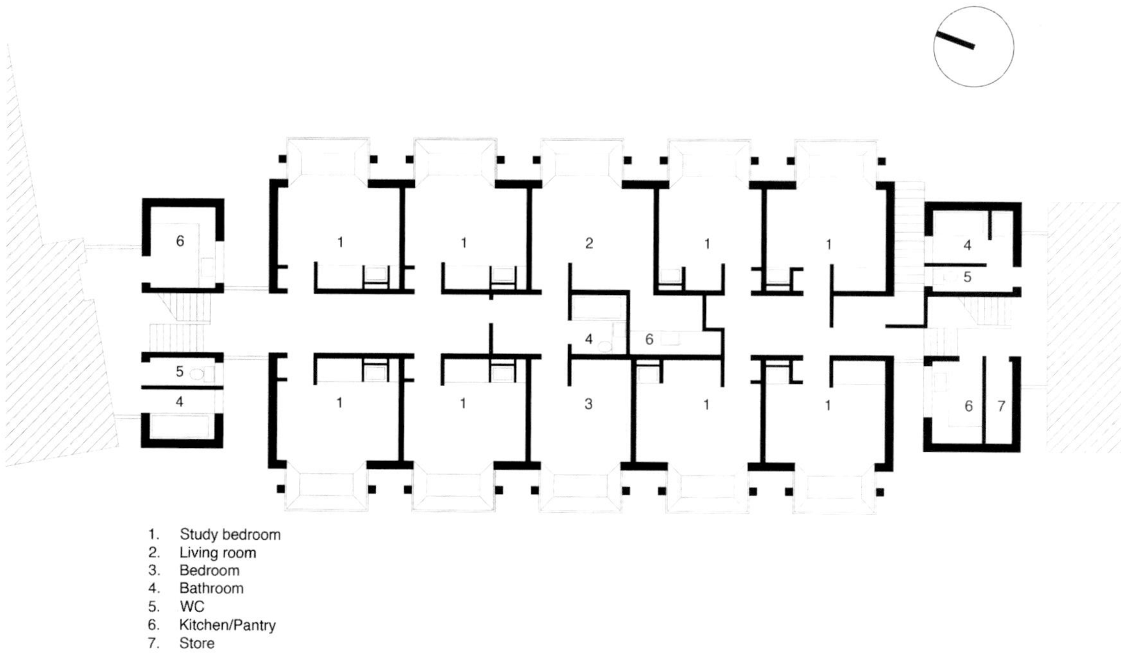

8.16 Somerville College, Oxford, Wolfson Building
8.17 Somerville College, Oxford, Wolfson Building. Upper floor plan

provide accommodation for postgraduate students at Corpus Christi College, Cambridge. It was designed as two pavilions of four and five storeys respectively, positioned to avoid as many existing trees as possible and to give each room a garden view (fig.8.25). The two were linked by a service block containing stairs, services and service rooms such as kitchens and bathrooms (fig.8.18). The architectural language followed that developed at Somerville College in Oxford, with a concrete exoskeleton in front of a glazed facade. The link block was clad in brick to emphasise the separation of functions into servant and served spaces, and to match the red brick of the adjacent Victorian house. Although the building was completed in 1964, the same year as the first Somerville building, and adopted the same vocabulary, it represented an advance by using a repetitive, storey-high, precast concrete H-frame to construct the exoskeleton, rather than the cast-in-situ concrete used at Oxford (fig.8.19).

Arup received the commission after a lengthy selection procedure, when it was noted that Dowson was 'deeply interested in the interior arrangements of residences for graduates or undergraduates'.[37] That approach paid dividends, and the result was hailed as 'one of Cambridge's best post-war buildings in every way: planning, structure, economy and social sensibility, [showing] a real understanding of student sociology in its grouping of rooms around the service areas . . .'[38]

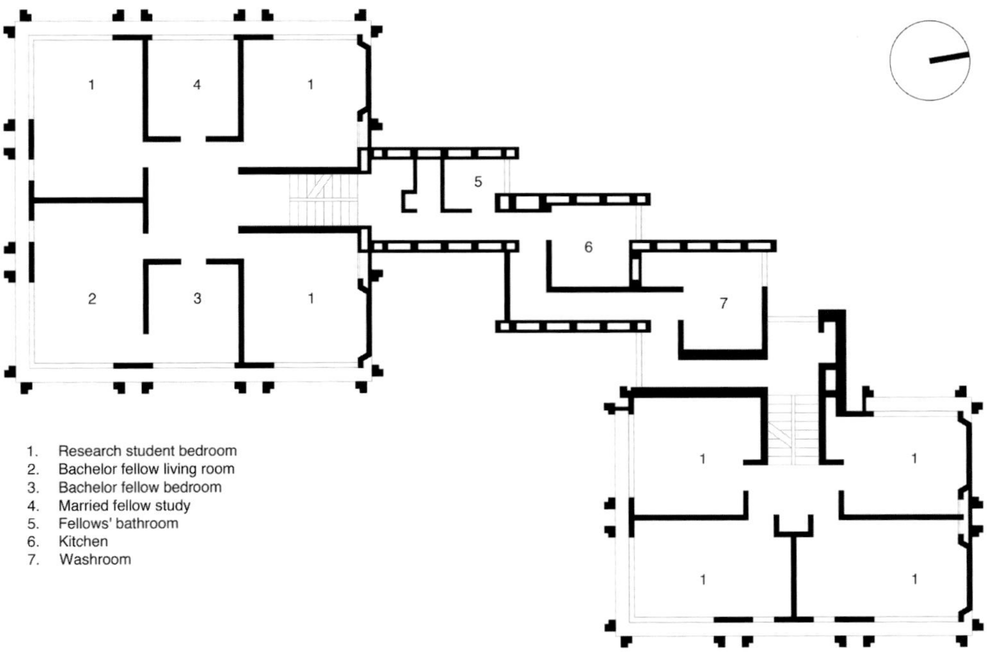

8.18 Corpus Christi College, Cambridge, George Thomson Building. Upper floor plan

8.19 Corpus Christi College, Cambridge, George Thomson Building

Trinity Hall, Cambridge, Boulton House, 1966–8
Just as the Wolfson Building at Somerville College, Oxford was a development of the Fry and Vaughan buildings, with individual bays projected out beyond the structural frame, so Boulton House at Trinity Hall was a development of the George Thomson Building at Corpus Christi, using the same H-frame, precast units but projecting glazed bays out beyond them (fig.8.20).

8.20 Trinity Hall, Cambridge, Boulton House

St John's College, Oxford, Sir Thomas White Building, 1970–75

The Sir Thomas White Building represents the culmination of the ideas explored in the projects described above. Like the George Thomson Building, it was organised as a series of pavilions linked by service towers that housed stairs and shared service spaces. The precast concrete exoskeleton was further developed to include corner units cranked at 90 degrees to address the issue of shading for projecting bay windows (fig.8.21). Tim Sturgis, who had worked on the earliest examples at the Fry and Vaughan buildings, called it 'the most assured and convincing of all the schemes for student rooms, the culmination of a long learning process. It seemed to incorporate both how to build with an exposed precast concrete structure and how students wanted to live'.[39] Dowson saw it as the most complete attempt to create 'a place of work and sleep, a retreat and a place to entertain, a place of privacy yet identifiably part of a larger community' (fig.8.22).[40]

8.21 St John's College, Oxford, Sir Thomas White Building

The project was Arup Associates' most ambitious for Oxford University and was bedevilled by an expanding brief and rising costs, for which client and architect each held the other responsible. In the end, a reduced scheme was built for an L-shaped development of 156 student rooms, arranged in 11 pavilions, linked by service blocks and connected by a colonnaded cloister at ground floor that housed set-back bars and common rooms (fig.8.23).[41]

The layout and finishes were reminiscent of Powell and Moya's development of Blue Boar Quad at Christ Church College, especially the use of stone-clad towers and the relationship to an existing stone wall that formed the site boundary along Lamb and Flag Passage (fig.8.24). Unlike Arup's other projects for Oxbridge colleges, the Sir Thomas White Building sought context not only in the use of Gothic structure but also by adopting materials that were seen as being more sympathetic to its central Oxford location. The line between abstract contextualism based on a modern reinterpretation of ideas and a more literal adoption of historical motifs is a thin one.

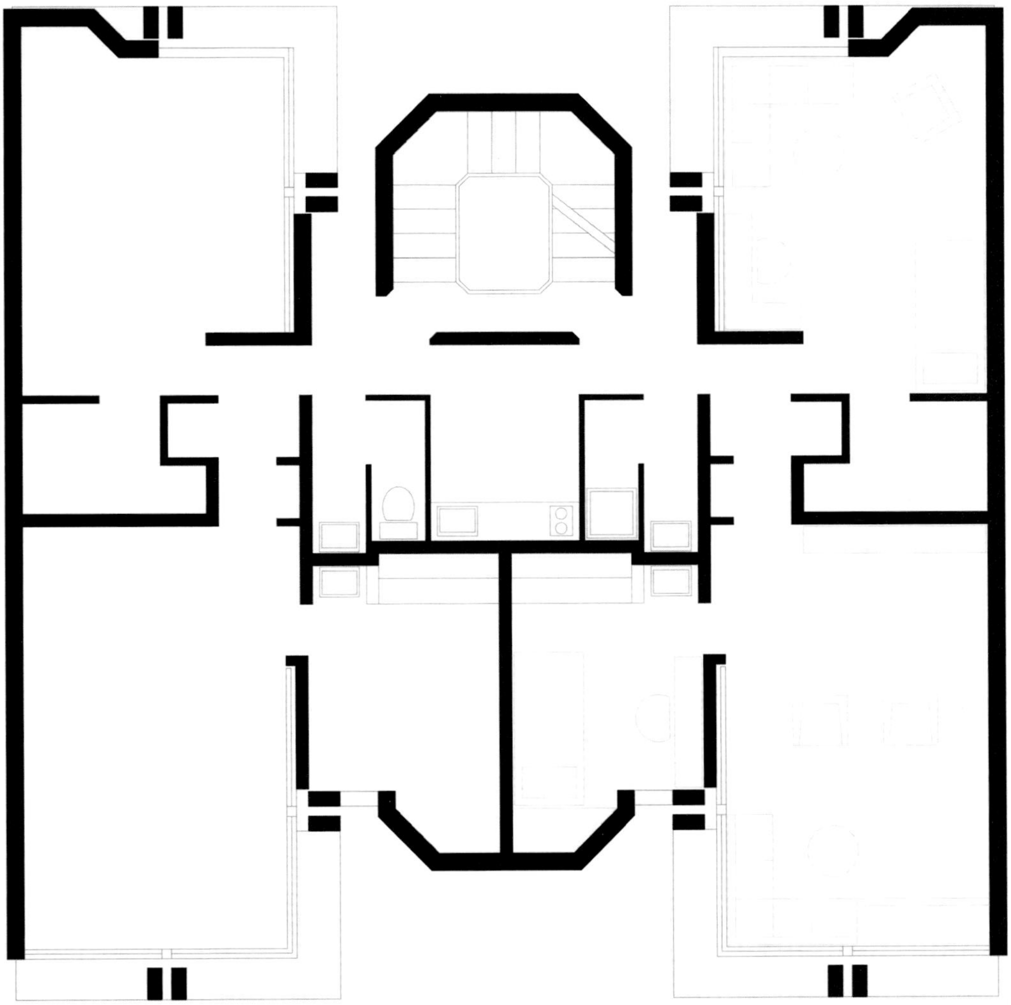

8.22 St John's College, Oxford, Sir Thomas White Building. Typical grouping of rooms

8.23 St John's College, Oxford, Sir Thomas White Building. The cloister, an almost medieval use of materials

8.24 St John's College, Oxford, Sir Thomas White Building. View from Lamb and Flag Passage

8.25 Corpus Christi College, Cambridge. George Thomson Building on the left, Leckhampton House on the right

9 The Missionaries
Architects' Co-Partnership
Alison and Peter Smithson

There was, in early modernism, a missionary zeal to make the world a better and fairer place after the horror of the First World War. The intensity of that desire had become diluted, only to be reignited in a new generation of architects in the aftermath of the Second World War and its landscape of ruin. 'Where it survives it is a sign of the wish to serve.'[1]

Architects' Co-Partnership

Architects' Co-Partnership (ACP) were of the generation that spanned the ideals of early modernism in the 1930s and those of the Welfare State that emerged after 1945. Well known and well regarded in the 1950s and 1960s, their reputation has been eclipsed by architects of the generation that followed. This might be due to their decision to adopt an anonymous title for their practice, making them a less attractive subject for publication in an industry that promotes the cult of personality. The founders claimed that the choice of name was an attempt to depart from 'prima donna' architecture, but they were equally intent on associating themselves with a political stance and with the Co-operative movement. They originally named the practice Architects' Co-operative Partnership and changed to Architects' Co-Partnership in 1953 when it appeared that the left-wing associations of the original title were discouraging potential clients. Kenneth Capon, one of the founding partners, recalls that the selection of partners was driven largely by personal friendships, but also by an assessment of political and personal commitment.[2] In 1938, while still students at the AA, some of the future partners were involved in production of the magazine *Focus*, which reflected their political views. The first issue declared that:

> We were born in war. Much that follows in this journal can be orientated to that one fact. We were born into a civilisation whose leaders, whose ideals, whose culture has failed. They are still in power today. But we, the generation that follow, cannot accept their domination. They lead us always deeper into reaction that we are convinced can only end in disaster.[3]

That kind of earnest prose, coupled with their middle-class backgrounds, prompted this retrospective and slightly mocking piece in *The Observer*:

9.1 Durham University, Dunelm House

GREAT COFFEE

> Left-wing, public school, they were all students together at the best and most expensive architectural school in the country, the Architectural Association . . . One can imagine them in those days just around the corner from Bedford Square [the location of the AA], lunching at Bertorelli's together, talking Spanish Civil War.[4]

The chance to put their ideals into practice came quickly. In 1945 they were asked by Jim Forrester (Lord Forrester and fourth Earl of Verulam) to design the Brynmawr Rubber Factory as a subsidiary to his family's Enfield Cable Works in the Welsh valleys. Forrester was the kind of well-intentioned if paternalistic landowner who 'looked after his people', and the project was backed by a government initiative to regenerate industrial communities where large-scale unemployment had become endemic. It fitted ACP's aspirations perfectly, allowing them to put their socialist principles and egalitarian ideals into practice – 'the perfect expression of their social engagement [and] an expiation of the guilt of being middle class and public school-educated in a world that they wanted to change'.[5] Michael Powers, one of the partners, recalled the pleasure of 'staying in a miner's cottage and meeting a wide variety of local people'.[6]

The project was an architectural and engineering tour de force, described as 'arguably the most spectacular interior of an industrial workplace in the history of British architecture' and 'one of the most impressive interiors in Britain since St. Paul's'.[7] However, it was a commercial failure and was sold to Dunlop Rubber within three years. There was no suggestion that the failure was related to the design but rather to the business model, and to other members of Forrester's family being unenthusiastic in their support.

The Brynmawr Rubber Factory was a major piece of architecture in the immediate post-war period, but it did not lead to further industrial projects for ACP. Instead, they moved into school design in a big way, completing around 40 projects overall. At that time many schools were designed by in-house local authority architects, and it is surprising, given their political views, that the partners did not individually take that route. They seem to have concluded that they were better placed to effect radical change independently. They were in favour of anonymous, 'non-prima donna' authorship, but only to an extent.

Their first university building was 'the Beehive', a set of student rooms for St John's College, Oxford. Completed in 1960, it was the first modern building to appear at an Oxford college. The plan consisted of three interlocking bands of stretched hexagons, where two opposing sides were longer than the other four. Following the traditional Oxbridge arrangement of rooms grouped around stairs, the central band contained stairs and ancillary rooms serving two outer bands of study bedrooms (fig.9.2). The hexagonal geometry allowed one wall of every room to be glazed, providing generous light and view whilst precluding overlook from adjacent rooms. The stair roofs were raised to form lanterns giving top light to the stairwells. External walls were faced in Portland stone and, together with pitched roofs over each hexagon, acknowledged traditional forms and materials (fig.9.3).

The interlocking hexagonal structure that gave the building its name reflected widespread interest amongst architects at that time with nesting forms whilst also expressing the cellular character of a hall of residence. At the same time, the resulting undulating facade was a modern take on the effect traditionally achieved with bay windows. Michael Powers, architect in charge for ACP, explained that the building's profile was a response to Oxford's 'spikey skyline, in which suddenly to insert a flat-roofed, flat-faced building would have been wrong'.[8]

The decision to appoint ACP was part of a policy to move away from tradition towards modernity that was being adopted across the Oxbridge colleges and the wider university sector. At the same time Queens' College, Cambridge was dismissing Stephen Dykes Bower in favour of Basil Spence (see Chapter 2) St John's College dismissed Sir Edward Maufe, an old member of the College, in favour of ACP. It marked a direction of travel that was irreversible and was confirmed when the

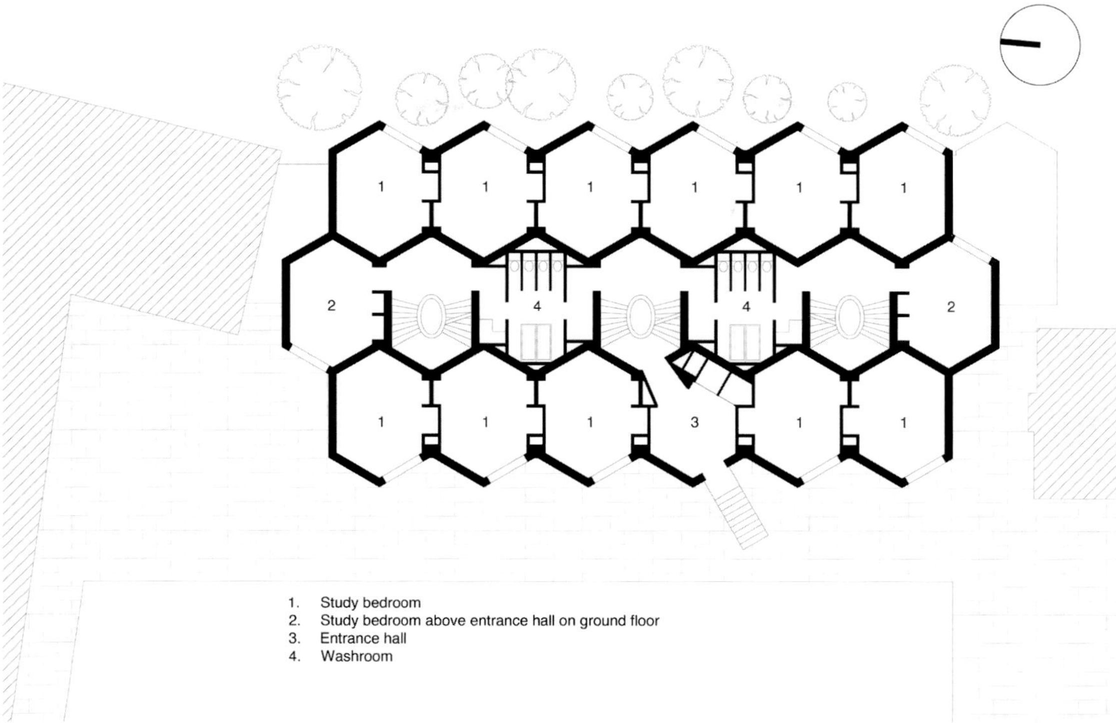

list of architects invited to participate in the design competition for Churchill College, Cambridge consisted of modernists only (see Chapter 1). ACP's entry to that competition was the only one to suggest high-rise point blocks for student residences. Their proposal was rejected, but they recycled the idea at Essex University, their biggest university project (see Chapter 3).

As ACP was completing the Beehive in Oxford, it began the design of student residences for King's College, Cambridge. The Market Hostel was not within the grounds of King's but in the town, just off the southwest corner of the market square. A concrete frame to the basement and ground floor housed a bank (now a shop). Above this, student rooms of brick cross-wall construction surrounded two sides of a raised courtyard above the bank. The design was well considered and unassuming. This was certainly not prima donna architecture; without close inspection it might easily be mistaken for a piece of commercial work by a hack designer (fig.9.4). What distinguishes it is its thoughtful planning, careful detailing and special, long, narrow, exceptionally regular, white bricks from Venlo in the Netherlands, which the architects specified, rather than use local Cambridge whites. Apparently, their aim was not to be contextual so much as to achieve a crisp, machine aesthetic in keeping with early modernism.

Function drove the design of the Wolfson Building for Trinity College, Cambridge. Another project for a student residence, it was like the Beehive in clearly expressing each individual room. Unlike the Beehive, it made no attempt to blend with its surroundings. An enormous whale of a building, stranded in the backyard to a city block of older shops and houses, it was only the fact that it was hidden from the surrounding streets that prevented it from overwhelming its neighbours. Rooms were stepped back in a ziggurat from a

9.2 St John's College, Oxford, The Beehive. Upper floor plan

lozenge-shaped plan that sat on top of a podium set about 4m (13ft) above street level (fig.9.5). The podium filled the site and abutted the backs of the existing buildings. Below it was a delivery and expansion area for the businesses that surrounded the site. Tim Rawle recorded the architects' initial intention to clad the building in vertically ribbed concrete to create an effect of 'soaring verticality'. It was the College which insisted on brick panels, giving the 'unintended impression of a pile of stacked boxes'.[9] The elevations repeated the Stonehenge-like simplicity of brick panels supporting visible slabs used by Lasdun at Fitzwilliam College and, like it, were ultimately influenced by Le Corbusier's Maisons Jaoul (see Chapter 4).

It is easy to dwell on the building's scale and lack of contextual sympathy while missing its

9.3 St John's College, Oxford, The Beehive

merits. It was an ingeniously practical solution to the difficult problem of housing a large number of students on a tight site. The stepped lozenge plan gave every room a view whilst avoiding overlook from other rooms. The stepped ziggurat section allowed ample daylight to penetrate the lowest level of accommodation, whilst two large rooflights illuminated the internal circulation spaces (fig.9.6). The space beneath the podium provided added value to the surrounding commercial premises which, in turn, hid the mass of the building from the street. I lived in Cambridge shortly after this building was completed and was unaware of its existence until researching this book.

Away from Oxford and Cambridge, ACP's university work followed a familiar path, from sharp, lightweight, early modernism influenced by Gropius and Mies to heavier concrete buildings influenced by Le Corbusier's post-war work. Their 1957 design for the Chemistry Building at Leicester University (now the George Porter Building) is an example of the former (fig.9.7). Essex University (see Chapter 3), begun in 1962, and Dunelm House at Durham University, 1965, are examples of the latter.

The Chemistry Building at Leicester completed Leslie Martin's masterplan and adopted a similar style to the buildings that he had designed for the site (see Chapter 2). The Essex and Durham designs pick up on ideas that were being developed at that time for mat buildings, which Alison Smithson later defined as a structure based on three parameters: interconnection; close-knit patterns of association; and possibilities for growth. Prominent examples were the Free University of Berlin by Candilis, Josic, Woods and Schiedhelm and Le Corbusier's proposal for the Venice Hospital. A characteristic of the mat building is a continuous horizontal development grid, best suited to a flat site. Both Essex and Durham were sited on river valleys, leading to the charge that the Essex design 'obliterated' the valley (see Chapter 3). At Durham, the mat is draped over the high riverbank and

9.4 King's College, Cambridge, Market Hostel

9.5 Trinity College, Cambridge, Wolfson Building

9.6 Trinity College, Cambridge, Wolfson Building. Surrounding buildings of existing city block in background

the building cascades down to the water's edge (fig.9.8). In both cases, the architectural language, in particular the use of randomly spaced concrete window mullions, is reminiscent of Le Corbusier's Convent of La Tourette (fig.9.9).

ACP was established as a non-hierarchical co-operative of equals and began life with 11 partners, although by 1947 that had reduced to eight. This arrangement begs the question as to how expansion was to be accommodated. Would every recruit become an equal partner? That was clearly not feasible and ACP soon became like other practices, with partners and staff. Even so, in order to support so many partners, the practice sought work overseas in previously colonised countries and opened an office in Nigeria in 1954. They were not the first to take that route and followed in the footsteps of Jane Drew and Maxwell Fry. Hannah Le Roux and Ola Uduku argue that there was a conveyor belt of modernist architects moving between centres of colonial power like London and colonies or ex-colonies in West Africa. Not only did the architects come from the colonising powers but the literature and analyses on which they based their designs were written from the perspective of the colonisers. The Building Research Establishment, at that time a UK government body, produced technical guides published as 'Colonial Building Notes'.[10]

The flow of architects from Europe carrying the word of modernism to ex-colonies bears uncomfortable comparisons with previous waves of preachers carrying the word of God to the unenlightened. In that respect, ACP can be seen as missionaries, determined to 'do good' in less advantaged communities, whether in the mining villages of Wales or the towns and villages of West Africa. There is no doubt that ACP produced intelligent and thoughtful buildings. Whether they were always culturally appropriate is another matter and there is little evidence that the architects consulted the communities for which they were intended. As with all missionaries, there was an assumption that they knew better than the recipients what was good for them.

9.7 Leicester University, Chemistry Building
9.8 Durham University, Dunelm House

9.9 Durham University, Dunelm House. View across the river to Durham Cathedral, bridge designed by Ove Arup and Partners

Alison and Peter Smithson

If ACP was on a mission to change the world, the Smithsons were on a mission to change British architecture. They saw the achievements of post-war architecture and planning in Britain as 'so feeble that for the ordinary person it was not possible to feel that any attempt to build the dreamed-of post-war world was being made . . . and this was not the result of practical restrictions, it was a true bankruptcy of sustaining notions'.[11] They were dissatisfied with everything from the 'ideas of the Garden City movement to the rationalism of the thirties'.[12] They argued that 'the very success of CIAM's campaigning [had created] inhuman conditions of a more subtle order than the slums'.[13] Along with other likeminded European architects of their generation they formed Team 10 as an alternative to CIAM. They were also members of the Independent Group of London-based artists, photographers, designers and writers that was centred around the Institute of Contemporary Arts (ICA). Key members included the architectural critic Reyner Banham, the artist and photographer Nigel Henderson, artists Eduardo Paolozzi and Richard Hamilton, and arts critic Lawrence Alloway.[14]

Some of the urban planning ideas the Smithsons explored were similar to those promoted by Jane Jacobs in the US: a granular hierarchy of house, street, district, city, although they abandoned those terms as 'too loaded with historical overtones' and replaced them with the idea of the 'cluster'.[15] Where they differed from Jacobs was in their assumption that previous failures were caused by the theories of the planners in charge and could be solved by a new set of planners with different theories. Jacobs argued that the system of top-down planning itself was the problem, where 'the right to have plans of any significance belonged only to the planners in charge'.[16]

The Smithsons were unusual in British architecture, operating simultaneously as practitioners, theorists, writers and educators. Their circle of friends included Theo Crosby, and when he became editor of the magazine *Architectural Design* (*AD*) in 1953 he gave them almost unlimited access to its pages for the next 20 years, providing an unprecedented and seemingly uncritical platform to publish both their ideas and their work.[17] They were widely read and discussed in architectural circles but their built output was modest.

The most prominent example of their urban planning theories was their entry for the Golden Lane housing competition, won by Chamberlin Powell and Bon (see Chapter 6). Here the Smithsons demonstrated their ideas about identity, mobility and horizontal connectivity at all levels throughout the city via their 'streets in the air'.[18] Similar solutions were being examined by Kenzo Tange, Arata Isozaki and the Metabolist Group in Japan, which the Smithsons visited in 1960.[19] The closest they came to a built example was at Robin Hood Gardens in Poplar, London, where two linear blocks of housing each demonstrated the idea of streets in the air but lacked any further horizontal connectivity either between or beyond themselves. The Smithsons' vision prioritised urban form and mobility over exhaustive design of every aspect of the buildings, which were left as basic as possible so that the inhabitants could develop them in ways that suited their individual needs and preferences. By their own admission, Robin Hood Gardens was a failure in that respect. It is not clear whether they blame the architecture or the inhabitants for this.

> The architect should stop at a point but make an offering which makes occupation possible. From then onwards it's up to you, the occupier, to say whether the building does or doesn't work. It certainly hasn't worked well at Robin Hood Gardens: the building has simply been vandalised.[20]

The Smithsons' big architectural idea was the New Brutalism, a label that was subsequently applied to the work of many architects of their generation, even if the architects themselves rejected it. Its meaning is difficult to pin down and may in part have been chosen as a tongue-in-cheek denial of

9.10 St Hilda's College, Oxford, Garden Building

the New Empiricism, the Scandinavian-influenced modernism that was adopted by many in the previous generation of British architects.[21] Banham announced its arrival in the *Architectural Review* and defined it as a 'mood' shared by a small number of artists in London with no particular unity of programme or intention but who had common interests.[22] The artists in question were the members of the Independent Group and their common interests included urban communities – influenced by Henderson's documentary photographs of London's East End – and the Neo-Dadaist use of 'as-found' objects and anti-aesthetic agenda.[23] They also embraced pop culture, with which the Smithsons tried, unconvincingly, to forge a connection. Had punk existed at that time, it would have provided a better home for their ideas about kicking over the old order and replacing it with something much rawer and, ostensibly, unaffected.

The first built example was Hunstanton School in Norwich, which the Smithsons won in competition while working in the schools' division of the GLC. The design owed much to the simplicity and potential of ordinary, off-the-shelf materials displayed in the work of Mies in the US, but had none of what Mark Crinson called the 'suavity' of its detailing. Instead, the Smithsons celebrated the roughness of manufactured parts as they emerged from fabrication, producing 'a lesson in honesty, a manifesto of plain-speaking materials and structural integrity'.[24] The Smithsons acknowledged their debt to Mies as 'so great it is difficult to disentangle what are our own thoughts, so often have they been the result of insights received from him'.[25] The 'Brutalist' element of the New Brutalism, however, they attributed to the Japanese 'respect for materials . . . which was at the root of our way of seeing and thinking about things that we called New Brutalism'.[26]

The Smithsons were perhaps being disingenuous in diminishing the influence of Le Corbusier, at the very least in the name of the new movement. 'Brutalism' was the description given to Le Corbusier's post-war, *béton brut* buildings with their rough and direct expression of massive concrete. The New Brutalism was a similar intellectual exercise, even if stylistically different and using different materials.

The strongest expression of these ideas lies in an unbuilt design for the Smithsons' own house and office in London. It was a simple, exposed brick, terraced house for a gap site in Fitzrovia which explored 'an idea about the relation between building technique and the form of domestic and working life that it allowed to develop, untrammelled by conventions of architectural finish, once the building was inhabited'.[27] The design was published as 'House in Soho', presumably to sound more edgy than Fitzrovia. The use of a gap site created by wartime bombing relates to their interest in 'as found', particularly the ordinary and even the ruined or the discarded. Henderson introduced them to London's East End and a 'way of looking' that included study and appreciation of the detritus of bomb sites.[28] There are parallels between the Smithsons' approach and the Japanese architect Takamitsu Azuma's childhood exploration of bomb sites in Osaka, his 'joy of finding things imperfect', his promotion of the 'aesthetics of imperfection' and his contention that 'an architect shouldn't define how to live . . . rather an architect should provide several possibilities from which users can choose . . .'[29] All are echoed in the Smithsons' theories.

The Smithsons submitted a high-profile but unsuccessful entry to the design competition for Sheffield University in 1953, based on their urban planning theories. They completed several buildings at Bath University between 1978 and 1990. But their only built university project in the 1960s was the Garden Building at St Hilda's College, Oxford, designed in 1967 and completed in 1970.

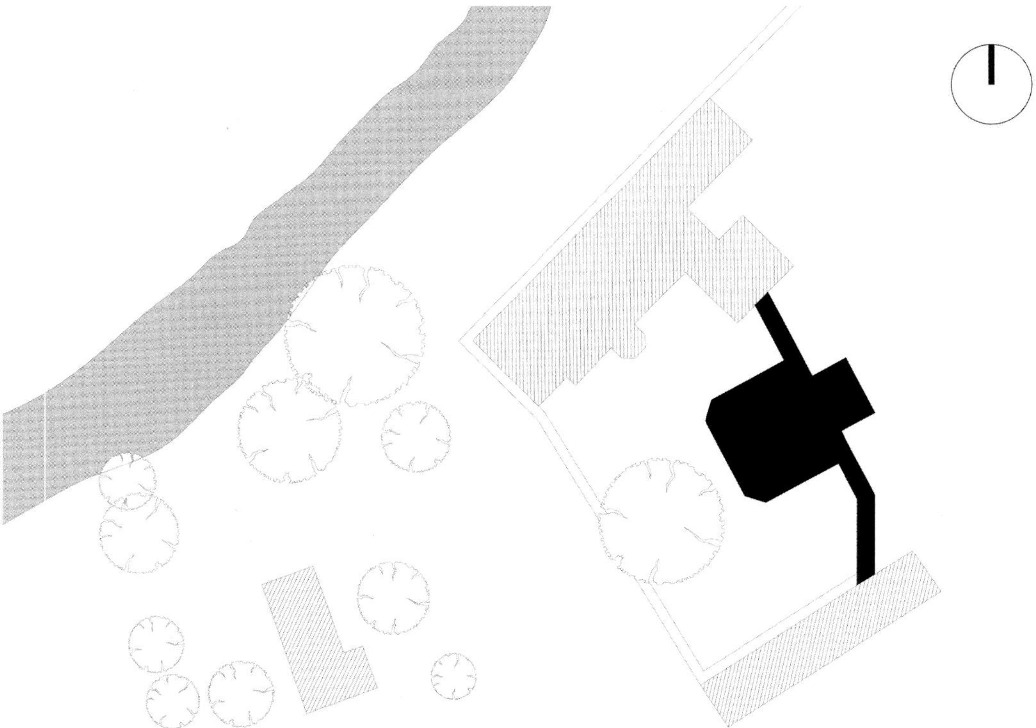

9.11 St Hilda's College, Oxford, Garden Building. Site plan

St Hilda's was one of the first women's colleges to be founded during the latter part of the 19th century. It consisted of several small, disparate buildings. The Garden Building was one of several additions that were made as funds became available.[30] It provided accommodation for female students, sitting within an existing garden that ran down to the River Cherwell and dominated by a mature copper beech. Instead of placing the building on the river's edge, as Stirling did with a contemporaneous design for Queen's College, Oxford (see Chapter 12), the Smithsons located it in the middle of the garden, adjacent to the beech tree, and used the tree's natural form as a foil to the strong geometry of the building's chamfered cuboid shape (fig.9.10). Covered walkways linked it with existing buildings to each side, co-opting them as wings in a grander composition. The plan was rather like an English country house, sitting foursquare, with wings that created a forecourt, and set back from the river with a lawn running down to the water's edge and some specimen trees (fig.9.11).

The architectural expression was the same as the group of buildings the Smithsons designed for the *Economist* in central London and completed in 1964. Both in plan and elevational treatment the Garden Building resembled the Economist Tower. The plan comprised three sides of accommodation wrapped round a service core that was exposed to a service yard at the rear, leaving the other three sides free to enjoy views over the garden (fig.9.12). The elevations were simple, alternating horizontal bands of almost room-height glazing and concrete panels. In front of this tight, controlled, facade they placed a heavy and rustic oak trellis

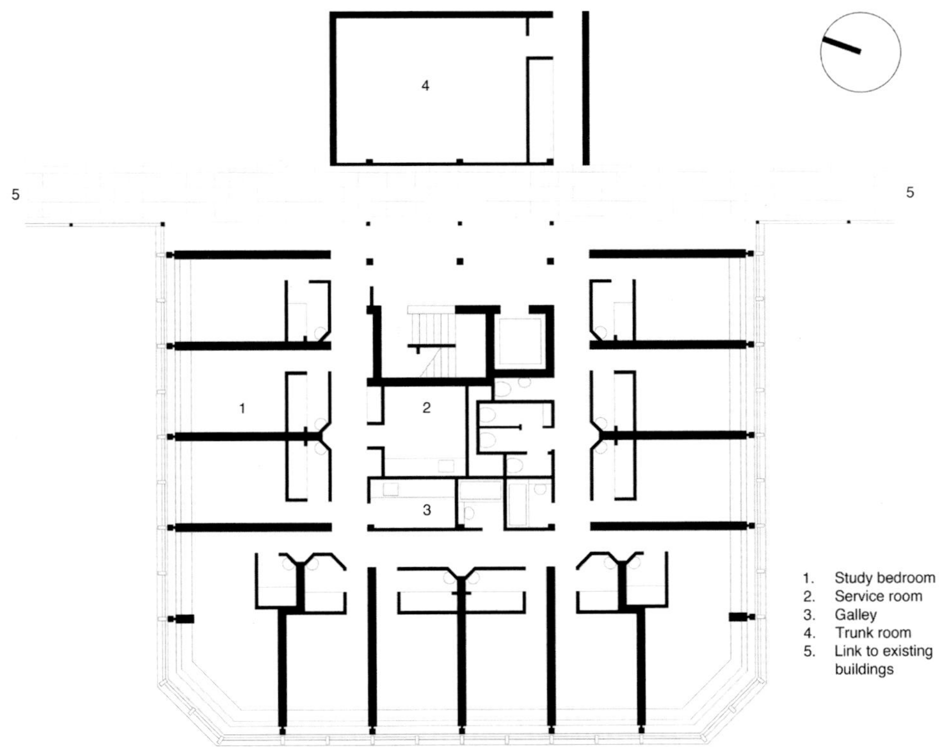

9.12 St Hilda's College, Oxford, Garden Building. Ground floor plan

with diagonal bracing that resembled a traditional half-timbered building.

They justified the presence of the timber screen on both quantitative and qualitative grounds: it provided screening to fully glazed rooms; it provided support for climbing plants; it recalled the 'memory' of garden trellises; and the seasonal growth of the plants symbolically marked the passage of time and invited the user to complete the building by adding their own 'layer of habitation'.[31] Writing later, the Smithsons argued that 'St Hilda's . . . found one way of inviting the occupiers into the game of architecture; one particular language of invitation, that of layers'.[32] They also referred to the screen as a 'yashmak'.[33]

It is characteristic of the Smithsons' theoretical and intellectual approach to describe the decision in those terms when a simpler, more pragmatic reason was available – that the building was too stark in its naked form and the screen was added to soften it and help settle it in its garden location. John Prestwich, who was a member of the Building Committee at Oxford, said that the Smithsons appeared arty, pretentious and rhetorical in conversation and appearance, but turned out to be sensible and efficient.[34] Certainly the Garden Building was judged by critics to be sensible and efficient: it was described as 'plain, square and dumpy' and 'an ordinary, straightforward and efficient building . . . the only unusual feature is the applied timber screen'.[35] In practice the screen has provided none of its hypothetical benefits and the occupants have 'joined the game of architecture' by introducing their own, more effective, 'yashmak' of net curtains which, in many photographs of the building, are fully closed in every room.

The Smithsons argued that the new has to be 'seen in the context of the existing patterns of association' and claimed that the New Brutalism 'finds its closest affinities not in past architectural style, but in peasant dwelling forms, which have style and are stylish but were never modish: a poetry without rhetoric'.[36] Whether their admiration for untutored peasant forms extended to the more middle-class 'patterns of association' conjured up by net curtains is unrecorded.

The episode of the net curtains is characteristic of the tendency for people to rebel against good intentions and leads to a wider questioning of those intentions. Are missionaries really interested in the problems, let alone the views, of their flock or in imposing their doctrines for the sake of their own glorification? The Smithsons and ACP are open to that criticism and to the charge that the doctrine was more important than the problems it was attempting to address. However, whilst the architects might be seen as elitist and the work might be criticised as dull and uninspiring, it could be thoughtful and practical. It could be more than that: the Economist group of buildings designed by the Smithsons is arguably the finest piece of urban design to be produced in 20th-century Britain. It eschewed the picturesque and was unafraid of simplicity and repetition, but marshalled planning, proportion, materials and detail to produce a quietly dignified and appropriate design that has stood the test of time (fig.9.13). Such issues raise the question of what we want from architecture, and that is a question that is not widely discussed in Britain. It is possible to question their motivation and criticise perceived pretensions, but the missionaries tried to stimulate that discussion.

9.13 The Economist group of buildings, London

10 The Structuralists

Arup Associates

HKPA

In previous chapters we have seen architecture presented as individual vision or collaborative teamwork, localised context or universal 'truth', social endeavour or top-down urban restructuring. Each of these described a broad attitude towards the provision of architecture. This chapter looks at a more specific approach to the design of buildings generated by consideration of structure.

Arup Associates

Given the origins of its foundation and philosophy, it is unsurprising that Arup Associates considered structure to be an integral part of building design. In Chapter 8, we saw how Arup's architects used structure to visually connect with the context of the ancient Oxbridge colleges. In other locations, where they did not feel the weight of history pressing so heavily, they used structure as an organising force behind the planning and operation of buildings.

An early example, and their first use of a 'tartan grid', was the laboratories for the Department of Mining and Metallurgy at Birmingham University. A series of parallel but offset grids for structure, services and partitions provided the framework for the design of the building and the integration of structure, services and functional spaces. The stimulus for this more systematic approach came primarily from the US and architects such as Mies; Skidmore, Owings & Merrill; and, in particular, Louis Kahn and his interest in the interplay between served and service elements to create a distinctive architectural language.[1]

At Birmingham, the tartan grid was based on 20ft (6m) square modules set out with gaps between them and supported by a column at each corner. Where four modules came together, the space left between the columns was used for vertical services distribution, whilst main horizontal distribution ran in the gaps between the modules (fig.10.2). The grid was expressed on the facade of the building, where columns were exposed and the bays between them clad in patent glazing, and at roof level, where extract vents formed a housing over each cluster of four columns (fig.10.3).[2]

The building was also layered vertically, with heavy equipment and lecture theatres on the ground floor, other teaching spaces and offices on the first floor, and laboratories and research facilities on the top floor.

10.1 Birmingham University, Department of Mining and Metallurgy

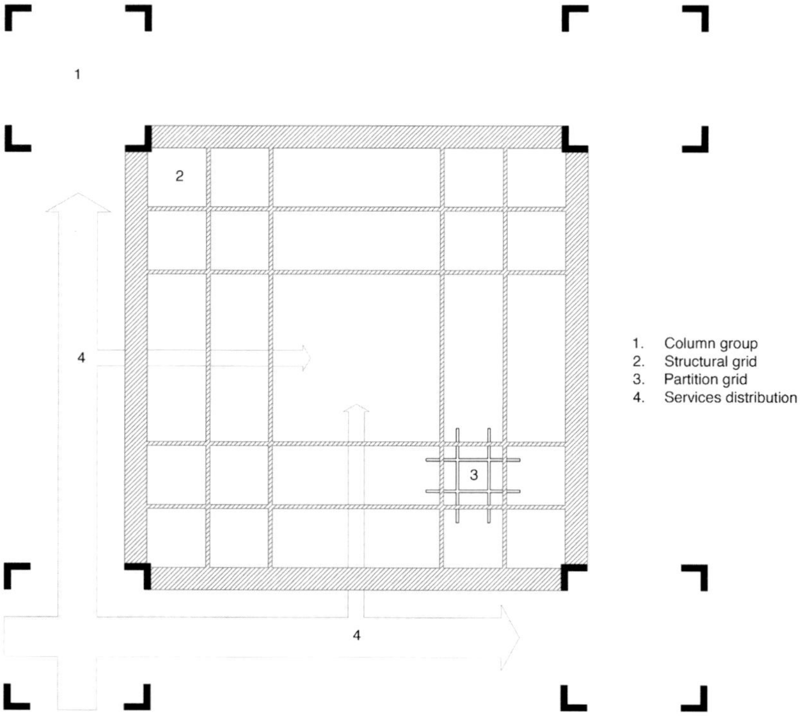

The decision to relegate style and almost let the building emerge from a systematic analysis of its inner workings, far from producing a dry and lifeless diagram, resulted in an elegant and timeless piece of architecture. Of course, the result was not automatic and was due in large part to the aesthetic judgement of the designers and the quality of their detailing and specification. It stands as a testament to Ove Arup's belief in the power of the integrated design team to produce 'total' architecture, 'architecture in depth so to speak – not just artificially imposed formalism or applied make-up – as well as efficient function and economy . . .'[3]

Arup designed other buildings at Birmingham University, the most notable being the Arts and Commerce Building (Muirhead Tower). The project responded to a rise in the number of arts students attending the University and to Casson and Conder's masterplan, which called for a landmark tower on the campus. It was Arup's most controversial building for the University and was dominated by its structural expression. A massive exoskeleton of columns and beams, like a giant, concrete Meccano set, supported floors that were slotted into it like drawers in a sequence of one 'dark' floor for every two 'light' floors (fig.10.4). Dark floors had few windows and housed lecture spaces; light floors were fully glazed and contained tutorial rooms and offices.[4] Conceptually, the design had parallels with the megastructure proposals of Isozaki and the Metabolist group in Japan, and with Tange's Yamanashi Press and Broadcasting Centre. Formally, it had a similar structural expression to Tange's proposal to redevelop the Tsukiji area in Tokyo which, like his Yamanashi Press building, was designed around the same time as Muirhead Tower.[5]

10.2 Tartan grid

At Loughborough University, Arup investigated the possibilities for extending the tartan grid beyond individual buildings to encompass an entire masterplan. Originally established as a college of education during the First World War, with an emphasis on aero- and auto-engineering, Loughborough was later designated a College of Advanced Technology (CAT) and expanded to designs by Sheppard Robson (fig.10.5). When it gained university status in 1966, it was further expanded by Arup Associates.[6]

H.L. Haslegrave, the Vice-Chancellor, had spoken against 'impressive, palatial buildings [and] highly specialised facilities [that would be] unsuitable for other purposes without a large expenditure of effort and money'. What he wanted was flexibility and the ability to expand continuously as demand rose and money was made available, whilst ensuring that the campus always appeared attractive and apparently complete.[7]

Arup determined that 'the problem of devising methods to allow for the growth and change of the University lies at the very heart of its masterplan'. They concluded that they must 'develop a pattern or discipline which will ensure a sense of order and continuity . . . but which will be flexible enough to provide the framework within which future requirements can be met'. Their solution was to develop 'a three-dimensional geometry of multiple but not coincident grids' and a basic, square unit of teaching space that could be agglomerated in both directions within the grid to cater for spaces of different sizes and for expansion.[8] In other words, a tartan grid (fig.10.6).

Other Arup buildings that were driven by a systematic approach to the design of structure, services and function include the Nuclear Physics Laboratory for Oxford University and the New Museums Building for Cambridge University. Both buildings were controversial because, unlike Arup designs for Oxbridge colleges, they seemed to ignore the context of those ancient cities.

10.3 Birmingham University, Department of Mining and Metallurgy

10.4 Birmingham University, Muirhead Tower

The Nuclear Physics building was one of several science buildings that were developed in a piecemeal fashion on a triangular site to the north of the city centre that was previously occupied by Victorian villas. With the demolition of the original buildings, there was little immediate context and the building was planned for efficiency. Efforts were made to visually reduce its bulk by deeply recessing the middle floor and cladding the top floor in glass that reflected the sky. The element that most clearly signalled its purpose was also the most visible and criticised – a large, freestanding, fan-shaped tower that housed a linear accelerator (fig.10.7).

The New Museums Building derives its name from the Zoological Museum that, together with workshops and loading bays, formed a plinth over which other departments were housed in a line of five towers, joined together by cores containing services and circulation. Offices were put in two hexagonal towers that docked onto the east and west sides of the main building, from which they were visually differentiated. The whole assemblage was shoehorned into the narrow street pattern in this densely packed part of central Cambridge. Whilst the building was described as 'cool, competent, elegant', it was also criticised as 'brutal and clumsy in its context'.[9]

The issue of scale is inherent in a situation where a large, modern and technical building is inserted into a medieval city plan of narrow streets and small buildings. Tim Rawle described the standard of university expansion in Cambridge as 'generally poor', although he felt that the colleges had, 'with a few exceptions, handled their modern development and expansion most successfully'.[10] Rawle's criticism was based largely on the destruction of vibrant and picturesque narrow streets of housing and shops to make way for new university or local authority developments in the city centre. His comments highlight the fact that many colleges could build on their own land without disrupting the fabric of the city, whilst the University

10.5 Loughborough University, Herbert Manzoni Building. Designed by Sheppard Robson

10.6 Loughborough University, Mechanical, Electrical and Manufacturing Engineering

10.7 *Oxford University, Nuclear Physics Laboratory. Linear accelerator in foreground*

10.8 *Cambridge University, New Museums Building. One of the office towers is just visible in the background to the left*

and local government often could not. A previous proposal for the New Museums site by Lasdun was for a series of freestanding towers that would have dwarfed the nearby King's College Chapel. One solution to the problem of scale would have been for the University to place the buildings further out of town, as they did with other faculty buildings at the Sidgwick site, for example. However, that course was often fraught with the difficulty of acquiring land from the Colleges (see Chapter 2).

Arup applied the same rational logic to the problem of location as they did to the functioning of the building. By successively stepping out upper floors they maintained street width whilst also maximising floor area. The top floor had the greatest area and housed laboratories arranged around three internal courtyards that provided daylight to the core of the building and valuable amenity space for staff in a tight urban setting.[11] It was a logical solution but heightened the impression that the building was looming over the narrow streets (fig.10.8).

Howard Killick Partridge and Amis

In his foreword to Geraint Franklin's book on HKPA, Norman Foster argued that their architecture was based on 'readable' structure, structure that we immediately grasp and which articulates space for us. He quotes Howell on the feel-good factor generated by beamy cottages, King's College Chapel, Japanese houses, old boats and planes, and the Crystal Palace, because they feed an unconscious human desire to be held.[12] Arup tapped into that desire in the design of student residences, where the structure of a room delineated discrete 'nesting' areas for sleep, study or conversation (see Chapter 8). HKPA's approach to structure was more emotional that Arup's, beginning with their entry to the Churchill College competition.

Bill Howell, John Killick and Stan Amis met as students at the AA and went to work at the LCC, where they encountered John Partridge. The four worked on a Le Corbusier-inspired design for housing at Roehampton Lane before Howell and

Killick left to set up practice. They were joined by Partridge to work on the Churchill College competition and later by Amis.[13]

Their entry to the competition placed second and was favoured by many commentators. It was seen by some as a quintessentially English take on modernism, channelling Nash crescents as well as the exoticism of his Brighton Pavilion and the English tradition of eccentricity.[14] Equally, it had more than a hint of German Expressionism. Like other unsuccessful entrants to the competition, they did not abandon the ideas but recycled them in other projects. Most noticeable were the highly sculpted facades that featured protruding, truncated-pyramid window surrounds that reappeared in many of their university designs.

The first of these was the Faculty of Commerce and Social Science at Birmingham University. The initial proposal consisted of a gently curving, two-storey linear building that shielded the site from traffic noise on an adjacent ring road, and a seven-storey building with a snail-shell plan and a central rotunda that housed tutorial and staff rooms (fig.10.10). These are known as the Strathcona and Ashley Buildings respectively.[15] Both buildings were faced with sculptural concrete brises soleil that were reminiscent of Oscar Niemeyer's work in Brasilia. The proposal was approved but cost overruns led to the removal of the brises soleil, to be replaced by simple concrete panels on the Strathcona Building and truncated-pyramid window cowls like those featured in the Churchill competition on the Ashley Building (fig.10.9). Other changes included a simpler plan for Strathcona, a reduction in the height of Ashley from seven to five storeys, and flipping the Ashley plan so that its 'tail' now helped enclose a garden between the two buildings.[16] The design of the Ashley and Strathcona Buildings was begun in 1961 and was quickly followed by a commission for St Anne's College, Oxford in 1962.

10.9 Birmingham University. Ashley Building on left, Strathcona on right. Arup Associates' Muirhead Tower in background

10.10 Birmingham University, Ashley Building. Central rotunda

St Anne's was 'the youngest, largest, and probably the poorest' women's college at Oxford according to its Principal in 1959.[17] It received its royal charter in 1952 and full self-governing status in 1959. After the University's annual quota of female students was lifted in 1957, numbers rose and the College sought to build new student accommodation. HKPA were appointed in 1960 and proposed a 'necklace' of five residential blocks strung around the edge of an artificial lake and terminated with a 12-storey tower. Construction would be phased as funding became available. In the event, only two beads of the necklace were constructed and named after their funders, the Wolfson and Rayne foundations. Ironically, as opportunities increased for women students and men's colleges began to take women, demand for the original women's colleges failed to expand as envisaged. That turn of events, combined with continuing difficulties in securing funding and in acquiring freehold over existing villas that were to be replaced by the new residences, meant that the College decided not to continue with further building.[18]

The St Anne's designs were not based on structural articulation but provided a link between the expressionism of HKPA's early projects and those that followed. Each building took the gentle curvature of the Strathcona Building and mirrored it to create two sets of student rooms enclosing a thin, oval atrium that housed an open circular stair in the centre, an enclosed escape stair at one end and kitchens at the other end (fig.10.11). Each room had a small window for ventilation and full height sliding glass doors that gave access to balconies that were contained within precast concrete cowls first seen in the Churchill competition and then at the Ashley Building (fig.10.12).

Another project begun in 1960 at the nearby St Antony's College saw the practice begin to use structure as a distinct element in the definition

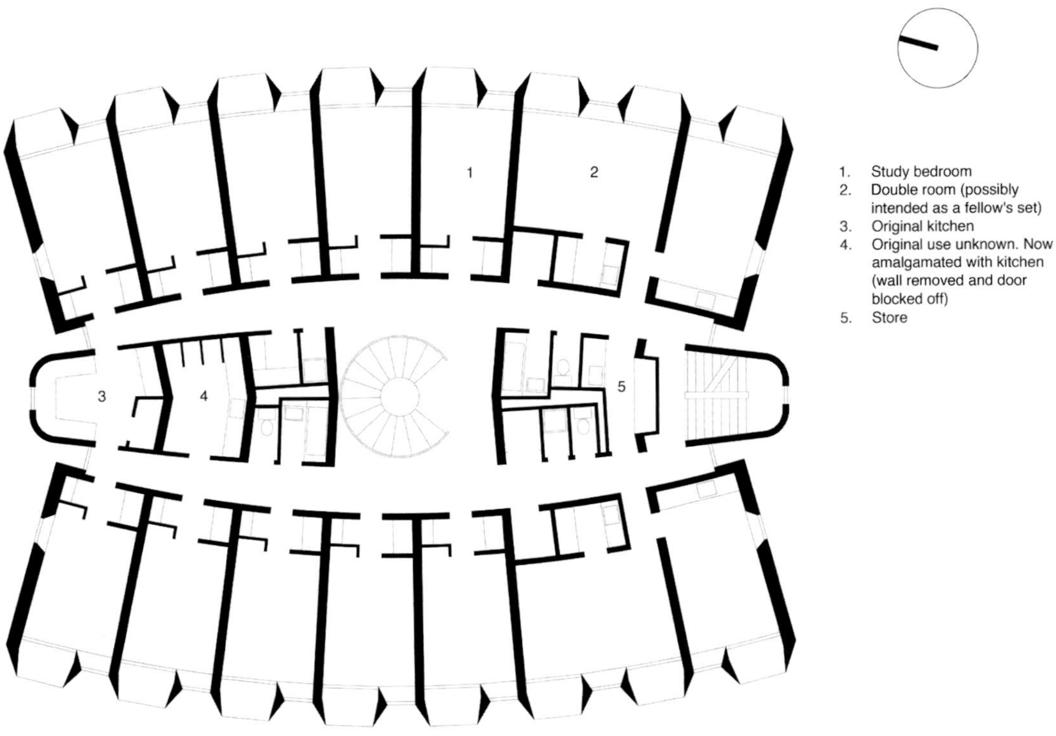

10.11 St Anne's College, Oxford, Wolfson and Rayne Buildings. Typical upper floor plan

10.12 St Anne's College, Oxford, Wolfson and Rayne Buildings

of space. In 1947 the Aden-based businessman Antonin Besse decided to endow an Oxford college. It was to be dedicated to St Antony of Egypt and focus on the study of international relations, to which later were added studies in Russia, Europe, Latin America, the Middle East and, most recently, Japan. A site was purchased from St John's College in 1950, and in 1960 HKPA submitted a masterplan that would allow phased construction of a college that included student residences, a hall and other communal facilities, teaching spaces and a library.[19]

Once again raiding their competition design for Churchill College, HKPA proposed highly sculpted facades that featured their now trademark window surrounds to the residential units and highly sculpted walls and prismatic roofs to the library and hall. After failing to secure funding for the library or teaching block, the College decided to focus on the construction of a larger hall and common rooms that would provide an initial social hub to the College. The result was the Hilda Besse Building (fig.10.13).[20]

10.13 St Antony's College, Oxford, Hilda Besse Building

The plan was simple and monumental. Two equal, rectangular volumes were separated by an atrium with stairs at either end. One half of the ground floor contained the entrance lobby and a casual dining space and the other housed private dining rooms. The ground floor was set back behind the perimeter columns to create a covered colonnade around the building (fig.10.15). Above, on one side of the atrium, a double height space held the main dining hall, whilst the other side contained kitchens at the lower level with senior and combined junior and middle common rooms above. Each of the major spaces was cradled in a framework of delicate and clearly delineated structural elements: slender hexagonal columns with six-inch (150mm) faces were set apart from external walls by six-inch (150mm) vertical slits of glass and supported a precast, post-tensioned diagrid roof structure. Each cell of the diagrid was surmounted by a truncated pyramid rooflight – a horizontal equivalent to the truncated pyramid units around windows (fig.10.14). The overall effect was an uncompromisingly modern rendering of a medieval hall.[21]

The Hilda Besse Building showcased several ingredients that would inform HKPA's work going forward: the separation and delineation of parts; the articulation of cladding panels as applied, non-structural elements; the use of splayed corners to help define individual volumes; and the formal demarcation of servant and served spaces.

All of these ingredients were present in HKPA's 1963 design for the Cambridge University Centre. The expansion of the University to the Sidgwick site and the new colleges (see Chapters 2 and 4) moved

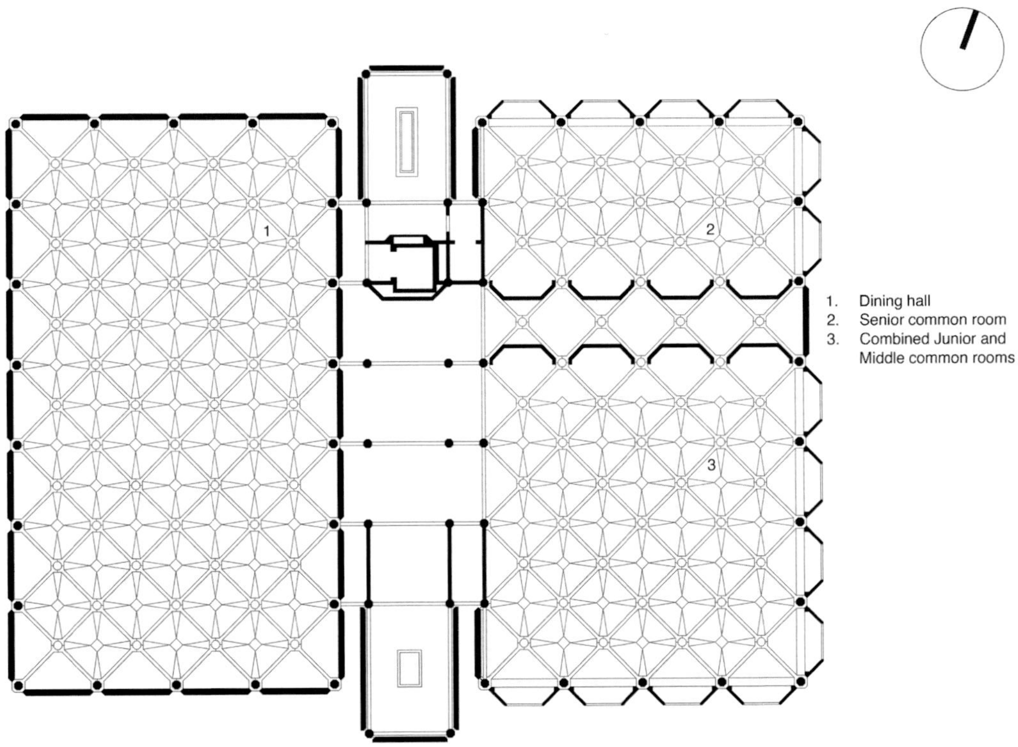

10.14 St Antony's College, Oxford, Hilda Besse Building. Reflected ceiling plan at upper level

10.15 St Antony's College, Oxford, Hilda Besse Building

its centre of gravity and created a body of research graduates and visiting academics who did not enjoy College membership and the social facilities that came with it. HKPA was commissioned to carry out a planning study for an extensive site at Granta Place that became available when the University Press moved. One element of that study was a graduates' club, and that became the focus of the University's attention. Funding was secured from the Wolfson Foundation and HKPA prepared designs for what would be known as the University Centre.[22]

The plan, whilst not symmetrical, was otherwise similar to the Hilda Besse Building. A linear atrium of vertical circulation separated a three-bay common room on one side from a three-bay common room and a large dining hall with associated service spaces on the other. The common room bays were not physically separated but were delineated by splayed corners and inboard columns forming a 'cage' that marked each bay as a discrete social space. The splayed corners further increased the possibilities for smaller 'private' spaces by creating a series of alcoves along the inner wall and a series of bay windows along the outer wall (fig.10.16). The expression of external cladding as an applied skin was accentuated by using small stone panels with gaps between that were fixed to the structure by exposed, stainless-steel bolts. The effect was reminiscent of Otto Wagner's 1905 Postal Savings Bank in Vienna. Some critics felt that the determination to separate parts and articulate joints loaded too much onto a small structure in pursuit of visual effect.[23]

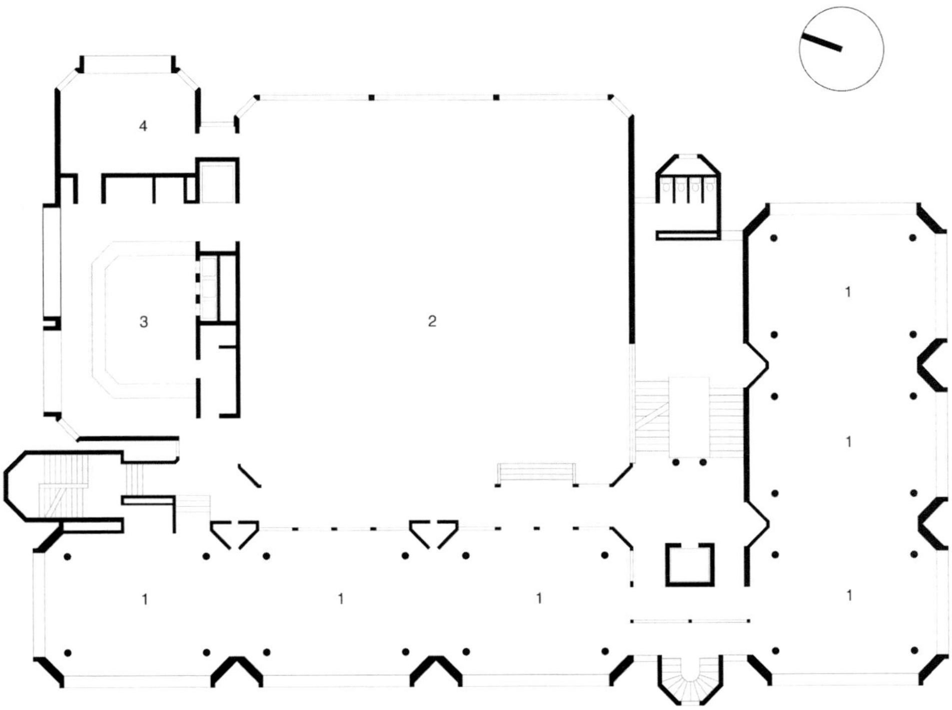

1. Common room
2. Dining hall
3. Servery
4. Washing up

10.16 University Centre, Cambridge. Plan at upper level

Those criticisms could be multiplied for the Senior Combination Room that HKPA designed for Downing College, Cambridge in 1965, a tiny building that is all articulated structure and separated parts. Downing College was originally designed by William Wilkins in the early 19th century in the Greek Revival style, with later additions by E.M. Barry in 1873 and Sir Herbert Baker from 1929 onwards. By the 1960s the College needed to expand and improve its dining and socialising arrangements because the restricted size of the dining hall and its rudimentary kitchens precluded any increase in student numbers. The College considered a longlist of 16 potential architects, which was narrowed down to the traditionalist Raymond Erith and HKPA, with HKPA winning the appointment.[24]

The hall in the Wilkins building was too small; by removing the Senior Combination Room (SCR) and kitchens, HKPA expanded it to fill the ground floor and located the new SCR as an independent pavilion to the west. Between the two they provided a stone-paved, south-facing terrace and added a new two-storey service wing that ran behind all three elements and provided kitchens, serveries, storage and offices, as well as a formal corridor that linked the dining hall and the SCR (fig.10.17). The outer wall of the corridor – stone-clad and blank save for one vertical opening – provided a quiet backdrop to the terrace and a visually balancing link between the hall and the SCR (fig.10.18).

The SCR building was a small jewel-like 'temple' with a perfectly square plan and identical, broken-pediment elevations on its three visible sides; the fourth side abutted the link block. A concrete post and beam structure, which was simple in origin but elaborate in execution,

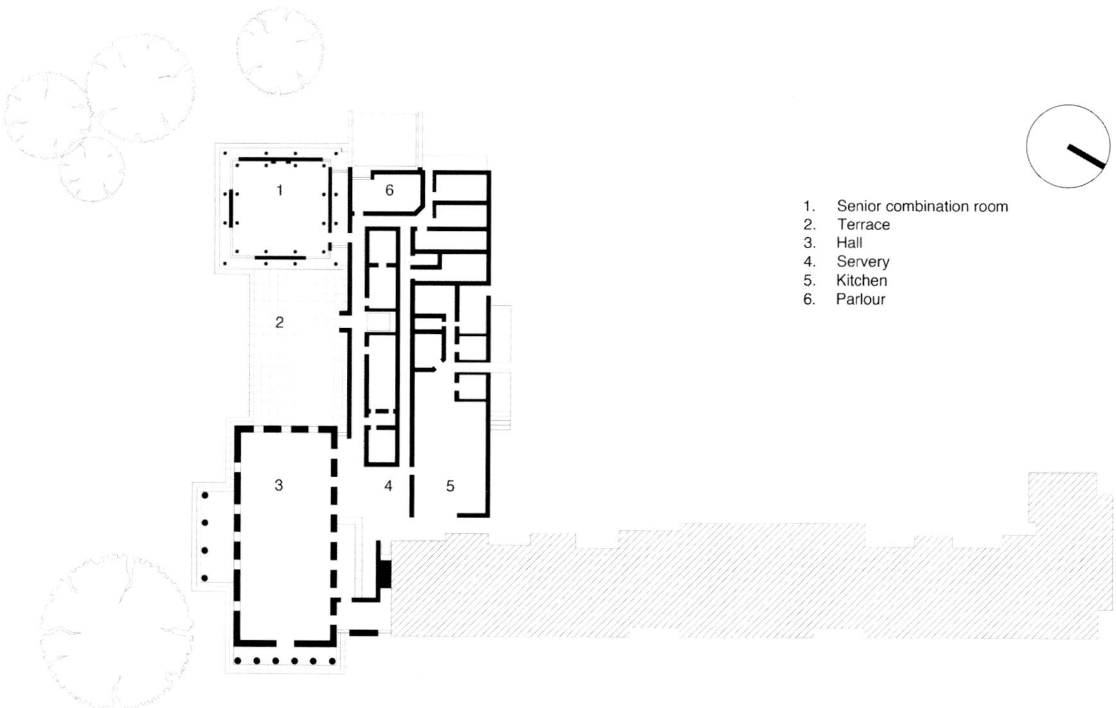

10.17 Downing College, Cambridge, hall, kitchens and Senior Combination Room. Ground floor plan

was left exposed and visually separated from the building envelope at both roof and walls. Freestanding columns were located both inside and outside the external walls, beams continued beyond column heads, and beam ends crossed at corners in imitation of timber detailing (fig.10.19). The sole purpose of this extravagant structure was to support visually distinct, inclined planes of lead-clad roof and a large central lantern (fig.10.21). The building envelope of stone walls and full-height, timber-framed windows that could slide open behind the stone panels was self-supporting and located in the zone between internal and external freestanding columns.

The inspiration for the design has been debated. As a post-and-beam structure it had historical precedent in both Greek and Japanese architecture. The practice had an interest in Japanese architecture and in 1958, Howell and Killick designed the North House, a private dwelling that was clearly based on the traditional Japanese house.[25] Some commentators saw Japanese influences in the imitation of timber detailing at the SCR. At the same time, the use of stone, the Classical detail in the broken pediments and, above all, the presence of Wilkins's Greek Revival building next door also led to the conclusion that it was a modern, deconstructed interpretation of the Greek temple.[26]

HKPA's last university building, the Faculty of Urban and Regional Studies at Reading University, had unmistakable Japanese influences, but they were modern rather than traditional. Designed in 1967, it owed a clear debt to Tange's 1958 design for the Kagawa Prefectural Government Offices. Both designs employed concrete to replicate timber structure and detailing, and both are open to scrutiny on the validity of representing

10.18 Downing College, Cambridge. Senior Combination Room on left, hall on right

the construction techniques of one material by using another material that requires quite different methods and skills.[27] In Tange's case it might be argued that he was referencing traditional Japanese precedent. HKPA's case is more difficult to explain and illustrates their progression from the emotional expressionism of the Churchill competition, through the rational use of structure to define space whilst simultaneously offering the possibility of historic or contextual references in the Hilda Besse Building, to the romantic expression of structure for its own sake (fig.10.20). The last approach invites the separation of structure from its role within the wider organism of the building and stands in contrast to Ove Arup's goal of 'total', integrated architecture. What both approaches showed is that structure, used deliberately, can be more than the technical device that holds up a building. For those seeking to make architecture more accessible, it offered a way in that we seem hard-wired to understand.

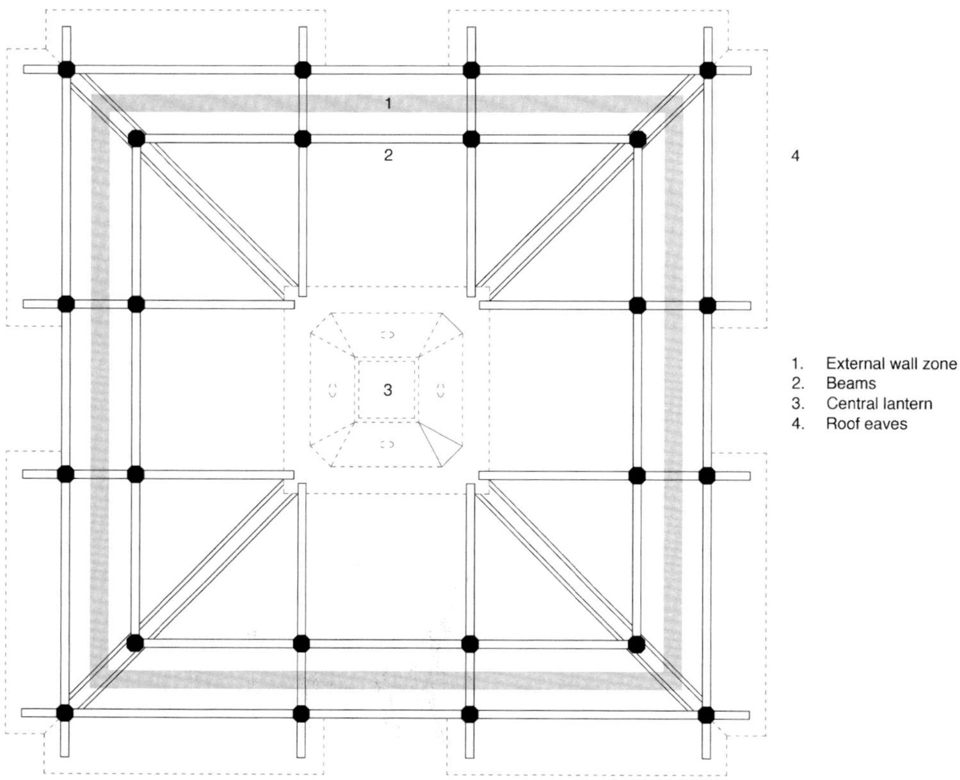

10.19 Downing College, Cambridge, Senior Combination Room. Reflected ceiling plan

10.20 *Reading University, Faculty of Urban and Regional Studies*

10.21 Downing College, Cambridge. Interior of Senior Combination Room

10.22 St Antony's College, Oxford, Hilda Besse Building. Interior of Senior Common Room

11 The Prefabricators

Arup Associates
HKPA
Denys Lasdun
James Stirling

Ideas for prefabrication had existed before the Second World War. 'Light and dry' construction techniques, bringing together components for rapid assembly, were well advanced in Germany and advocated by Gropius when he came to Britain. Meanwhile, Leslie Martin was involved, along with Richard Llewelyn-Davies, in developing prefabricated stations for London Midland and Scottish Railways before his move to the LCC (see Chapter 2). In 1944, Churchill announced a target to build 500,000 temporary homes from steel, later reduced to 150,000. Several types of prefabricated homes were developed, including the Arcon system and the AIROH house that was made on the production line that built Spitfire fighter planes during the war. The AIROH house was mass-produced but ultimately proved more expensive than a traditional house. It was in the schools' programme that prefabrication really took off, led by the architects' department at Hertfordshire County Council under the Chief Education Officer, John Newsom, and Stirrat Johnson-Marshall. The schools designed at Hertfordshire began to feature in the architectural press from 1946, and the system developed there spread nationally. Some of those engaged in its development joined the Ministry of Education, to which Johnson-Marshall transferred in 1948.[1]

There never was a programme for prefabrication in the higher education sector and the only university to adopt a widely used system that involved mass production was York, designed by Johnson-Marshall and Andrew Derbyshire using a refinement of the CLASP system that had been developed for schools (see Chapter 3). That is not to say that other architects did not turn to prefabrication – many did and for a variety of reasons. For some, prefabrication formed part of the modernist dream of equality and progress through the harnessing of technology. For others, it offered the benefits of quality control and, for many, the opportunity for design control. Unlike the mostly anonymous architects who worked collaboratively to develop the schools' systems, many architects in the university sector saw prefabrication as an opportunity to extend their control over the design of not only the building but every component and its means of assembly and connection.

11.1 St Andrews University, Andrew Melville Hall

Arup Associates

In Chapter 8 we saw how Arup's earliest university designs, the Fry and Vaughan buildings at Somerville College, Oxford, expressed structure as an unbroken exoskeleton grid that framed and delineated the boundaries of the residential rooms that sat behind it. The Wolfson Building that followed on the same site broke the structure down into individually articulated elements: the glazed bays that punched through the structure appeared to hang from pairs of projecting beams that, in turn, were fixed to the sides of freestanding columns. From articulation of individual structural elements, it was a short step to prefabricated production of a kit of structural parts.

The external structure of the George Thomson Building at Corpus Christi College, Cambridge can be read as a direct descendant of Fry and Vaughan that has been resolved into a prefabricated, repetitive H-shaped frame that incorporates both columns and edge beam and spans from mid-height of a room to mid-height of the room above. Visual articulation of each piece of structure is further enhanced by use of recessed joints between adjoining units (fig.8.19). The clever move here was the positioning of the joint at mid-height, reducing the number of joints required and simplifying them. Rather than make a special unit for the top storey, the architects maintained the standard prefabricated unit and, in a nod to historical context, allowed the narrow columns to project above the roof line like finials on a Gothic building.

If the George Thomson Building was a descendant of Fry and Vaughan, then Herrick and Boulton Houses at Trinity Hall, Cambridge were descendants of the Wolfson Building, with bay windows supported on projecting beams and clear articulation of each element, but utilising the same prefabricated, H-shaped structural frames as the George Thomson Building (fig.8.20).

The Sir Thomas White Building at St John's College, Oxford marked the culmination of the line of enquiry that the architects pursued through the series of projects described above. To the standard H-shaped structural module they added a version that was cranked through 90 degrees to allow the formation of projecting bay windows that were held within the structural frame as if cupped in a hand (fig.8.21). It was the epitome of what Michael Brawne described as Arup Associates' 'very deliberate outlining of space', where structure created habitable niches that defined and made a 'usable space'.[2]

Howard Killick Partridge and Amis (HKPA)

HKPA's use of prefabrication was largely restricted to cladding panels and, in particular, the truncated-pyramid concrete units they used on several university buildings (see Chapter 10). These performed a number of functions: the articulation of cladding as an attached 'skin'; hooded window surrounds that provided shade within and delineated framed views out from the building (fig.10.22); expressive three-dimensional facade modelling that created a feeling of depth and weight using thin, lightweight materials (fig.10.15). These shapes could only be cleanly and uniformly achieved using a prefabricated mould.

Structure was predominately cast in-situ, with occasional use of some precast elements. The exception was the Senior Combination Room at Downing College, Cambridge (see Chapter 10). Here, an elaborate structure that supports the roof was made entirely of precast elements whilst the external walls consisted of hand-built stone panels sitting between and separate from two layers of structural columns. There is no reason that a building of this size should require such an extravagant duplication of structure, which seems to have been designed solely for the purpose of expressing the separation of structure and envelope both inside and outside the building (fig.10.19). It is as if the architects were determined that anyone encountering the building, whether as user or passer-by, should not miss the effort that went into designing its prefabricated structure, an aspect that is accentuated by the emphasis on half-checked and articulated joints between members (fig.10.21).

Denys Lasdun

Barnabas Calder makes the argument that Lasdun's use of concrete, and in particular prefabricated concrete, was a 'central part of his career-long effort to establish and defend his creative prerogative as an artist'.[3] Such a description puts him squarely in the category of those architects who chose prefabrication as a way to exert more control over every aspect of building design. He was antagonistic to the anonymous, multi-disciplinary teamwork and generic systems approach of the schools' programme, for example, and quarrelled publicly with Derbyshire over this.[4] As noted above, Derbyshire had been heavily involved in the schools' programme and in the design of York University, using the CLASP system.

Lasdun's early use of precast was as permanent shuttering, into which in-situ concrete was then poured. This was clearly a technique designed to maximise control over the appearance of the finished surface and stands in stark contrast to the New Brutalist preference for 'as found' materials, or the concept, borrowed from Japan, of the 'aesthetics of imperfection'.[5] Lasdun, similarly, had little sympathy with the Smithsons' theoretical approach. 'There are clearly plenty of modes of thought about today, but it is difficult to see that most of them have much relevance for architecture.'[6]

His first structural use of precast concrete at scale was at the University of East Anglia. The design was put out to competitive tender at the cost planning stage and found to be more expensive than a load-bearing brick, cross-wall structure. However, the architects and structural engineers continued to press for the use of precast panels, citing logistical concerns and a lack of available labour.[7] Whether those concerns were legitimate or reflected the design team's wish to use precast for ideological reasons is open to question.

Calder called UEA 'Lasdun's full and gleeful leap into producing an entire landscape of exposed, often structural concrete surfaces' and highlights his use of different types of concrete (in-situ, precast, blockwork) for different purposes within the same project.[8]

> The infinite variety of colour in the valley landscape makes the choice of external materials and colour of particular importance. Of all the suitable materials available today concrete in its natural grey state appears to enhance the colours of the landscape to greatest advantage. It is important, therefore, that there should be a predominance of this material with its range of neutral colours depending on whether it is precast, in situ or in the form of concrete blocks.[9]

Both the teaching wall at UEA and the Charles Wilson Building at Leicester University featured an in-situ core for stability, surrounded by peripheral precast structure and cladding. Thereafter, Lasdun moved more and more towards the use of precast because of the control it gave him over the appearance of the final product. His use of board-marked in-situ concrete for the National Theatre on London's South Bank is a major exception for a large, public project (fig.7.1).[10]

At Christ's College, Cambridge Lasdun repeated the stepped section used at UEA but, where the UEA design emphasised the overall form of the ziggurats, at Christ's he articulated a precast kit of parts and drew a clear distinction between precast and in-situ parts of the structure (fig.7.3). The entire rear of the building was cast in-situ and expressed in yellow, shutter-marked and monolithic concrete, while the student rooms were formed of white precast panels that glittered from the inclusion of quartz aggregate.

James Stirling

Stirling showed little interest in prefabrication except as an intellectual exercise. His resolution for 1954 was to design four houses: one in mass concrete, one in precast and pre-stressed concrete, one in steel and one in brick.[11] He did not complete that wish list, but it is possible that he transferred it to his university buildings. In 1964, shortly after completing the Leicester Engineering Building in mass concrete, he was appointed to design student residences at St Andrews University and said:

> The new buildings for St Andrews are in the north of Scotland where there is no local building material (not even bricks) or workmen (who have all come south) . . . The only method which seemed possible was to design a kit of precast concrete elements to be manufactured elsewhere.[12]

Stirling was often guilty of revising or at least exaggerating the facts in order to support his design decisions (see Chapter 12). The residents of St Andrews would have been surprised to find their town relocated to the north of Scotland and would have wondered how on earth any buildings were being constructed elsewhere in a country devoid of building materials and workmen. It seems more likely that Stirling wanted to experiment with precast, a possibility that is reinforced by his use of it at the Olivetti Training Centre in Haslemere, Surrey and in public housing at Runcorn New Town, Cheshire, neither located anywhere in Scotland.[13] His decision may also have been a response to Lasdun's acclaimed use of precast panels at UEA, where similar arguments were deployed to justify their use.

Following his critical success at Leicester, Stirling was appointed without having to go through a competitive process. The site occupied a slope with views towards the sea, although these have been obscured by later tree planting. There were to have been four residences, each consisting of two splayed, linear blocks that stepped down the slope and were joined at the top end. These were arranged in mirrored pairs,

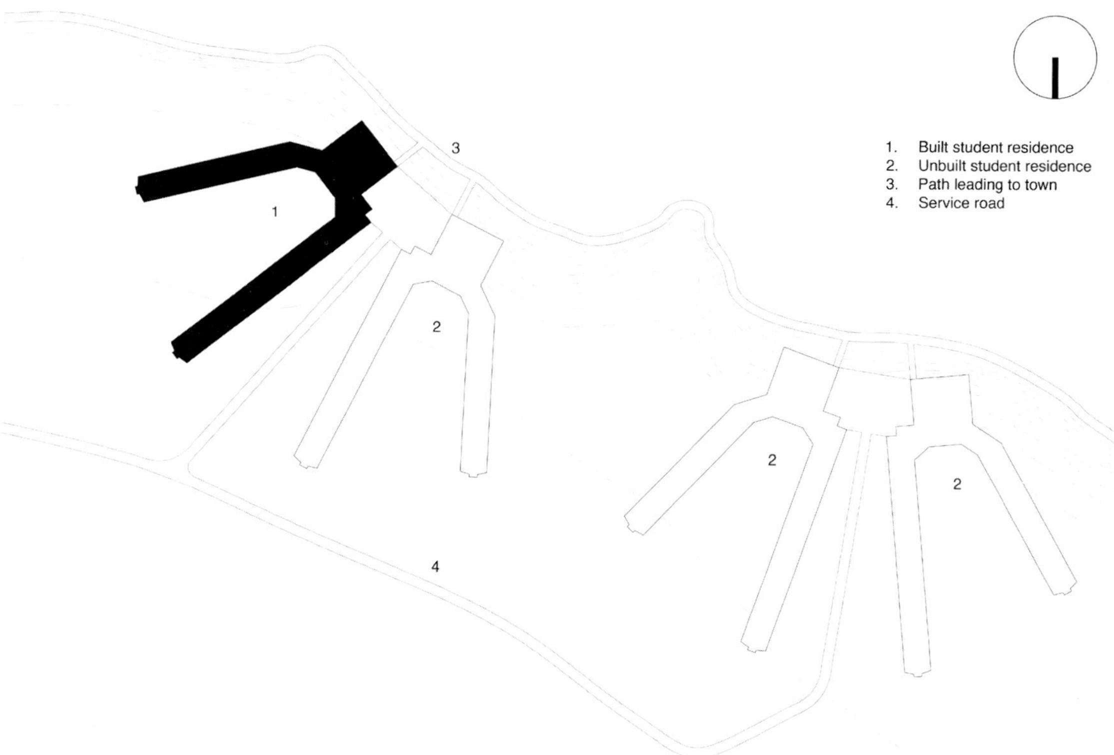

11.2 St Andrews University, Andrew Melville Hall and other proposed residences. Site plan

forming two sets of four linear blocks, spread like the fingers of two hands (fig.11.2).

The fingers contained prefabricated student rooms, stacked to follow the slope and angled to give every room a view towards the sea, resulting in a sawtooth profile in plan. A glazed promenade ran at mid-level along the inside of each finger, from which stairs ascended and descended to the rooms above and below (fig.11.1). The promenades met at the web between fingers, where communal rooms were situated (fig.11.3). From there bridges crossed to the crest of the hill and joined a path leading to the town.

The construction tenders proved too expensive for the University Grants Committee which approved the construction of one residence (Andrew Melville Hall). It did so on condition that subsequent residences on the site be designed to obviate its high cost. Stirling maintained that the initial cost of setting up prefabrication would have been offset by re-use in subsequent phases, but only one residence was ever built.[14]

Whether the cost savings claimed by Stirling would ever have been realised remains a moot point, but the episode is indicative of the economic difficulties posed when prefabrication means custom-designed units for use on only one project. That was the case on most university designs that used prefabrication and suggests that it was an intellectual choice by architects who wished to experiment with it or use it to extend their design control. Very few were prepared to adopt a universal, mass-produced system as RMJMP did at York University.

11.3 St Andrews University, Andrew Melville Hall

12 The Disruptors

James Stirling and James Gowan

Unusually for the architects featured in this book, neither James Stirling nor James Gowan studied at the AA, although Gowan taught there later. Nor did they work at the LCC under Leslie Martin, although he was to promote their inclusion on university shortlists on several occasions. Stirling studied architecture at Liverpool University and Gowan at the Mackintosh School of Art in Glasgow before they both made their way to London, where they met while working at Lyons Israel Ellis. They formed their partnership in 1956 and worked together until 1963 before disagreeing and going their separate ways. During that time, they produced around nine works that had a significant impact on the world of British modern architecture. By far the most significant was the Engineering Building at Leicester University.[1]

The Engineering Building arrived with the bracing shock of cold water thrown over the heated discussion about British modern architecture and the path it should take. Everyone had been looking in another direction when Stirling and Gowan crept up and kicked them from behind. The design seemed completely new and yet somehow familiar. Stirling and Gowan had not discovered new ideas; they put existing ideas together in new and productive ways. They had little interest in context, if context is restricted to the immediate physical or cultural environs of the site, as in the examples shown in Chapter 8. Instead, they channelled the idea of modernism, notions of Britain's industrial heritage, wider cultural references, and mixed them with both Classical and Gothic sensibilities. At Liverpool – perhaps the only school other than the AA to take up modernism at that time – Stirling was influenced by the Classical view of history promoted by his tutor, Colin Rowe, who placed modernism in an historical context rather than seeing it as a complete break with the past. Gowan's education at the Mackintosh School of Art was more technological and he developed an interest in the way buildings are put together, which he saw as closer to the Gothic tradition. He was later to say that it was the constant tension between Stirling's Classical and his own Gothic tendencies that injected vitality into their designs.[2]

It is possible that their status as outsiders to the London gang revolving around the AA and LCC was instrumental in their development of alternative ideas. It may be no coincidence that the other *enfants terribles* of Sixties architecture, the

12.1 Leicester University, Engineering Building

Smithsons, had also been educated in the North, at King's College Durham, before moving to London. Perhaps all of them felt a need to assert themselves in the face of a cliquish London architecture scene. The Smithsons quickly became leading members of the MARS Group and later Team 10, as well as the Independent Group. Stirling associated with these groups and picked up ideas from them but was not an active member. Gowan was a thinker but appears to have been more of a loner.

The Smithsons were intent on developing generalised theories that would result in replicable archetypes.[3] Stirling and Gowan believed in finding the right 'style for the job'. Those differences were plainly visible when Stirling presented the design for the Leicester Engineering Building to a meeting of Team 10 members. Alison Smithson, who seems to have disliked Stirling on a personal level, was particularly dismissive, complaining that this 'little building' tells us nothing about 'Stirling's general theory' or about how it relates to what he has done in the past or informs what he will do in the future.[4] Despite Smithson's criticism, the 'style for the job' served Stirling and Gowan well on the Leicester project.

As mentioned previously, when Leslie Martin was appointed Professor of Architecture at Cambridge University, he enjoyed a position of influence in recommending architects for several universities. He brought Stirling and Gowan into the Churchill College competition, where their shortlisted submission attracted much attention. Their proposal evoked the fortified enclosures of English castles and possessed an unbending rigour that sat in contrast to the looser, winning design by Sheppard Robson and Partners (see Chapter 1). Martin again recommended them for a new residential building at Selwyn College, which was never built (see Chapter 2). Finally, in 1959, he was successful in persuading Leicester University to commission them to design a new engineering building as part of an overall masterplan he had prepared.[5]

Martin's masterplan was an arrangement of linear buildings in loose courtyards somewhat reminiscent of Casson's plan for the Sidgwick site in Cambridge (see Chapter 2). The Engineering Building was assigned an awkward, left-over corner separate from the rest of the site. He suggested that it could 'stand on its own feet', with no requirement to match other buildings or to 'build fragments of possible futures'.[6] John McKean suggests that this was intentional on Martin's part. 'Fully aware that his own ideas . . . were quite different [he] expected Stirling and Gowan to bring to their isolated site an architecture of formal assertion.'[7] One wonders if this precedent encouraged Stirling to take a similar approach in his design of the History Faculty within Casson's Sidgwick masterplan (see Chapter 2).

Edward Parkes was brought in as Professor and Head of Department. At 33, he was the same age as Gowan and two years younger than Stirling. Frank Newby, the structural engineer, was also 33 years old. It was a young team with radical ideas. Parkes prepared a brief that outlined the functional requirements of the building and left it to the designers to decide how those should be achieved.[8]

Stirling later argued that the design emerged almost entirely from rational consideration of the site and the client's technical requirements, as if no other solution would have been possible. Hence, the small area left after accommodating workshops meant that other parts had to go vertical, and the requirement for a water tank positioned at least 100 ft (30m) above ground level required an office tower that the tank could sit on top of (fig.12.2). Meanwhile the client's insistence that workshops be lit by northlight, combined with a site that was not orientated north–south, led to the most noticeable element in the design: a sea of serrated roof lights that run at an angle to the workshops below (figs 12.3, 12.5).[9]

The contextual references were wide-ranging and layered. On the surface lay a machine-like quality that recalled the early modernist vision, whilst the choice of red bricks and patent glazing conjured images of 19th-century factory buildings and Britain's industrial heritage. Beyond the surface impression, the visual expression of the raked and cantilevered lecture theatres referenced Russian

12.2 Leicester University, Engineering Building
12.3 Leicester University, Engineering Building

Constructivism through Konstantin Melnikov's Rusakov Workers' Club, while the slender columns and spiral stair ascending into the belly of the cantilever recall his Makhorka Tobacco Pavilion for the 1923 All-Russian Agricultural and Handicraft Exposition in Moscow (fig.12.4).[10] At a subliminal level these references had the power to prompt half-remembered images of Soviet propaganda posters featuring muscular workers fashioning pieces of heavy metal. Similarly, Stirling's proposal to replace the 'white architecture' of early modernism with his 'post-white' alternative of red brick and tile might have stirred thoughts of Red and White Russians and revolution. Or perhaps it was a tongue-in-cheek reference to redbrick universities, as the technical universities that were created in contrast to the ancient universities were known.

Stirling never explicitly acknowledged any of these potential references. Just as he maintained that the form of the building was the inevitable result of a rational analysis of its site and functions, so he argued that the 'exploitation of local materials and methods is perhaps the only alternative to the conventional or the "contemporary" left open to the European architect faced with a minimum budget'.[11]

All these factors together produced an intensely satisfying design. Once seen, it was difficult to imagine any other solution. And yet, other solutions were clearly available and some are illustrated in Stirling and Gowan's own interim proposals. Meanwhile, some of the assumptions, which seem so obvious at first sight, require further scrutiny.

The bricks were 'local' only in as much as they were English, but they were not Leicestershire bricks and the tiles were Dutch. Red engineering bricks were brought from the heartland of the industrial revolution in the northwest and seem designed to evoke those associations rather than to cut costs or conform to any local context. Stirling had criticised Le Corbusier's unintelligent and anti-mechanistic use of brickwork at the Maisons Jaoul, and he and Gowan had partly addressed that issue at Ham Common (see Chapter 2). At Leicester they went further and combined brickwork with matching red tiles to coat the building in a homogenous, tight skin that reinforced its appearance as a piece of machinery.

However, whilst appearing machine-like and constructed of standardised components, the building was put together using labour-intensive traditional skills: the in-situ concrete frame, the brickwork and tiling were all labour-intensive; the 'off-the-peg' patent glazing system was used in such a bespoke way that many of the aluminium sections had to be cut and fitted on site; and deflection in the workshop roof trusses meant that each roof light had to be measured and fitted individually.[12]

These factors have led to suggestions that the design was not so much the inevitable result of rational decisions but that the narrative was reverse engineered to justify the consequences of the architects' aesthetic preferences. Joining his wife in criticising the design, Peter Smithson said: 'I don't think you arrived at this [solution] *a priori*. It was just that you solved it in a certain way, and in order to bring it under artistic control, you opted for this way of doing it.'[13]

Other questions arise over the type of technology being represented. It was rooted in a 19th-century, object-based engineering of structures and machines. It made no concession to the growing importance of electrical engineering and systems that could neither be seen nor touched.[14] In that sense it can be viewed as backward, not forward, looking. Nonetheless, the image was compelling and, when compared with Lasdun's adjacent Charles Wilson Building, it marks a step-change from heavy and static to taut and energised (figs 12.6, 12.7).

The Leicester Engineering Building was the most famous architectural design of its time, both nationally and internationally, and continues to divide opinion. One view of its success is that Stirling was able to 'transform programmatic needs into the kind of visual poetry that would make his buildings "sing"'.[15] Another argues that the most shocking thing was the implication that architecture could be all about form and not much else.[16] Whichever view one subscribes to, its fame proved to be a double-edged sword. It led to more high-profile university

12.4 *Leicester University, Engineering Building*

12.5 Leicester University, Engineering Building

commissions, but Stirling became seduced by its appearance, to the detriment of finding the 'style for the job'. This would contribute to his split with Gowan.

In 1963, shortly before the Leicester project was completed, Stirling and Gowan were awarded the commission for the History Faculty at Cambridge University, but split soon afterwards, with Stirling retaining the job. They were selected from a shortlist of three. Once on the shortlist, Stirling and Gowan quite easily convinced the faculty of the merits of their design, but it had taken tenacious lobbying by Martin to get them there.

The site sat within Casson and Conder's masterplan for the Sidgwick site, and although the University stressed that it remained satisfied with their plan and their work on the southern part of the site, a reduction in the land available for the northern part opened the possibility of a redesign and an opportunity to involve other architects (see Chapter 2). It was rumoured that, although publicly silent on the matter, Martin was unconvinced by what he had seen so far.

Martin and Casson were each asked to suggest potential candidates for the design of the History Faculty and came up with numerous names. Martin suggested HKPA, ACP and Powell and Moya, but added other names that he felt were worth considering, including Stirling and Gowan. Casson also suggested ACP and Powell and Moya, along with several other British and overseas names, but not Stirling and Gowan. The committee approached six architects but not Stirling and Gowan. No clear front-runner emerged and the committee decided to widen its net and add more names, including several Nordic architects, but not Stirling and Gowan. This longlist was gradually whittled down but no final decision was reached and Martin restated his confidence in HKPA and ACP but reiterated that Stirling and Gowan should also be considered. More names were added but not Stirling and Gowan. Then, in November 1962, the committee met, with Martin in attendance, and a final shortlist of three was decided: ACP, David Roberts (who the committee had included from

12.6 Leicester University, Engineering Building

12.7 Leicester University, Charles Wilson Building

the beginning), and Stirling and Gowan.[17] How this result was arrived at is unknown, but it seems clear that the only person pushing for Stirling and Gowan's inclusion was Martin, and that somehow he prevailed.

Once on the shortlist, Professor Geoffrey Elton, who was on the selection committee, attributed the success of their proposal to the fact that 'it developed from a genuine (and accurate) conception of what the History Faculty is – a body of men [*sic*], teachers and students, concentrating their lives upon their library'.[18] The design consisted of an L-shaped building containing seven floors of student and staff lounges, seminar rooms and offices, holding a reading room between its two arms with a glazed roof that cascaded down between them like an enormous, crystalline glasshouse (fig.12.8). Two levels of open book stacks curved around the outer edge of the reading room. Aesthetically, the design followed the language of red engineering bricks, red tiles and patent glazing developed at Leicester, but it was not the appearance of the building that attracted the committee; it was the plan, which read like a perfect diagram of how the building should operate (fig.12.9). Stirling's ability to create plans that seemed so self-evidently 'right' is something to which I will return. The two elements of the History Faculty plan that most appealed to the committee were the radial arrangement of bookstacks that allowed complete supervision from a central control desk, and the integration of books, reading room and other faculty functions within a single volume.[19] Everything revolved around a central space for books and study, like a cathedral of knowledge, surely a very satisfying metaphor for serious academics (fig.12.10).

Gowan was not so easily convinced. He objected to the design on both ideological and practical grounds, and his objections were so strong that he left when Stirling refused to address them. The story that had been appropriate for a department of engineering in Leicester was not, he felt, appropriate for a department of history

12.8 Cambridge University, History Faculty

in Cambridge. It was not the right 'style for the job'. Also, there had been technical problems at Leicester – which Gowan had to deal with – and he felt there would be worse problems at Cambridge, where the technology was being pushed beyond its known limits. There were critics who agreed on both counts.

Pevsner declared: 'Here is anti-architecture. Here is an intelligent and resourceful architect making it his business to design a building which fulfils all the functional demands and yet is actively ugly . . .'[20] Meanwhile, Banham likened it to a machine that would require 'mechanical literacy and competence' to operate and suggested that, like any machine or technology, it would ultimately become redundant.[21] He was referring to the machine-like quality of the building, rather than the actual technology used, and was simply extending a metaphor. In fact, the technology was found to be faulty or inadequate, validating Gowan's misgivings.

In theory it looked convincing. The glass roof would admit ample natural light for reading. The issue of potential glare would be answered by constructing a double-skin roof, the inner skin being translucent to cut out glare and provide a diffuse light. The space between the two layers would be ventilated by three large extract fans located at the apex of the roof that would draw off warm air and pull in cool air from around the perimeter to prevent overheating in the reading room below (fig.12.11). However, the fans were not effective when run at lower speeds, and when turned up to full speed, they were so loud that the readers below could not concentrate and they had to be switched off, leading to severe overheating

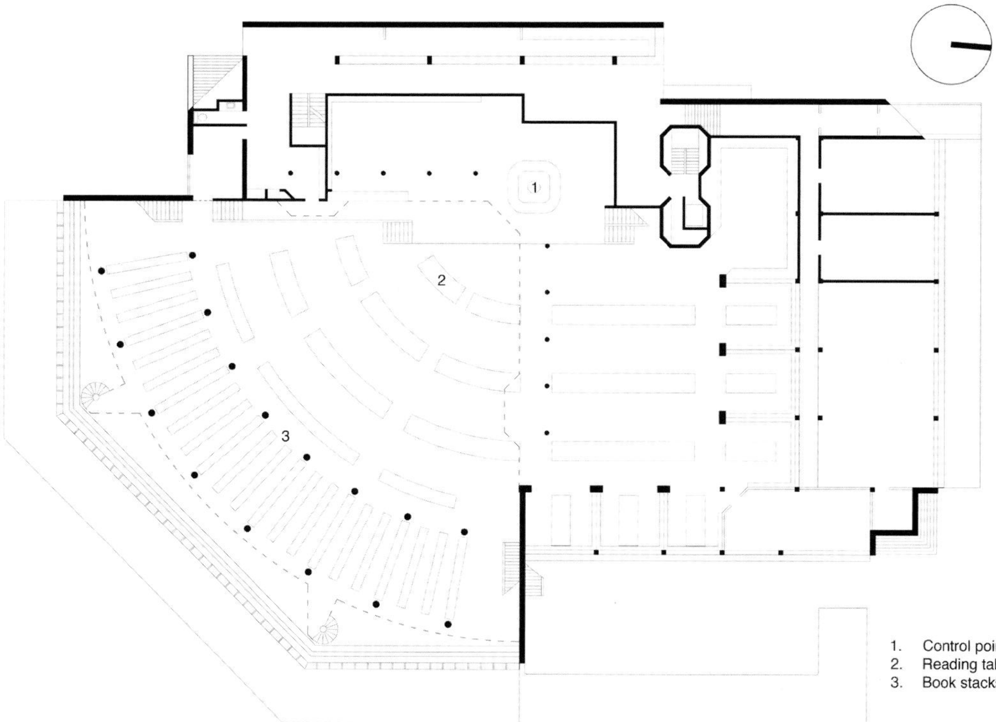

12.9 Cambridge University, History Faculty. Ground floor plan

12.10 Cambridge University, History Faculty. Interior of reading room

12.11 Cambridge University, History Faculty. Glazed roof to reading room

on sunny days. In addition, the patent glazing system leaked and a new method for fixing the tile cladding failed, causing tiles to fall off after a few years.

It was a simple matter for Stirling to shrug off Pevsner's criticism, especially as he had made several factual errors in his remarks about Leicester, allowing Stirling to observe that 'when Professor Pevsner approaches a building which he THINKS he should not like he closes his eyes'.[22] In any case, Stirling seemed happy in the role of renegade, as his remark about the History Faculty being designed to 'fuck Casson' made clear (see Chapter 2). It was not such a simple matter to ignore the technical failures, which were severe enough for the University to consider demolition in 1983, after less than 20 years of service.

It was the photographer Richard Einzig's dramatic images of the Leicester and Cambridge buildings that established Stirling's reputation in the UK and around the world.[23] It was the technical failures that caused commissions to dry up after 1969 and leave him without any work for 11 years in the UK and eight years overseas.[24]

Shortly after being appointed at Cambridge, Stirling received the commission to design student residences at St Andrews University (see Chapter 11), and in 1966, at Queen's College, Oxford. The former was a direct appointment; the latter, known as the Florey Building, was won after an interview in competition with three other practices. The Florey Building shared much with the Cambridge History Faculty: the aesthetic, the technical failings and a plan that seemed irrefutable.

Le Corbusier said:

> To make a plan is to determine and fix ideas . . . It is so to order those ideas that they become intelligible . . . it is essential therefore to exhibit a precise intention . . . A plan is to some extent a summary like an analytical contents table . . . In a form so condensed that it seems as clear as crystal . . . it contains an enormous quantity of ideas and the impulse of an intention.[25]

Stirling's plans always seem so obviously right that we experience that 'of course' moment where any other solution seems impossible – a diagram of how the building works that the viewer can immediately grasp. The big idea is always clear whilst accommodating complexity and sophistication. Moreover, Stirling had the ability to preserve that clarity throughout the trials and tribulations of design development, which is why his buildings made such powerful statements. The downside is that functional requirements often took a back seat or may not even have entered his thinking. The Florey Building was a prime example of all these factors.

The site, on the River Cherwell, is around 700 metres walking distance from the College. The brief called for the provision of student accommodation, with an allowance for a kitchen and communal breakfast room but nothing that would detract from a policy that required students to study and take their main meals in the College.[26] The project was to be part of a larger development of student dormitories linked by a walkway along the riverbank. The other buildings never materialised, leaving the Florey Building rather isolated and defeating some of the decisions that drove the design.[27] Student rooms and a central, social space that should have been connected to a lively footpath and wider student community now overlook an empty stretch of dark, overgrown and uninviting riverbank (fig.12.17).

Single aspect student rooms were stacked like a grandstand or amphitheatre to create a raked-back profile that was extruded, like a stick of rock, around a semi-octagonal plan that focused all views on a central courtyard and the adjacent river (fig.12.12). The building was raised on sloping columns to create a continuous covered cloister around the courtyard, which was itself raised over a ground-floor kitchen and breakfast room. The breakfast room was top-lit by a lantern that protruded through a corner of the courtyard (figs 12.13, 12.14). The diagram is similar to Leslie Martin's student residence at Harvey Court (see Chapter 2) but the architectural expression is radically different. Perhaps Stirling was making

12.12 Queen's College, Oxford, Florey Building

a point of contrasting Martin's polite, contextual treatment with his own unapologetically industrial, machine aesthetic, as if saying, *this* is modern architecture.

Once again, Stirling's plan is utterly convincing when taken in the abstract. In reality, whilst it set up a satisfying relationship with the river, it literally turned its back on the surrounding neighbourhood, presenting a blank facade, ignoring the existing street pattern and looming over the domestic-scale buildings with its overhanging mass (fig.12.15). And then there were the familiar technical failings: student rooms were too cold in winter and too hot in summer; there were issues of overlooking and visual privacy between facing rooms, and acoustic privacy between adjacent rooms. As with the Cambridge History Faculty, the client has considered demolition, and when I visited the site in 2022 the building was empty and sealed off, its undercroft and yard used for car parking.

The three buildings featured in this chapter are known as the 'red trilogy'. Each one sent shockwaves through the architectural world and have been admired and condemned in equal measure: admired as powerful architectural statements that offered a fresh view of modern architecture; condemned as 'over-dramatic, aggressive and highly individual' buildings that did not offer a replicable model, and for their technical failings.[28] It is instructive to unpick some of that with the benefit of hindsight.

Although they are often seen as a group, there is a significant difference between the Leicester Engineering Building and the other two. At Leicester, Stirling and Gowan attempted to reset

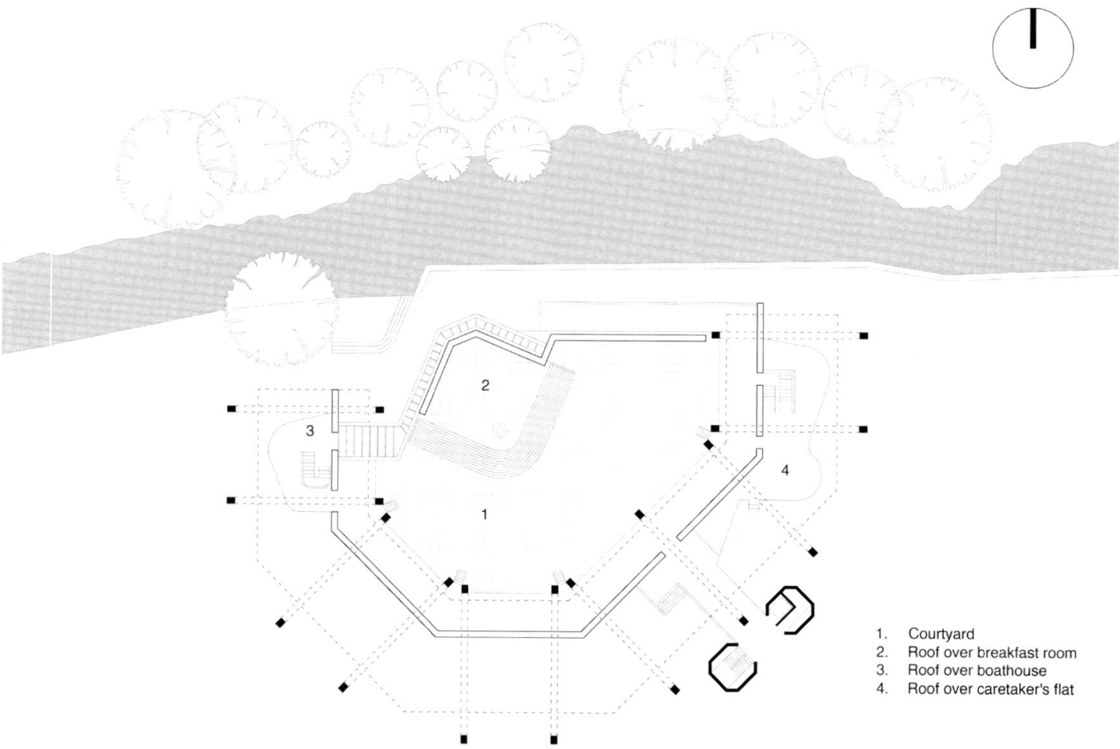

12.13 Queen's College, Oxford, Florey Building. Plan at courtyard level

modernism, not as a complete break with the past but as a continuation. In doing so, they broadened the definition of context from the immediate physical and historical context of the site to include hints and memories drawn from a wide range of past events. This worked at Leicester because the allusions were appropriate and convincing. It failed at Cambridge and Oxford because they were not. As the American architect, Peter Eisenmann wrote:

> Despite recent critical pronouncements, which would have us place Leicester, Cambridge and Oxford in an historical continuum, it is my contention that Leicester remains seminal and singular in this context . . . Cambridge and Oxford are not polemical. They seem to be merely borrowing on the iconic charge given by the use of similar materials and building methods developed at Leicester.[29]

Stirling seemed to have fallen into the same trap as the early modernists, where a set of principles descended into style.

After visiting several of Le Corbusier's early 'white' buildings, Stirling noted that, whilst they appeared machine-like, they were constructed using traditional materials and techniques. It is likely that his use of untried techniques or, at least, materials that had previously been used in other situations, was an attempt to produce buildings that not only looked mechanistic but also used industrial techniques and components. Traditional techniques rest on a base of experience, knowledge and mastery. Neither Stirling nor his contractors had any of these with regard to

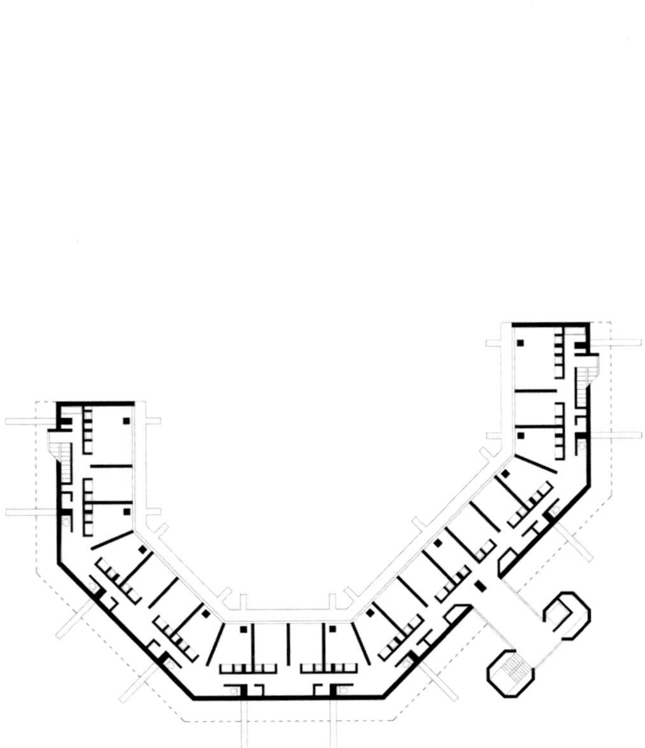

12.14 Queen's College, Oxford, Florey Building. Typical upper level plan

the technologies he used. He paid the price in reputational damage; the building users paid the price in physical discomfort.

Whilst the buildings at Cambridge and Oxford may not have been tuned into appropriate reference points in the way that Leicester was, they were significant in marking the direction of travel for university education, where living and learning were increasingly separated into specialised buildings. Despite the shortcomings noted above, in their clarity of planning these buildings attempted to develop models that recognised the new reality.

12.15 Queen's College, Oxford, Florey Building. The building turns its back on the local context

12.16 Queen's College, Oxford, Florey Building

12.17 Queen's College, Oxford, Florey Building. Plans for a lively riverside walkway never materialised

13 Interlude
Less R&B, More R&D

All three of Stirling's Red Trilogy buildings have been threatened with demolition at some time because of user dissatisfaction, as have several of the buildings by other architects featured in this book. Some have been saved only because they were listed by English Heritage as being of special architectural or historic interest, curtailing owners' freedom of action. How do we arrive at such a situation, where a modern building is considered to be of special consequence but does not meet the basic requirements of its users? In the case of buildings featured in this book, the issues have mostly been technical: too hot, too cold, leaking roofs, leaking windows, underperforming services installations.

Such failures imply an underperforming construction industry in its widest sense, from design through fabrication to assembly. It was not only the construction industry that was underperforming in the 1960s, however. Despite Harold Wilson's promise of a new era forged in the white heat of technology, British industry remained inefficient and underproductive. By 1967, Dean Rusk, the U.S. Secretary of State, recorded that Britain had few friends and no future course that promised success, and had never cut a less impressive figure.[1]

Meanwhile, British popular culture in the 1960s was incredibly successful, not only at home but also overseas. British popular music was seen as world-leading, and the 'British Invasion' of pop and rhythm and blues bands like The Beatles, The Rolling Stones, The Animals and The Yardbirds storming the US has been well documented. For many of these bands, success was based on their ability to take American musical genres, particularly black music, and tweak it to create a more commercial sound that appealed to a white audience (R&B). British industry would have done well to follow the example of the bands and adopt certain American practices, in particular a willingness to invest in Research and Development (R&D). Failure to adequately invest in R&D was not only a feature of the 1960s; it has continued to be the case.

Department of Trade and Industry (DTI) statistics reveal a continuing problem. Investment in research by UK industry as a whole lags behind other major European countries, and well behind countries like the US, Japan or South Korea. Within the UK, the construction industry lags far behind

13.1 Cambridge University, History Faculty

every other industry. The UK construction industry accounts for a vanishingly small share of an already small investment in applied research by UK industries compared to other advanced economies.

This situation, combined with a confrontational construction industry which prioritises contractual arrangements that pass responsibility to others over collaboration to ensure technical competence, contributed in large part to the technical failures of the 1960s and continues to do so. At their most devastating, the lack of R&D and a contractual approach to design and construction contributed to situations like the partial collapse of the Ronan Point tower block in 1968 and the Grenfell Tower fire in 2017. The latter also illustrates a failure to learn lessons from history. In the wake of the Summerland Leisure Centre fire of 1973, where 50 people died and 80 were seriously injured, and which was the result of flammable cladding and inadequate escape provisions, the Building Regulations governing those issues were tightened. However, they were subsequently diluted, or at least made less prescriptive, and the onus for ensuring compliance was gradually shifted from government to an ill-prepared industry. These same issues contributed in large part to the catastrophic results of the fire at Grenfell Tower.

My own experience of working as an architect in the UK and Japan is instructive. The exams that grant entry to the profession in the UK primarily assess knowledge of contract conditions and legal matters. The professional exams in Japan are a series of rigorous technical tests. And whilst the professional body in the UK (the RIBA) is essentially a members' club that any qualified architect can join by paying a fee, the equivalent body in Japan (the Architectural Institute of Japan) is a learned society where membership is based on research output. The primary function of the former is to support and promote the profession; the purpose of the latter is the pursuit of knowledge. A glance at the monthly journal issued by each body quickly reveals the difference in approach – not many glossy pictures in the AIJ's journal but a great deal of text, charts, graphs and data.

There have been numerous attempts to address both the lack of R&D and the lack of collaboration in the UK construction industry, notably in the 1990s. Studies were conducted and reports were published, some of which looked directly at the Japanese model. Amongst the major reports of the period were:

1994 Constructing the Team [The Latham Report]
1994 Construction (Design and Management) Regulations
1995 Time for Real Improvement, Learning from Best Practice in Japanese Construction R&D: Report of the DTI Science and Technology Expert Mission to Japan
1998 Rethinking Construction: The Report of the Construction Task Force [The Egan Report]
2002 Rethinking Construction, Innovation and Research: A Review of Government R&D Policies and Practices [Sir John Fairclough]
2002 Rethinking Construction, Accelerating Change: Strategic Forum for Construction [Egan II]

Meanwhile, in the early 2000s, the Office of Government Commerce (OGC, established in 2000, closed in 2011) published several guides aimed at obtaining 'value for money' in the construction industry including:

- Essential Requirements for Construction Procurement Guide
- Value for Money in Construction Procurement
- Appointment of Consultants and Contractors
- Teamworking, Partnering and Incentives
- Procurement Strategies
- Financial Aspects of Projects
- Whole Life Costs
- Project Evaluation and Feedback
- Benchmarking

Organisations that contributed to the debate included:

- Rethinking Construction
- Movement for Innovation

- The Housing Forum
- The Local Government Task Force
- The Construction Industry Training Board
- The Office of Government Commerce
- The Confederation of Construction Clients
- The Commission of Architecture and the Built Environment
- The Construction Research and Innovation Strategy Panel

More than ten years of talking that produced a plethora of committees, reports and alternative procurement regimes, but no improvement in technical performance. The issue that all these danced around and failed to address is one of attitude. I have written elsewhere that what Japanese architects, engineers and contractors do is essentially no different from their UK counterparts, but the atmosphere within which they work is completely different. Their willingness to invest in R&D and to work collaboratively as a team, along with clients who are prepared to pay a fair price in order to receive the desired building, on time, on cost and defects-free, creates a definition of 'value for money' that has yet to be grasped in the UK.[2]

13.2 Cambridge University, History Faculty. Perimeter of lower-level book stacks

14 The New Knights
Ahrends Burton and Koralek

The title of this chapter is a joke. Peter Ahrends, Richard Burton and Paul Koralek were never knighted. It was unlikely that they ever would be after the heir to the throne took a violent and public dislike to their work. In December 1981, a competition was launched to design an extension to the west of the National Gallery on London's Trafalgar Square. In December 1982, after a judging and shortlisting process followed by a public vote, ABK's proposal was announced as the winner. Some of the gallery trustees were unhappy with the result and there followed a year of amendments that resulted in a much changed and compromised design, which was then called in by the Environment Secretary for a public inquiry. The inquiry found in favour of the design, but then Prince Charles intervened.

The prince had been invited to attend a celebration of the 150th anniversary of the Royal Institute of British Architects (RIBA) at a dinner at Hampton Court. He chose the occasion to lambast modern architecture in general, and ABK's design for the National Gallery Extension in particular. One of the changes to the original design was the addition of a tower fronting onto Trafalgar Square, and the prince described the proposal as 'a kind of vast municipal fire station, complete with the sort of tower that contains the siren . . . like a monstrous carbuncle on the face of a much-loved and elegant friend'.[1]

In the wake of the speech, and despite the lengthy selection process that the proposal had been through, including a public vote and approval from a public inquiry, the Secretary of State used his powers to refuse planning permission and the ABK design was never built.

The Hampton Court episode demonstrated the continued existence in Britain of a class-ridden society that deferred to those at the top. The apparent relaxation of social barriers that had occurred in the Sixties had increased some personal freedoms but had not changed the overall social order in any meaningful way. Some individuals from humble backgrounds – in particular some musicians, actors, fashion designers, models and photographers involved in popular culture – had been able to move up the social ladder, but the ladder was still in place. Sandbrook argues that:

> . . . far from being open and classless, the swinging scene was essentially the province of a self-satisfied elite. In some ways this tight,

14.1 Keble College, Oxford

> incestuous world was an advantage, fostering a spirit of cooperation . . . and thereby creating a sense of synthesis between the worlds of art, music and fashion. But it is hard to deny that the swinging elite simply replaced one form of snobbery with another.[2]

No, Ahrends, Burton and Koralek were not knighted, but their work represents a link from the modernism of the 1960s to the 'high-tech' modernism of the next generation of architect knights: Sir Norman Foster, Sir Richard Rogers (later Lord Foster and Lord Rogers), Sir Michael Hopkins and Sir Nicholas Grimshaw. Like Foster and Rogers after him, Koralek had spent time in the US and was influenced by the way modern architecture had developed there.

It was a university project that allowed ABK to set up in practice when Paul Koralek won the competition to design the New Library at Trinity College, Dublin in 1960. The initial design was to be achieved in precast concrete but, following comments from the assessors that it appeared too lightweight for its historic surroundings and doubts that any Irish contractor could handle such a large requirement for precast at that time, a revised design was prepared. The new proposal was for a more massive, hand-built and monumental building.

Other Irish university work followed, with the Arts Building and extension at Trinity College begun in 1968, before their first British university project: the Centre for Management Studies for Oxford University, begun in 1969 and followed by residences for Keble College, Oxford in 1972.

The commission for the Centre for Management Studies (later known as Templeton College and now part of the Said Business School) was secured when Powell and Moya turned it down due to an already heavy workload. They had been approached by the centre's first director, Norman Leyland, who had been bursar at Brasenose College when they designed residential accommodation there (see Chapter 8). Burton had worked for Powell and Moya as project architect at Brasenose and so ABK was suggested. The design made use of a tartan grid of structure and service routes to allow for incremental growth in a controlled fashion over a development period that lasted nearly 30 years.[3]

A feature of the design was sloping patent glazing to the study bedrooms. Some have seen this as a reference to the sloping glass facades at Stirling's Florey Building for Queen's College, Oxford (see Chapter 12). That is entirely possible as the Florey Building began three years earlier and featured another device adopted by ABK – the use of double-height study bedrooms with sleeping on one level and study on the other.

The early phases of the Centre for Management Studies overlapped the start of work at Keble College, which also made use of sloping glass facades to the student rooms. There the resemblance ends; whilst the former was designed as an extendable system that allowed for unforeseen future requirements, the latter was a very specific response to its site and surroundings.

Keble was a new college founded in 1870 with the aim to make an Oxford education available to 'gentlemen wishing to live economically'.[4] The original buildings were designed by William Butterfield and were differentiated from traditional Oxford colleges in two major respects: rooms accessed by corridors rather than stairwells, and the use of polychromatic brickwork. The residences designed by ABK reversed both those moves, using monochromatic buff brickwork and reverting to stairwell access to a pair of rooms on each level. This resulted in a high number of stair towers, which were visually expressed on the street and, in combination with almost windowless walls, created a protective, fortress-like perimeter to the site (fig.14.2). In contrast, the facade to the interior of the site was completely glazed, overlooking an enclosed garden and facing the existing college buildings (fig.14.3).

The long, narrow site originally housed a row of Victorian semi-detached houses owned by the College. The architects' first proposal was to keep these as student accommodation, infill the gaps between them and provide a continuous glazed link along the rear, which would contain social facilities and open onto the garden. However, the College wanted a new building that would be the

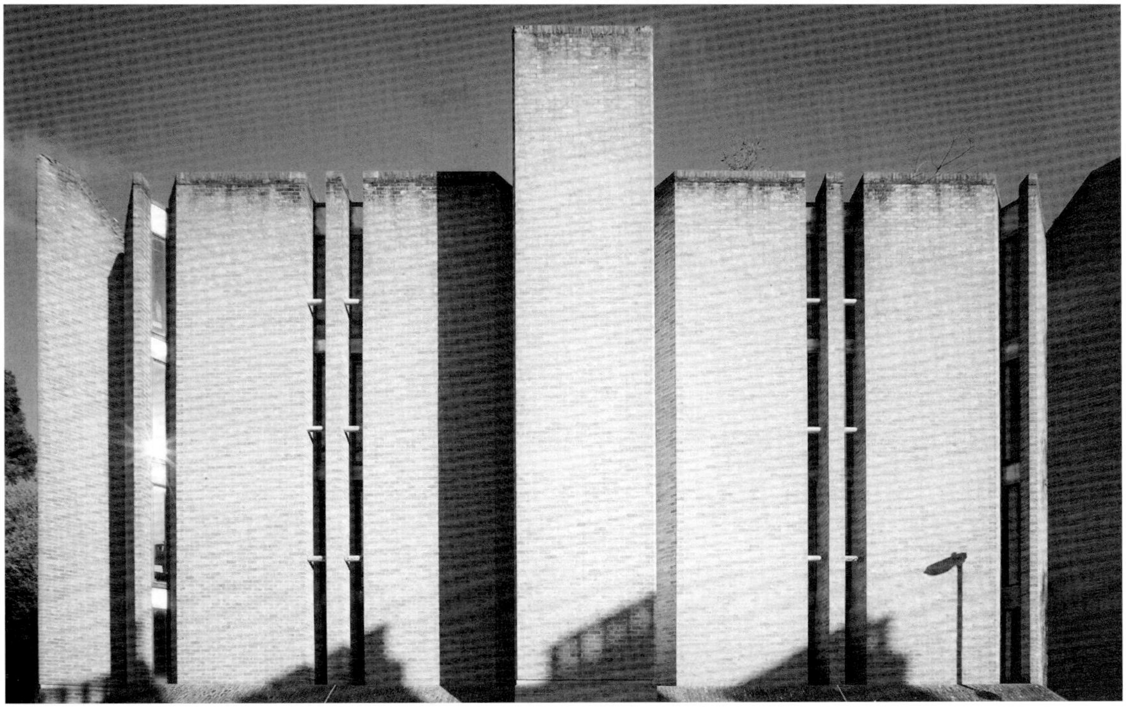

14.2 Keble College, Oxford. Street facade
14.3 Keble College, Oxford. Garden facade

equal of those recently built by other colleges.[5] The architects' solution was to propose a long, snaking building, one room deep and pushed hard against the street edge (fig.14.4). All rooms were single aspect, overlooking the garden from behind an entirely glazed facade. A feature retained from the original proposal was a continuous corridor that ran along the garden side of the building at ground level, concealed by grass banking and protected by a glass roof, a device that the architects also used at the Arts Building for Trinity College Dublin (fig.14.1). This corridor provided covered access to the stairwells and college bar and common room, the last two also concealed behind grass banking. The sloping glass roof over the corridor morphed into the sloping glazing to the bar and common room so that together they formed a seamless curving edge to the garden (fig.14.5).

The cascading glass facade had precedent in the Centre for Management Studies, but both were preceded by Stirling's Florey Building, which also adopted a solid exterior wrapped around a protected, glazed interior with views to a central court. Those similarities led to understandable comparisons between the two. Stirling's design may well have been the inspiration for the general concept of a hard exterior protecting a sloping, glazed interior facade, but the fortress-like towers of the street wall seem to owe more to Kahn's Richards Medical Research Laboratories at the University of Pennsylvania, whilst the use of load-bearing brick is strongly reminiscent of his architecture.

Despite similarities with Stirling's Florey Building, ABK's design feels less assertive, more sympathetic to its surroundings. This might be due to its simple, loadbearing construction as opposed to the Florey's

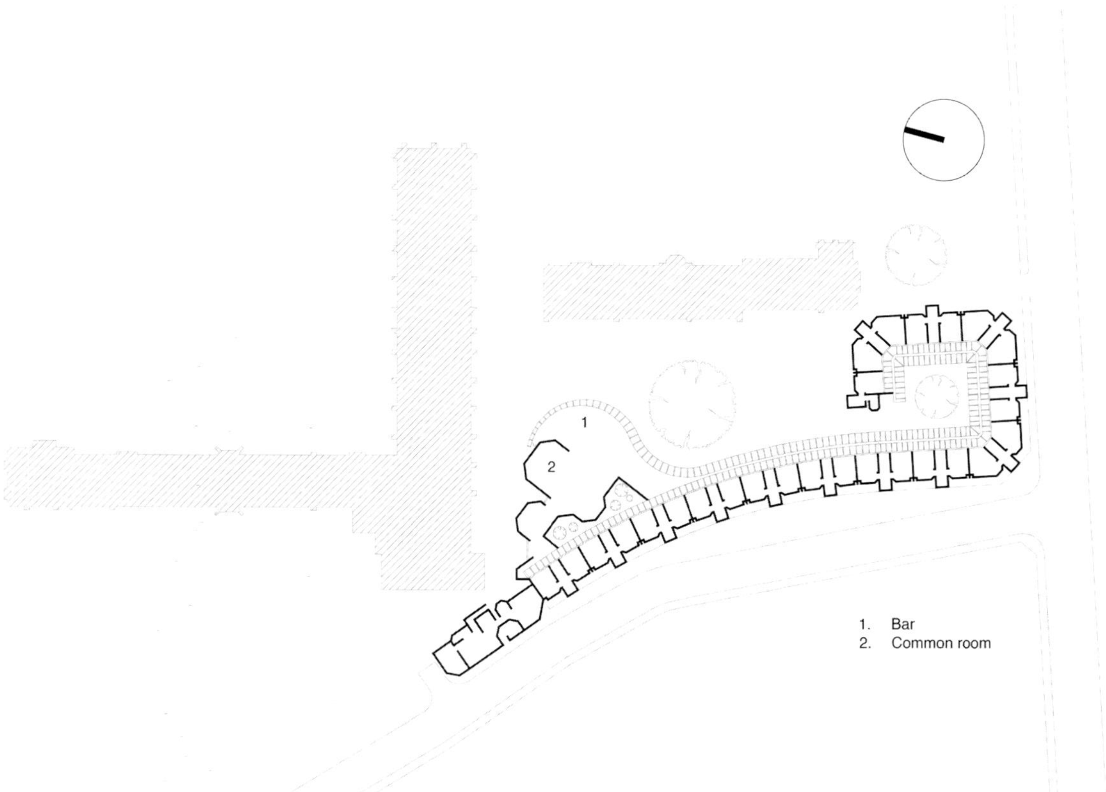

14.4 Keble College, Oxford. Site plan

more aggressive, inclined structural frame blasting out through the wall of the building as if propping it up to prevent collapse. Or it might be due to ABK's building following the existing street line where Stirling's appears to ignore and erase any pre-existing street pattern. Keble certainly seems to be more loved than the Florey, better maintained. That might mean that it is more soundly detailed, with fewer technical problems, but it is hard to escape the feeling that it is just better liked by its owner. On the Florey project, there was friction between client and architect from the beginning and the College seems to have formed an early dislike for the building. Had it not been protected as a building of special architectural interest, the College may well have demolished it some time ago.

Perhaps because the three partners all retained an equal design input, ABK's work exhibited a number of styles and influences. One of those was an increasing interest in lightweight, industrialised structures as seen in the Cummins factory at Shotts, the Sainsbury store at Canterbury, the unbuilt Post Office headquarters in London and the infamous tower addition to their unbuilt design for the extension to the National Gallery.

ABK and Stirling are convenient representatives for the routes that British architecture would take after the Sixties. Stirling moved into a post-modern style, albeit one that was more thoughtful, informed and literate than most of the architecture that came under that heading. ABK, although never fully embracing it, provided a link with the lightweight, industrialised modernism that would become known as high-tech, and which would propel its most accomplished proponents onto the world stage in a way that exceeded any previous British architect.

14.5 Keble College, Oxford

15 Back to the Future

I began this book by describing British university buildings in the Sixties as representing a Golden Age in British modern architecture. At the same time, I introduced an alternative description of the Sixties as 'the most disastrous decade in modern architecture'. The latter view is widespread, certainly amongst the public.

Britain, and especially England, was never going to welcome international modernism. In 1963, the French wartime hero, President Charles de Gaulle, vetoed the UK's attempt to join the Common Market (the precursor to the European Union) on the grounds that Britain would never fit, as it was culturally and politically different from continental Europe, with distinctive habits and traditions. His words proved prophetic when a sense of losing national identity, rather than any tangible issue, seemed to prevail as the UK voted to leave the EU in 2016, promoted by the slogan 'Take Back Control'.

Meanwhile, the British wartime hero, Sir Winston Churchill, proclaimed the importance of science and technology and pushed for the construction of a British MIT, but wanted a Neoclassical building. Of course, MIT was largely Neoclassical in design and there are many examples of modern technology housed in older buildings. This is not simply, or perhaps even primarily, a matter of practicability; it is a matter of attitude. What kind of country and society do we want? What are our values and how should our architecture reflect them? 'Take Back Control' – but to what end?

The Labour governments of 1945 and 1964, along with most architects entering the profession after the war, were clear about what kind of society they wanted: open, egalitarian, light-filled (in a metaphorical as well as literal sense). For the architects, this was best achieved by modern architecture, but there was no history of a British modernism and no consensus on how one might be achieved. Earlier ideas on modern architecture had been imported from the continent and were widely perceived as unsuited to the British habits and traditions identified by De Gaulle.

Even the much-touted liberalism of the Swingin' Sixties had less impact than its legendary status would suggest. It was largely London-centric and based on a synergy that arose amongst those involved in the fashionable industries of clothing, music, film and photography, creating a new elite rather than a more equal society. Meanwhile, attitudes towards gender equality, sexual freedom, homosexuality, race and immigration were still deeply conservative amongst a majority of the public.

The charge of London-centrism and elitism can also be levelled at many of the architects who designed the university buildings of the Sixties. And yet, they cannot be blamed for coalescing around the centres of influence and opportunity. They reacted to a centralised hierarchy that revolved around royalty and the bestowing of honours in a society where these were seen as the ultimate mark of success.

The best hope for a more equal society lay in education, and there was political consensus around the need to create more university places in order to have a wider and more varied student population. This was seen as a benefit to society and was paid for by the state. The fact that student numbers doubled, whilst their social profile barely changed, suggests that social barriers were more potent than economic factors.

These were the conundrums faced by British post-war architects. There was a desire for a more equal society, and yet the architecture that had grown out of that desire in the 1920s and 1930s was widely perceived as elitist and contrary to the culture of a country that was still deeply wedded to its traditional institutions. The preceding chapters describe a variety of approaches to resolving that situation and it is for readers to decide on their relative merits. What I would say is that none of them were cynical. They may have been paternalistic at times, or wrongheaded, but they represent a period when issues were seriously discussed by architects who were genuinely concerned to help create a better society.

I am not clear what alternative is offered by those who decry the period as an architectural disaster. Is it a return to an era when magnificent buildings were erected for the wealthy by highly skilled craftsmen and were only affordable because those craftsmen were paid a pittance while working and living in unacceptable conditions? Is it that kind of architecture, which was achieved through everyone knowing their place and staying there?

In many ways Britain is still class-ridden, with a centralised establishment largely drawn from a small and privileged section of a society that seems to have become less, not more, equal. In those respects, the aspirations of the Sixties appear to have failed. Where did it all go wrong?

Many of the failures of post-war architecture involved external factors: the political necessity to build quickly and cheaply; the attempts to replace communities ravaged by war damage or by slum conditions that failed to consider the measures necessary to retain community life; the lack of ongoing investment in maintenance and repair. All those forces played a part, and it can be difficult to separate out the specific role of architectural decisions in any such failures. The study of university buildings offers an opportunity to assess architectural decisions to a large extent free from the social, economic and management factors that have dogged other sectors.

One failure the university buildings of the Sixties cannot avoid, however, is the technical failure that blighted many of them and reflected the refusal of the UK industry to invest in research and development. That had wider ramifications for the perception of Sixties' architecture. Without diminishing the seriousness of such technical failures, more than one commentator has suggested that the outcry was overblown and that those making the loudest complaints were indulging in the common human trait of exaggerating the problems of something that offended their taste.[1]

Whatever the reasons, a reaction against the ideas of the Sixties led to a change in direction that had critical consequences for both architecture and universities. A new political climate valued the individual over the collective, the private sector over the public sector, and profit above all else. It is difficult to see what we have gained, but quite clear what we have lost. In the early 1970s, at the tail end of what can culturally be defined as the Sixties, I was a newlywed postgraduate student, living in Cambridge in a modern council maisonette, ten-minutes' walk from the city centre and the Market Square, where I worked in the City Architect's Department alongside a group of talented and dedicated architects who were committed to providing high-quality, affordable, inner-city housing. None of that would be possible now. It is unlikely that I could afford a university education; the City Architect's Department was disbanded, its staff retired or moved to private practice; most council housing was sold off under 'right to buy' legislation; and affordable housing does not exist anywhere near the city centre, or perhaps anywhere in Cambridge.

There was a shortage of affordable housing after the war; there is a shortage of affordable housing now. The difference is that, after the war, there was a serious discussion about solutions in which architects were involved. There was a skills shortage after the war; there is a skills shortage now. The difference is that, after the war, there was a consensus on the benefits and purpose of free university education in addressing the issue.

Some of the buildings featured in this book were more successful than others, but looking back on them now, I believe many of them to be genuinely impressive works of architecture. However, the lessons to be learnt from the successes and failures concern ideas about the kind of society we want and what role architecture might play in helping to achieve it. Just as there is now no clear vision for the purpose of universities beyond money-making businesses, so there is no clear vision for the purpose of architecture within society. The last time these issues were seriously discussed was in the Sixties, and I believe we can look to the period for ideas that are of relevance today. The university buildings may have been a Golden Age for British modern architecture, but more importantly, they represent a period of serious thought, discussion and commitment to build a better society for the benefit of its citizens individually and collectively.

15.1 St Catherine's College, Oxford. Interior of the hall

Notes

Introduction

1 Lord Lionel Robbins, *Higher Education: Report of the Committee*, Cmnd. 2154, HMSO, London, 1963.

2 Eric Hobsbawm, *Age of Extremes: The Short Twentieth Century 1914–1991*, Abacus, London, 1995, pp 6 and 258.

3 Hobsbawm, *Age of Extremes*, p.185.

4 Arthur Marwick, *The Sixties: Social and Cultural Transformation in Britain, France, Italy and the United States, 1958–74*, Oxford University Press, 1998.

5 Dominic Sandbrook, *White Heat: A History of Britain in the Swinging Sixties*, Abacus, London, 2007.

6 Mark Donnelly, *Sixties Britain: Culture, Society and Politics*, Routledge, London, 2005; Robert Hewison, *Too Much: Art and Society in the Sixties, 1960–75*, Methuen, London, 1986.

Prelude

1 David Kynaston, *Austerity Britain 1945–51*, Bloomsbury, London, 2007, p.64.

2 Kynaston, *Austerity Britain*.

3 Dominic Sandbrook, *White Heat: A History of Britain in the Swinging Sixties*, Abacus, London, 2007, p.56.

4 Sandbrook, *White Heat*, pp 3–17.

5 Steven Fielding, *The Labour Governments 1964–1970, Volume 1: Labour and Cultural Change*, Manchester University Press, Manchester, 2003, p.1.

6 Lord Lionel Robbins (Chairman), *Higher Education: Report of the Committee*, Cmnd. 2154, HMSO, London, 1963; Ourania Filippakou and Ted Tapper, *Creating the Future? The 1960s New English Universities*, Springer Briefs in Education, Cham, Switzerland, 2019, p.4.

7 Filippakou and Tapper, *Creating the Future?*, p.vii.

8 Filippakou and Tapper, p.4.

9 Filippakou and Tapper, p.7.

10 Filippakou and Tapper, p.vii.

11 Filippakou and Tapper, p.27.

12 David Fowler, *The First Teenagers: The Lifestyle of Young Wage-Earners in Interwar Britain*, Woburn Press, London, 1995, pp 93–111.

13 Fielding, *The Labour Governments 1964–1970*, p.15.

14 Sandbrook, p.xviii.

15 Sandbrook, p.46.

16 Sir William Beveridge, *Social Insurance and Allied Services*, Cmd. 6404, HMSO, London, 1942 [Parliamentary Archives BBK/D/495].

17 Geraint Franklin, *Howell Killick Partridge and Amis*, Historic England, Swindon, 2017, p.xiii.

18 Piers Gough's foreword to Elain Harwood, *Chamberlin, Powell & Bon: The Barbican and Beyond*, RIBA Publishing, London, 2011, p.viii.

19 Mark Girouard, *Big Jim: The Life and Work of James Stirling*, Chatto & Windus, London, 1998, p.27.

20 Mark Crinson (ed.), *James Stirling: Early Unpublished Writings on Architecture*, Routledge, London and New York, 2010, p.74.

21 Eric Hobsbawm, *Age of Extremes: The Short Twentieth Century 1914–1991*, Abacus, London, 1995, p.179.

22 Crinson, *James Stirling: Early Unpublished Writings*, p.23.

1 Winning the Peace

1 Mark Goldie, *Churchill College: The Guide*, Churchill College, Cambridge, 2009, p.10.

2 Rt Hon. Lord Eustace Percy (Chairman), *Higher Technological Education: Report of a Special Committee Appointed in April 1944*, HMSO, London, 1945.

3 Sir Allan Barlow (Chairman), *Scientific Manpower: Report of a Committee Appointed by the Lord President of the Council*, HMSO, London, 1946.

4 Mark Goldie, 'History of Churchill College: Contexts', 2014, https://www.chu.cam.ac.uk/about/churchill-identity/history-of-the-college/contexts/.

5 Mark Goldie, 'History of Churchill College: Origins', 2014, https://www.chu.cam.ac.uk/about/churchill-identity/history-of-the-college/origins/.

6 Goldie, 'Contexts'.

7 Mark Goldie, 'History of Churchill College: The Cultural Revolution', 2014, https://www.chu.cam.ac.uk/about/churchill-identity/history-of-the-college/the-cultural-revolution/.

8 Goldie, 'History of Churchill College: The Cultural Revolution'.

9 Mark Goldie, *Corbusier Comes to Cambridge: Post-War Architecture and the Competition to Build Churchill College*, Churchill College, Cambridge, 2012, pp 13–14.

10 Goldie, *Corbusier Comes to Cambridge*, p.7.

11 *Architects' Journal*, 30 April 1959.

12 Goldie, *Corbusier Comes to Cambridge*, p.15.

13 Colin Rowe, 'The Blenheim of the Welfare State', *Cambridge Review*, vol.81, no.1964, October 1959, pp 89–92, cited in Amanda Reeser Lawrence, *James Stirling: Revisionary Modernist*, Yale University Press, New Haven and London, 2012, p.57.

14 Charles McKean, in Stephen Hitchins (ed.), *Sheppard Robson: Architects*, Lund Humphries, London, 1983, p.9.

15 Nikolaus Pevsner, *The Buildings of England: Cambridgeshire*, Penguin, Harmondsworth, 1970, p.185.

16 Elain Harwood, 'The Churchill College Competition and the Smithson Generation', in Louise Campbell (ed.), *Twentieth Century Architecture and its Histories*, Society of Architectural Historians of Great Britain, London, 2000, p.44.

17 Terry Jones (dir.), *Life of Brian*, Handmade Films, London, 1979.

18 *Architectural Design*, vol.26, no.12, December 1956, cited in William J.R. Curtis, *Denys Lasdun: Architecture, City, Landscape*, Phaidon, London, 1994, p.207.

19 Pevsner, *Buildings of England: Cambridgeshire*, p.42.

2 The Old Knights

1 Peter Davey, 'Hugh Casson, 1910–1999', Obituary in *Architectural Review*, vol.206, no.1232, October 1999; Jose Manser and Fiona McCarthy, 'Obituary: Sir Hugh Casson: Festival of Britain architect who opened the Royal Academy of Arts to a wider public', *The Guardian*, 17 August 1999; 'Sir Hugh Casson: Obituary', *The Times*, 17 August 1999.

2 Manser and McCarthy, 'Obituary'.

3 Michael Frayn, 'Festival', in Michael Sissons and Philip French (eds), *Age of Austerity*, Oxford University Press, 1986, pp 307–8.

4 Andrew Saint, 'James Stirling, the architect who divides opinion', *The Guardian*, 2 April 2011.

5 Nicholas Taylor and Philip Booth, *Cambridge New Architecture*, Leonard Hill, London, 1970, pp 170, 174–8.

6 https://www.sidgwick.sitedevelopments.cam.ac.uk/background.

7 Taylor and Booth, *Cambridge New Architecture*, p.174.

8 Taylor and Booth, p.177.

9 Alistair Fair, 'An Ideal Campus: The Sidgwick Site, Cambridge', in Elain Harwood, Alan Powers and Otto Saumarez Smith (eds), *Twentieth Century Architecture, No.11, Oxford and Cambridge*, Twentieth Century Society, London, 2013, pp 102–21.

10 Fair, 'An Ideal Campus', p.109.

11 Taylor and Booth, p.178.

12 Taylor and Booth, p.176.

13 Nikolaus Pevsner, *Buildings of England: Cambridgeshire*, Penguin, Harmondsworth, 1970, p.217.

14 Taylor and Booth, p.42.

15 Louise Campbell, Miles Glendinning and Jane Thomas (eds), *Basil Spence: Buildings and Projects*, RIBA Publishing, London, 2012, pp 128–9.

16 For a comprehensive overview of Spence's work, see Campbell, Glendinning and Thomas, *Basil Spence*.

17 Mark Crinson (ed.), *James Stirling: Early Unpublished Writings on Architecture*, Routledge, London and New York, 2010, pp 51–3.

18 Campbell, Glendinning and Thomas, p.130.

19 John Twigg, *A History of Queens' College, Cambridge 1448–1986*, Boydell Press, Woodbridge, 1987, pp 402–3.

20 Twigg, *A History of Queens' College*, pp 406–8.

21 Steven Fielding, *The Labour Governments 1964–1970, Volume 1: Labour and Cultural Change*, Manchester University Press, Manchester, 2003, pp 16–17.

22 Twigg, p.394.

23 'State School Admissions are Rising at Oxford and Cambridge', *The Economist*, 11 March 2023.

24 Peter Carolin, 'Forty Years of Public Acclaim', *Architects' Journal*, vol.194, no.15, 9 October 1991, cited in Peter Carolin and Trevor Dannatt, *Architecture, Education and Research, The Work of Leslie Martin: Papers and Selected Articles*, Academy Editions, London, 1996, p.31; Leslie Martin, *Buildings and Ideas 1933–83: From the Studio of Leslie Martin and His Associates*, Cambridge University Press, 1983, pp 14–19.

25 Martin, *Buildings and Ideas*, pp 130–31.

26 Tim Rawle, *Cambridge Architecture*, Trefoil Books, London, 1985, p.160.

27 Taylor and Booth, p.156.

28 Rawle, *Cambridge Architecture*, p.104.

29 Taylor and Booth, p.159.

30 Taylor and Booth, p.155.

31 Geoffrey Tyack, *Oxford: An Architectural Guide*, Oxford University Press, Oxford and New York, 1998, p.311.

32 Taylor and Booth, p.41.

33 Interview with Spence in *The Guardian*, 21 October 1970, cited in Campbell, Glendinning and Thomas, p.279.

3 The New Universities

1 Michael Brawne (ed.), *University Planning and Design: A Symposium*, Lund Humphries for the Architectural Association, London, 1967, p.12.

2 Ourania Filippakou and Ted Tapper, 'Policymaking and the Politics of Change in Higher Education: The New 1960s Universities in the UK, Then and Now', *London Review of Education*, vol.14, no.1, April 2016, pp 11–22.

3 Elain Harwood, *Space, Hope and Brutalism: English Architecture 1945–1975*, Yale University Press and Historic England, London, 2016, p.256.

4 Brawne, *University Planning and Design*, p.25.

5 Brawne, p.27.

6 Louise Campbell, 'Drawing a New Map of Learning', in Philip Long and Jane Thomas (eds), *Basil Spence: Architect*, National Galleries of Scotland, Edinburgh, 2007, pp 97–103.

7 'Influences of Greek and Roman architecture in the proposed Sussex University', *Architect and Building News*, 13 April 1960, p.471, cited in Campbell, p.103.

8 Minutes of the Joint Committee for the Proposed University of Sussex, 10 October 1958, Stone papers, Box 12, cited in Louise Campbell, Miles Glendinning and Jane Thomas (eds), *Basil Spence: Buildings and Projects*, RIBA Publishing, London, 2012, p.157.

9 Interview with Spence in *Interior Design*, 1960, p.73, cited in Campbell, p.103.

10 Letter to R.F. Jordan, 18 April 1958, RCAHMS MS 2329/X/19/5/52, cited in Campbell, Glendinning and

Thomas, *Basil Spence: Buildings and Projects*, p.130.

11 Campbell, Glendinning and Thomas, *Basil Spence: Buildings and Projects*, p.169.

12 Maurice Howard, 'Ancient Spaces in Modern Dress', in Christopher Breward, Fiona Fisher and Ghislaine Wood (eds), *British Design: Tradition and Modernity After 1948*, Bloomsbury Academic, London and New York, 2015, p.102; Tony Birks and Michael Holford, *Building the New Universities*, David and Charles, Newton Abbot, 1972, p.54.

13 Birks and Holford, *Building the New Universities*, p.60.

14 Alan Powers, 'Architects Co-Partnership: Private Practice for Public Service', in Breward, Fisher and Wood, *British Design*, pp 113–14.

15 Jules Lubbock, 'Something Fierce: Brutalist Historicism at Essex University Library', in Breward, Fisher and Wood, pp 128–9.

16 Lubbock, 'Something Fierce', p.127.

17 Lubbock, p.129.

18 Brawne, p.48.

19 Kenneth Capon, in Brawne, *University Planning and Design*, p.49.

20 Birks and Holford, p.96.

21 Birks and Holford, p.60.

22 Charles Carter, quoted on the Lancaster University website, https://www.lancaster.ac.uk/about-us/our-history/campus-life/campus-construction/.

23 Birks and Holford, p.116.

24 Birks and Holford, p.117.

25 Stefan Muthesius, *The Postwar University: Utopianist Campus and College*, Yale University Press, New Haven and London, 2000, p.141, cited in Harwood, p.261.

26 William J.R. Curtis, *Denys Lasdun: Architecture, City, Landscape*, Phaidon, London, 1994, p.88.

27 Brawne, p.37.

28 Brawne, p.38.

29 Denys Lasdun & Partners, 'Development Plan for the University of East Anglia', *Development Plan III*, 1962, RIBA Archives Collections LaD/87/1.

30 Alison and Peter Smithson, *Without Rhetoric: An Architectural Aesthetic 1955–1972*, Latimer New Dimensions, London, 1973, p.30.

31 Birks and Holford, pp 74–5.

32 Birks and Holford, p.85.

33 Birks and Holford, p.86.

34 Birks and Holford, p.91.

35 Andrew Saint, *Towards a Social Architecture*, Yale University Press, New Haven and London, 1987, p.214.

36 Saint, *Towards a Social Architecture*, pp ix–x.

37 Saint, p.184.

38 Saint, p.215.

39 Saint, p.33.

40 Harwood, *Space, Hope and Brutalism*, p.259.

41 Saint, p.219.

42 Richard P. Dober, *The New Campus in Britain: Ideas of Consequence for the United States*, Educational Facilities Laboratories, New York, 1965, pp 59–60.

43 Birks and Holford, pp 105–7.

44 William Whyte, 'MARS group', *Oxford Dictionary of National Biography*, Oxford University Press, published online 4 October 2007.

45 Birks and Holford, pp 109–22.

46 Brawne, pp 98–100.

4 The New Colleges

1 Evan Grandidge de Paz, 'Living in the "Inhabited Wall": An Architectural Journey at Fitzwilliam College', *Varsity*, Cambridge, July 2023.

2 Nicholas Taylor and Philip Booth, *Cambridge New Architecture*, Leonard Hill, London, 2007, p.152.

3 Taylor and Booth, *Cambridge New Architecture*, p.152.

4 Denys Lasdun (ed.), *Architecture in an Age of Scepticism*, Heinemann, London, 1984, p.134.

5 Denys Lasdun and John H.V. Davies, 'Thoughts in Progress: Summing Up 3', *Architectural Design*, October 1957, cited in William J.R. Curtis, *Denys Lasdun: Architecture, City, Landscape*, Phaidon, London, 1994, p.215.

6 Elain Harwood, *Chamberlin, Powell & Bon: The Barbican and Beyond*, RIBA Publishing, London, 2011, p.57.

7 Harwood, *Chamberlin, Powell & Bon*, p.2.

8 Harwood, p.60.

9 Taylor and Booth, p.161.

10 Harwood, p.64.

11 Mark Donnelly, *Sixties Britain: Culture, Society and Politics*, Pearson Education, Harlow, 2005, pp 116–17.

12 Dominic Sandbrook, *White Heat: A History of Britain in the Swinging Sixties*, Abacus, London, 2008, p.199.

13 Tim Rawle, *Cambridge Architecture*, Trefoil Books, London, 1985, p.154.

14 Nikolaus Pevsner, *The Buildings of England: Cambridgeshire*, Penguin, Harmondsworth, 1970, p.193.

15 Elain Harwood, *Space, Hope and Brutalism: English Architecture 1945–1975*, Yale University Press and Historic England, London, 2016, p.210.

16 Michael Sheridan, *Room 606: The SAS House and the Work of Arne Jacobsen*, Phaidon, London, 2003, p.9.

17 Tobias Faber, *Arne Jacobsen*, Verlag Gerd Hatje, Stuttgart, 1964, pp v–vi.

18 St Catherine's College website, https://www.stcatz.ox.ac.uk/about-us/buildings-grounds/.

19 Geoffrey Tyack, *Oxford: An Architectural Guide*, Oxford University Press, Oxford and New York, 1998, p.310; David Reed and Philip Opher, *New Architecture in Oxford*, Urban Design, Oxford Polytechnic, 1977, unpaginated.

20 Simon Bradley and Nikolaus Pevsner, *The Buildings of England: Cambridgeshire*, Yale University Press, New Haven and London, 2014, p.82.

5 Interlude

1 From Lindsay Anderson (dir.), *If . . .*, Memorial Enterprises, London, 1968.

2 Ourania Filippakou and Ted Tapper, *Creating the Future? The 1960s New English Universities*, Springer Briefs in Education, Cham, Switzerland, 2019, p.3.

3 Harold Perkin, 'University Planning in Britain in the 1960's', *Higher Education*, vol.1, no.1, 1972, p.111.

4 Filippakou and Tapper, *Creating the Future?*, p.7.

5 Robert Berdahl, 'Academic Freedom: Autonomy and Accountability in British Universities', *Studies in Higher Education*, vol.15, no.2, 1990, pp 169–80.

6 Filippakou and Tapper, p.vii.

7 Research Excellence Framework (REF), *Research Excellence: The Results*, 2014.

8 Filippakou and Tapper, pp 33–5.

9 Berdahl, 'Academic Freedom', p.176.

10 Filippakou and Tapper, p.36.

11 Filippakou and Tapper, p.80.

12 Vicki Boliver, 'Misplaced Optimism: How Higher Education Reproduces Rather Than Reduces Social Inequality', *British Journal of Sociology of Education*, vol.38, no.3, 2017, p.424.

13 Labour Party, *Let's Go with Labour for the New Britain*, Labour Party, London, 1964.

14 Steven Fielding, *The Labour Governments 1964–1970, Volume 1: Labour and Cultural Change*, Manchester University Press, Manchester, 2003, p.88.

15 Fielding, *The Labour Governments 1964–1970*, p.90.

6 The Planners

1 David Kynaston, *Austerity Britain 1945–51*, Bloomsbury, London, 2008, p.31.

2 Kynaston, *Austerity Britain*, pp 29–30.

3 Kynaston, p.136.

4 Dominic Sandbrook, *White Heat: A History of Britain in the Swinging Sixties*, Abacus, London, 2008, p.171.

5 Sandbrook, *White Heat*, pp 86–100.

6 Alan Powers, *Britain: Modern Architectures in History*, Reaktion Books, London, 2007, pp 66–70.

7 Elizabeth Denby, *Europe Rehoused*, Allen & Unwin, London, 1938, p.275, cited in Powers, p.69.

8 Elain Harwood, *Chamberlin, Powell & Bon: The Barbican and Beyond*, RIBA Publishing, London, 2011, pp 27–38.

9 Harwood, *Chamberlin, Powell & Bon*, pp 99–122.

10 John Allan, 'Barbican: The Unique Urban Vision', in Stefi Orazi (ed.), *The Barbican Estate*, Batsford, London, 2018, p.9.

11 Harwood, pp 68–73.

12 Peter Chamberlin, *University of Leeds Development Plan*, University of Leeds, 1960, p.3.

13 Chamberlin, *University of Leeds Development Plan*, p.7.

14 Harwood, p.90.

15 Harwood, pp 86–9.

16 Harwood, p.3.

17 Andrew Saint, *Towards a Social Architecture*, Yale University Press, New Haven and London, 1987, p.216.

18 Saint, *Towards a Social Architecture*, p.217.

7 The Urbanists

1 Denys Lasdun, 'An Architect's Approach to Architecture', *RIBA Journal*, vol.172, April 1965, p.194; 'A Sense of Place and Time', *The Listener*, 17 February 1966, p.229, cited in Alan Powers, *Britain: Modern Architectures in History*, Reaktion, London, 2007, p.120.

2 Denys Lasdun, *A Language and a Theme: The Architecture of Denys Lasdun and Partners*, RIBA, London, 1976, p.9.

3 Denys Lasdun (ed.), *Architecture in an Age of Scepticism*, Heinemann, London, 1984, p.134.

4 Lasdun, *A Language and a Theme*, p.9.

5 Denys Lasdun and John H.V. Davies, 'Thoughts in Progress: Truth to Structure', *Architectural Design*, March 1957, cited in William J.R. Curtis, *Denys Lasdun: Architecture, City, Landscape*, Phaidon, London, 1994, p.208; Denys Lasdun and John H.V. Davies, 'Thoughts in Progress: Summing Up 1', *Architectural Design*, October 1957, cited in Curtis, p.214.

6 Paul Thomson, *Architecture or Social Service?*, Fabian Society, London, 1963, cited in Powers, p.90.

7 Stephen Hitchins (ed.), *Sheppard Robson: Architects*, Lund Humphries, London, 1983, p.130.

8 Hitchins, *Sheppard Robson*, p.92.

9 Michael Brawne (ed.), *University Planning and Design: A Symposium*, Lund Humphries for the Architectural Association, London, 1967, pp 82–4.

8 The Contextualists

1 Eric Hobsbawm, *Age of Extremes: The Short Twentieth Century 1914–1991*, Abacus, London, 1995, p.188.

2 The Master, Fellows and Scholars, *Selwyn College 1882–1973: A Short History*, Selwyn College, Cambridge, 1973.

3 Nikolaus Pevsner, *The Buildings of England: Cambridgeshire*, Penguin, Harmondsworth, 1970, p.198.

4 Reyner Banham, 'Nice, Modern and British', *New Society*, 18 July 1974, pp 160–61.

5 Alan Powers, *Britain: Modern Architectures in History*, Reaktion Books, London, 2007, p.92.

6 Kenneth Powell, *Powell and Moya*, RIBA Publishing, London, 2009, p.xi.

7 Kenneth Powell, *Powell and Moya*, pp xi and 2.

8 *New Oxford: A Guide to the Modern City*, Oxford University Design Society, 1961, cited in Kenneth Powell, *Powell and Moya*, p.60.

9 David Reed and Philip Opher, *New Architecture in Oxford*, Urban Design, Oxford Polytechnic, 1977, unpaginated.

10 Kenneth Powell, *Powell and Moya*, p.60.

11 Pevsner, *The Buildings of England: Cambridgeshire*, p.156.

12 Mark Girouard, *Big Jim: The Life and Work of James Stirling*, Chatto and Windus, London, 1998, p.148.

13 Pevsner, p.45.

14 Girouard, *Big Jim*, p.148.

15 Kenneth Powell, *Powell and Moya*, p.76.

16 Philip Powell, 'Architects' approach to architecture', *RIBA Journal*, March 1966, p.126, cited in Kenneth Powell, *Powell and Moya*, p.76.

17 Nicholas Taylor and Philip Booth, *Cambridge New Architecture*, Leonard Hill, London, 2007, pp 43–6.

18 Kenneth Powell, *Powell and Moya*, p.78.

19 Taylor and Booth, *Cambridge New Architecture*, pp 43–6.

20 Reed and Opher, *New Architecture in Oxford*, unpaginated.

21 'Blue Boar Quad', *Architectural Review*, November 1968, p.365, cited in Kenneth Powell, *Powell and Moya*, p.62.

22 Kenneth Powell, *Powell and Moya*, p.63.

23 Kenneth Powell, *Powell and Moya*, p.121.

24 Reed and Opher, unpaginated.

25 Reed and Opher, unpaginated.

26 Geoffrey Tyack, *Oxford: An Architectural Guide*, Oxford University Press, Oxford and New York, 1998, p.316.

27 Kenneth Powell, *Powell and Moya*, p.79.

28 Stephen Gardiner, 'Masterpiece by the Cam', *The Observer*, 11 May 1980.

29 Tom Sharpe, *Porterhouse Blue*, Secker and Warburg, London, 1974, p.139.

30 Tim Rawle, *Cambridge Architecture*, Trefoil Books, London, 1985, p.124.

31 Kenneth Powell, *Arup Associates*, Historic England, Swindon, 2018, p.xv.

32 'Art and Architecture', in Nigel Tonks (ed.), *Ove Arup: Philosophy of Design, Essays, 1942–1981*, Prestel, Munich, 2012, p.100, cited in Kenneth Powell, *Arup Associates*, p.xiii.

33 Jonathan Coulson, Paul Roberts and Isabelle Taylor, *University Planning and Architecture: The Search for Perfection*, Routledge, London and New York, 2011, p.7.

34 Reed and Opher, unpaginated.

35 Kenneth Powell, *Arup Associates*, p.30.

36 Taylor and Booth, p.147.

37 'George Thomson Building', *Corpus Christi College Archives*, cited in Kenneth Powell, *Arup Associates*, p.32.

38 Nicholas Hughes, Grant Lewison and Tom Wesley (eds), *Cambridge New Architecture*, self-published, 1964, p.100, cited in Kenneth Powell, *Arup Associates*, p.36.

39 Tim Sturgis, *Memories of the 1960s at Arup Associates*, an unpublished typescript sent to Kenneth Powell, cited in Kenneth Powell, *Arup Associates*, p.40.

40 Philip Dowson, 'A room of one's own', *Architectural Design*, vol.38, no.4, April 1968, p.164, cited in Kenneth Powell, *Arup Associates*, p.40.

41 Kenneth Powell, *Arup Associates*, pp 36–40.

9 The Missionaries

1 Nikolaus Pevsner, *The Buildings of England: Cambridgeshire*, Penguin, Harmondsworth, 1970, p.45.

2 Kenneth Capon, Introduction to 'Architects' Co-Operative Partnership: Memorandum of a Meeting held by the A.C.P at 4 Thurloe Street on the 14th November 1943', cited in Alan Powers, 'Architects Co-Partnership: Private Practice for Public Service', in Christopher Breward, Fiona Fisher and Ghislaine Wood (eds), *British Design: Tradition and Modernity After 1948*, Bloomsbury Academic, London and New York, 2015, pp 113–14.

3 Editorial, *Focus*, no.1, Summer 1938.

4 Pendennis [Anthony Sampson], 'Table Talk, The Men at the Back of the Buildings', *The Observer*, 17 September 1961, cited in Powers, p.113.

5 Powers, 'Architects Co-Partnership', p.116.

6 Anthony Cox, Michael Powers, Kenneth Capon, Cyril Mardall and Dan Lacey, 'The Brynmawr Rubber Factory', *AA Files*, no.10, Autumn 1985, pp 3–12, p.4.

7 Powers, 'Architects Co-Partnership', p.116; Reyner Banham, *Guide to Modern Architecture*, The Architectural Press, London, 1962, p.62.

8 Michael Powers, *Architectural Association Journal*, January 1961, p.193, cited in Elain Harwood, *Space, Hope and Brutalism: English Architecture 1945–1975*, Yale University Press and Historic England, London, 2016, pp 219–20.

9 Tim Rawle, *Cambridge Architecture*, Trefoil Books, London, 1985, p.94.

10 Hannah Le Roux and Ola Uduku, 'The Media and the Modern Movement in Nigeria and the Gold Coast', *Nka: Journal of Contemporary African Art*, no.19, 2004, pp 46–9.

11 Alison and Peter Smithson, *Ordinariness and Light: Urban Theories 1952–60 and their Application in a Building Project 1963–70*, Faber and Faber, London, 1970, p.9.

12 Alison and Peter Smithson, 'The Built World: Urban Re-identification', *Architectural Design*, June 1955.

13 Alison and Peter Smithson, *Urban Structuring*, Studio Vista, London, 1967, p.18.

14 Mark Crinson, *Alison and Peter Smithson*, Historic England, Swindon, 2018, p.21.

15 Alison and Peter Smithson, *Urban Structuring*, pp 33–47.

16 Jane Jacobs, *The Death and Life of Great American Cities*, Random House, New York, 1961, p.17.

17 Crinson, *Alison and Peter Smithson*, pp xi–xvii.

18 Alison and Peter Smithson, *Urban Structuring*, pp 14–27.

19 John Barr, *20th Century Japan in 20 Buildings*, Lund Humphries, London, 2022, pp 178–93.

20 Peter Smithson interviewed by Fouad Samara, 23 June 1994, reproduced in Helena Webster (ed.), *Modernism Without Rhetoric: Essays on the Work of Alison and Peter Smithson*, Academy Editions, London, 1997, pp 173–9.

21 Barnabas Calder, 'Unlearning Lessons: Denys Lasdun in the 1950s Part 1', *arq*, vol.11, no.3–4, December 2007, pp 301–10, p.308.

22 Webster, *Modernism Without Rhetoric*, p.24.

23 Webster, pp 23–4.

24 Crinson, p.4.

25 Alison and Peter Smithson, *Without Rhetoric: An Architectural Aesthetic 1955–1972*, Latimer New Dimensions, London, 1973, p.19.

26 Alison and Peter Smithson, *Without Rhetoric*, p.6.

27 Crinson, pp 13–14.

28 Crinson, pp 22–3.

29 Nobuaki Furuya, 'Interview with Takamitsu Azuma', translated by Yushin Toda, *INAX* Report 189, January 2012, cited in Barr, pp 154–67.

30 David Reed and Philip Opher, *New Architecture in Oxford*, Urban Design, Oxford Polytechnic, 1977, unpaginated.

31 Webster, p.65.

32 David Dunster (ed.), *A+P Smithson: The Shift*, Architectural Monograph 7, Academy Editions, London, 1982, p.73.

33 Crinson, pp 65–7; Harwood, *Space, Hope and Brutalism*, p.229; Marco Vidotto, *Alison and Peter Smithson: Works and Projects*, Gustavo Gill, Barcelona, 1997, p.128.

34 Mark Girouard, *Big Jim: The Life and Work of James Stirling*, Chatto & Windus, London, 1998, p.158.

35 Amanda Reeser Lawrence, *James Stirling: Revisionary Modernist*, Yale University Press, New Haven and London, 2012, p.128; Reed and Opher, *New Architecture in Oxford*, unpaginated.

36 Alison and Peter Smithson, *Without Rhetoric*, p.85 and p.6

10 The Structuralists

1 Kenneth Powell, *Arup Associates*, Historic England, Swindon, 2018, p.xviii.

2 Powell, *Arup Associates*, pp 42–3.

3 'Art and Architecture', in Nigel Tonks (ed.), *Ove Arup: Philosophy of Design, Essays 1942–1981*, Prestel, Munich, 2012, p.100, cited in Powell, p.xiii.

4 Powell, *Arup Associates*, p.45.

5 Rem Koolhaas and Hans Ulrich Obrist, *Project Japan, Metabolism Talks . . .*, Taschen, Cologne, 2011, pp 362–3.

6 Stephen Hitchins (ed.), *Sheppard Robson: Architects*, Lund Humphries, London, 1983, p.89.

7 Michael Brawne (ed.), *University Planning and Design: A Symposium*, Lund Humphries for the Architectural Association, London, 1967, pp 95–7.

8 Brawne, *University Planning and Design*, p.98.

9 Theo Crosby, 'The New Museums Building', *Architectural Review*, vol.155, no.924, February 1974, pp 75–6.

10 Tim Rawle, *Cambridge Architecture*, Trefoil Books, London, 1985, p.37.

11 Nicholas Taylor and Philip Booth, *Cambridge New Architecture*, Leonard Hill, London, 2007, p.54.

12 Geraint Franklin, *Howell Killick Partridge and Amis*, Historic England, Swindon, 2017, p.viii.

13 Franklin, *Howell Killick Partridge and Amis*, p.1.

14 Simon Henley, 'London Calling: British Modernism's Watershed Moment – The Churchill College Competition', https://www.archdaily.com/521417/london-calling-british-modernism-s-watershed-moment-the-churchill-college-competition.

15 Franklin, p.90.

16 Franklin, p.91.

17 Letter of 16 November 1959 from Lady Ogilvie (Principal of St Anne's College) to Lord Birkett (trustee of the Isaac Wolfson Foundation), 'St. Anne's College, bursars' papers, Wolfson grant folder', cited in Franklin, p.46.

18 Franklin, pp 47–51.

19 Franklin, p.52.

20 Franklin, pp 53–5.

21 Franklin, pp 57–60.

22 Franklin, p.67.

23 Ian Nairn, 'Meeting Point on the Cam', *The Observer*, 19 November 1967, cited in Franklin, p.73; Michael Manser, 'Appraisal', *Architect and Building News*, vol.233, no.10, 6 March 1968, cited in Franklin, p.73.

24 Taylor and Booth, *Cambridge New Architecture*, pp 18–19; Franklin, pp 79–81.

25 Franklin, p.125.

26 Rawle, *Cambridge Architecture*, p.140.

27 John Barr, *20th Century Japan in 20 Buildings*, Lund Humphries, London, 2022, p.117.

11 The Prefabricators

1 Alan Powers, *Britain: Modern Architectures in History*, Reaktion Books, London, 2007, pp 48–51; Andrew Saint, *Towards a Social Architecture: The Role of School-Building in Post-War England*, Yale University Press, New Haven and London, 1987, p.113.

2 Michael Brawne, *Arup Associates: The Biography of an Architectural Practice*, Lund Humphries, London, 1983, p.65.

3 Barnabas Calder, '"The sweetest music you will ever hear": Structural and Programmatic Uses of Concrete by Denys Lasdun and Partners', *The Journal of Architecture*, vol.20, no.3, 2015, pp 376–418, p.378.

4 Calder, 'The sweetest music', p.383.

5 John Barr, *20th Century Japan in 20 Buildings*, Lund Humphries, London, 2022, pp 160–62.

6 Denys Lasdun and John H.V. Davies, 'Thoughts in Progress: Summing Up 1', *Architectural Design*, October 1957, cited in William J.R. Curtis, *Denys Lasdun: Architecture, City, Landscape*, Phaidon, London, 1994, p.214.

7 Lasdun and Davies, 'Thoughts in Progress', in Curtis, pp 379–80.

8 Barnabas Calder, 'Concrete and Culture: A Material History', *The Journal of Architecture*, vol.18, no.5, 2013, pp 744–56, p.751.

9 Denys Lasdun & Partners, 'Development Plan for the University of East Anglia', *Development Plan III*, 1962, RIBA Archives Collections LaD/87/1, cited in Calder, 'Concrete and Culture', p.751.

10 Calder, 'The sweetest music', p.392.

11 Mark Crinson (ed.), *James Stirling: Early Unpublished Writings on Architecture*, Routledge, London and New York, 2010, p.23, taken from the 'black notebook'.

12 James Stirling, 'Anti-structure', a talk given at Bologna University, November 1966, reproduced in *James Stirling: RIBA Drawings Collection*, RIBA Publications, London, 1974, pp 37–57, p.48.

13 Mark Girouard, *Big Jim: The Life and Work of James Stirling*, Chatto & Windus, London, 1998, p.141.

14 Stirling, 'Anti-structure', p.50.

12 The Disruptors

1 Mark Crinson (ed.), *James Stirling: Early Unpublished Writings on Architecture*, Routledge, London and New York, 2010, p.4.

2 Geoffrey Baker, *The Architecture of James Stirling and his Partners James Gowan and Michael Wilford: A Study of Architectural Creativity in the Twentieth Century*, Ashgate Publishing, Farnham, 2011, p.37.

3 Crinson, *James Stirling: Early Unpublished Writings*, p.13.

4 Alison Smithson (ed.), *Team Ten Meetings (1953–84)*, held in the library of Delft University of Technology, 1991, cited in Crinson, p.97.

5 Mark Girouard, *Big Jim: The Life and Work of James Stirling*, Chatto & Windus, London, 1998, p.106.

6 John McKean, *Leicester University Engineering Building: James Stirling and James Gowan*, Phaidon, London, 1994, p.20.

7 McKean, *Leicester University Engineering Building*, p.58.

8 Girouard, *Big Jim*, pp 106–7.

9 Talk given by Stirling to Team Ten at their meeting at Abbaye Royaumont from 12–16 September 1962, reproduced in Crinson, pp 86–92.

10 Tom Heneghan, 'Leicester University Engineering Building', *A+U* 537, June 2015, pp 14–43.

11 McKean, p.36.

12 McKean, p.36.

13 Smithson, *Team Ten Meetings*, cited in Crinson, pp 94–5.

14 McKean, p.36.

15 Baker, *The Architecture of James Stirling*, p.31.

16 Alan Powers, *Britain: Modern Architectures in History*, Reaktion Books, London, 2007, p.104.

17 Alistair Fair, 'An Ideal Campus: The Sidgwick Site, Cambridge', in Elain Harwood, Alan Powers and Otto Saumarez Smith (eds), *Twentieth Century Architecture, no.11, Oxford and Cambridge*, pp 102–21, Twentieth Century Society, London, 2013, pp 117–18.

18 Girouard, p.140.

19 Nicholas Taylor and Philip Booth, *Cambridge New Architecture*, Leonard Hill, London, 2007, p.179.

20 Nikolaus Pevsner, *The Buildings of England: Cambridgeshire*, Penguin, Harmondsworth, 1970, p.217.

21 Reyner Banham, 'History Faculty, Cambridge', *The Architectural Review*, vol.144, December 1968, p.333, cited in Amanda Reeser Lawrence, *James Stirling: Revisionary Modernist*, Yale University Press, New Haven and London, 2012, p.143.

22 James Stirling, 'Letter to the Editor', *The Listener*, 12 January 1967.

23 Nicholas Ray, 'The Cambridge History Faculty Building: A Case Study in Ethical Dilemmas in the 20th Century', in Nicholas Ray (ed.), *Architecture and its Ethical Dilemmas*, Routledge, London and New York, 2005, pp 23–34.

24 Girouard, p.137.

25 Le Corbusier, *Towards a New Architecture*, Butterworth Architecture, Oxford, 1989, p.179.

26 Lawrence, *James Stirling*, p.122.

27 Lawrence, p.122.

28 Girouard, p.148.

29 Peter Eisenmann, 'Real and English', *Oppositions*, vol.4, October 1974, p.30, cited in Lawrence, p.120.

13 Interlude

1 Richard J. Aldrich, *The Hidden Hand: Britain, America and Cold War Secret Intelligence*, John Murray, London, 2001, p.644, cited in Dominic Sandbrook, *White Heat: A History of Britain in the Swinging Sixties*, Abacus, London, 2008, pp 511–12.

2 John Barr, *20th Century Japan in 20 Buildings*, Lund Humphries, London, 2022, pp 194–9; John Barr, 'Bad Attitude', *Prospect*, no.89, January/February 2003, pp 34–7.

14 The New Knights

1 Kenneth Powell, *Ahrends, Burton and Koralek*, RIBA Publishing, London, 2012, pp 97–101.

2 Dominic Sandbrook, *White Heat: A History of Britain in the Swinging Sixties*, Abacus, London, 2007, p.274.

3 Powell, *Ahrends, Burton and Koralek*, pp 26–8.

4 Keble College website, https://www.keble.ox.ac.uk/about/history/.

5 Powell, p.30.

15 Back to the Future

1 William Whyte, 'A Pastiche or a Packing Case: Building in Twentieth-Century Oxford and Cambridge', in Elain Harwood, Alan Powers and Otto Saumarez Smith (eds), *Twentieth Century Architecture 11: Oxford and Cambridge*, The Twentieth Century Society, London, 2013, p.27; Alan Berman (ed.), *Jim Stirling and the Red Trilogy: Three Radical Buildings*, Frances Lincoln, London, 2010, p.144.

Bibliography

Aldrich, Richard J., *The Hidden Hand: Britain, America and Cold War Secret Intelligence*, John Murray, London, 2001

Allan, John, 'Barbican: The Unique Urban Vision', in Stefi Orazi (ed.), *The Barbican Estate*, Batsford, London, 2018

Baker, Geoffrey, *The Architecture of James Stirling and his Partners James Gowan and Michael Wilford: A Study of Architectural Creativity in the Twentieth Century*, Ashgate Publishing, Farnham, 2011

Banham, Reyner, *Guide to Modern Architecture*, The Architectural Press, London, 1962

Banham, Reyner, 'History Faculty, Cambridge', *The Architectural Review*, vol.144, December 1968

Banham, Reyner, *The New Brutalism: Ethic or Aesthetic?*, Reinhold, New York, 1966

Banham, Reyner, 'Nice, Modern and British', *New Society*, 18 July 1974

Banham, Reyner, 'The Word in Britain: Character', *Architectural Forum*, vol.119, August–September 1964

Barlow, Sir Allan (Chairman), *Scientific Manpower: Report of a Committee Appointed by the Lord President of the Council*, HMSO, London, 1946

Barr, John, *20th Century Japan in 20 Buildings*, Lund Humphries, London, 2022

Barr, John, 'Bad Attitude', *Prospect*, no.89, January/February 2003

Beer, Samuel H., *Britain Against Itself: The Political Contradictions of Collectivism*, W.W. Norton and Co., New York, 1982

Berdahl, Robert, 'Academic Freedom: Autonomy and Accountability in British Universities', *Studies in Higher Education*, vol.15, no.2, 1990

Berman, Alan (ed.), *Jim Stirling and the Red Trilogy: Three Radical Buildings*, Frances Lincoln, London, 2010

Beveridge, Sir William, *Social Insurance and Allied Services*, Cmd. 6404, HMSO, London, 1942

Birks, Tony, and Michael Holford, *Building the New Universities*, David and Charles, Newton Abbot, 1972

Boliver, Vicki, 'Misplaced Optimism: How Higher Education Reproduces Rather Than Reduces Social Inequality', *British Journal of Sociology of Education*, vol.38, no.3, 2017

Bradley, Simon, and Nikolaus Pevsner, *The Buildings of England: Cambridgeshire*, Yale University Press, New Haven and London, 2014

Brawne, Michael, *Arup Associates: The Biography of an Architectural Practice*, Lund Humphries, London, 1983

Brawne, Michael (ed.), *University Planning and Design: A Symposium*, Lund Humphries for the Architectural Association, London, 1967

Breen, Richard, Ruud Luijkx, Walter Muller and Reinhard Pollack, 'Nonpersistent Inequality in Educational Attainment: Evidence from Eight European Countries', *American Journal of Sociology*, vol.114, no.5, 2009

Breward, Christopher, Fiona Fisher and Ghislaine Wood (eds), *British Design: Tradition and Modernity After 1948*, Bloomsbury Academic, London and New York, 2015

Calder, Barnabas, 'Concrete and Culture: A Material History', *The Journal of Architecture*, vol.18, no.5, 2013

Calder, Barnabas, '"The sweetest music you will ever hear": Structural and Programmatic Uses of Concrete by Denys Lasdun and Partners', *The Journal of Architecture*, vol.20, no.3, 2015

Calder, Barnabas, 'Unlearning Lessons: Denys Lasdun in the 1950s Part 1', *arq*, vol.11, no.3–4, December 2007

Campbell, Louise, Miles Glendinning and Jane Thomas (eds), *Basil Spence: Buildings and Projects*, RIBA Publishing, London, 2012

Carolin, Peter, 'Forty Years of Public Acclaim', *Architects' Journal*, vol.194, no.15, October 1991

Carolin, Peter, and Trevor Dannatt, *Architecture, Education and Research, The Work of Leslie Martin: Papers and Selected Articles*, Academy Editions, London, 1996

Chamberlin, Peter, *University of Leeds Development Plan*, University of Leeds, 1960

Coulson, Jonathan, Paul Roberts and Isabelle Taylor, *University Planning and Architecture: The Search for Perfection*, Routledge, London and New York, 2011

Cox, Anthony, Michael Powers, Kenneth Capon, Cyril Mardall and Dan Lacey, 'The Brynmawr Rubber Factory', *AA Files*, no.10, Autumn 1985

Crinson, Mark, *Alison and Peter Smithson*, Historic England, Swindon, 2018

Crinson, Mark (ed.), *James Stirling: Early Unpublished Writings on Architecture*, Routledge, London and New York, 2010

Crosby, Theo, 'The New Museums Building', *Architectural Review*, vol.155, no.924, February 1974

Curtis, William J.R., *Denys Lasdun: Architecture, City, Landscape*, Phaidon, London, 1994

Davey, Peter, 'Hugh Casson, 1910–1999', Obituary, *Architectural Review*, vol.206, no.1232, October 1999

Davies, Christie, *Permissive Britain: Social Change in the Sixties and Seventies*, Pitman Publishing, London, 1975

Dell, Edmund, *A Strange Eventful History: Democratic Socialism in Britain*, HarperCollins, London, 2000

Denby, Elizabeth, *Europe Rehoused*, Allen & Unwin, London, 1938

Dober, Richard P., *The New Campus in Britain: Ideas of Consequence for the*

United States, Educational Facilities Laboratories, New York, 1965

Domingo Calabuig, Débora, and Laura Lizondo Sevilla, 'Plateglass Universities: Spaces for a New Higher Education in Post-War Britain', in Jan Styk and Lia Bezerra (eds), *Education for Research, Research for Creativity*, Wydział Architektury Politechniki Warszawskiej, Warsaw, 2016

Donnelly, Mark, *Sixties Britain: Culture, Society and Politics*, Routledge, London, 2005

Dowson, Philip, 'A Room of One's Own', *Architectural Design*, vol.38, no.4, April 1968

Dunster, David (ed.), *A+P Smithson: The Shift, Architectural Monographs 7*, Academy Editions, London, 1982

Eisenmann, Peter, 'Real and English', *Oppositions*, vol.4, October 1974

Faber, Tobias, *Arne Jacobsen*, Verlag Gerd Hatje, Stuttgart, 1964

Fair, Alistair, 'An Ideal Campus: The Sidgwick Site, Cambridge', in Elain Harwood, Alan Powers and Otto Saumarez Smith (eds), *Twentieth Century Architecture, No.11, Oxford and Cambridge*, Twentieth Century Society, London, 2013

Fielding, Steven, *The Labour Governments 1964–1970, Volume 1: Labour and Cultural Change*, Manchester University Press, Manchester, 2003

Filippakou, Ourania, and Ted Tapper, *Creating the Future? The 1960s New English Universities*, Springer Briefs in Education, Cham, Switzerland, 2019

Filippakou, Ourania, and Ted Tapper, 'Policymaking and the Politics of Change in Higher Education: The New 1960s Universities in the UK, Then and Now', *London Review of Education*, vol.14, no.1, April 2016

Fowler, David, *The First Teenagers: The Lifestyle of Young Wage-Earners in Interwar Britain*, Woburn Press, London, 1995

Franklin, Geraint, *Howell Killick Partridge and Amis*, Historic England, Swindon, 2017

Frayn, Michael, 'Festival', in Michael Sissons and Philip French (eds), *Age of Austerity*, Oxford University Press, 1986

Furuya, Nobuaki, 'Interview with Takamitsu Azuma', translated by Yushin Toda, *INAX* Report 189, January 2012

Games, Stephen (ed.), *Pevsner on Art and Architecture: The Radio Talks*, Methuen, London, 2002

Gardiner, Stephen, 'Masterpiece by the Cam', *The Observer*, 11 May 1980

Girouard, Mark, *Big Jim: The Life and Work of James Stirling*, Chatto & Windus, London, 1998

Goldie, Mark, *Churchill College: The Guide*, Churchill College, Cambridge, 2009

Goldie, Mark, *Corbusier Comes to Cambridge: Post-War Architecture and the Competition to Build Churchill College*, Churchill College, Cambridge, 2012

Goldie, Mark, 'History of Churchill College: Contexts', 2014, https://www.chu.cam.ac.uk/about/churchill-identity/history-of-the-college/contexts/

Goldie, Mark, 'History of Churchill College: The Cultural Revolution', 2014, https://www.chu.cam.ac.uk/about/churchill-identity/history-of-the-college/the-cultural-revolution/

Goldie, Mark, 'History of Churchill College: Origins', 2014, https://www.chu.cam.ac.uk/about/churchill-identity/history-of-the-college/origins/

Grandidge de Paz, Evan, 'Living in the "Inhabited Wall": An Architectural Journey at Fitzwilliam College', *Varsity*, Cambridge, July 2023

Green, Jonathon, *All Dressed Up: The Sixties and the Counterculture*, Jonathan Cape, London, 1998

Hansen, Randall, *Citizenship and Immigration in Post-war Britain*, Oxford University Press, 2000

Harwood, Elain, *Chamberlin, Powell & Bon: The Barbican and Beyond*, Twentieth Century Architects, RIBA Publishing, London, 2011

Harwood, Elain, 'The Churchill College Competition and the Smithson Generation', in Louise Campbell (ed.), *Twentieth Century Architecture and its Histories*, Society of Architectural Historians of Great Britain, London, 2000

Harwood, Elain, *Space, Hope and Brutalism: English Architecture 1945–1975*, Yale University Press and Historic England, London, 2016

Heneghan, Tom, 'Leicester University Engineering Building', *A+U* 537, June 2015

Henley, Simon, 'London Calling: British Modernism's Watershed Moment – The Churchill College Competition', https://www.archdaily.com/521417/london-calling-british-modernism-s-watershed-moment-the-churchill-college-competition

Hewison, Robert, *Too Much: Art and Society in the Sixties, 1960–75*, Methuen, London, 1986

Hitchins, Stephen (ed.), *Sheppard Robson: Architects*, Lund Humphries, London, 1983

Hobsbawm, Eric, *Age of Extremes: The Short Twentieth Century 1914–1991*, Abacus, London, 1995

Holland, Charles, 'Penthouse and Pavement', in Stefi Orazi (ed.), *The Barbican Estate*, Batsford, London, 2018

Hughes, Nicholas, Grant Lewison and Tom Wesley (eds), *Cambridge New Architecture*, self-published, 1964

'Influences of Greek and Roman Architecture in the Proposed Sussex University', *Architect and Building News*, vol.217, 13 April 1960

Jacobs, Jane, *The Death and Life of Great American Cities*, Random House, New York, 1961

Jones, Terry (dir.), *Life of Brian*, Handmade Films, London, 1979

Kynaston, David, *Austerity Britain 1945–51*, Bloomsbury, London, 2007

Labour Party, *Let's Go with Labour for the New Britain*, Labour Party, London, 1964

Lasdun, Denys, 'An Architect's Approach to Architecture', *RIBA Journal*, vol.172, April 1965

Lasdun, Denys (ed.), *Architecture in an Age of Scepticism*, Heinemann, London, 1984

Lasdun, Denys, *A Language and a Theme: The Architecture of Denys Lasdun and Partners*, RIBA, London, 1976

Lasdun, Denys, and John H.V. Davies, 'Thoughts in Progress: Summing Up', *Architectural Design*, vol.27, no.10, 1957

Lasdun, Denys, and John H.V. Davies, 'Thoughts in Progress: Truth to Structure', *Architectural Design*, vol.27, no.3, 1957

Lasdun, Denys, & Partners, 'Development Plan for the University of East Anglia', *Development Plan III*, 1962, RIBA Archives Collections LaD/87/1

Lawrence, Amanda Reeser, *James Stirling: Revisionary Modernist*, Yale University Press, New Haven and London, 2012

Le Corbusier, *Towards a New Architecture*, Butterworth Architecture, Oxford, 1989

Le Roux, Hannah, and Ola Uduku, 'The Media and the Modern Movement in Nigeria and the Gold Coast', *Nka: Journal of Contemporary African Art*, no.19, 2004

Long, Philip, and Jane Thomas (eds), *Basil Spence: Architect*, National Galleries of Scotland, Edinburgh, 2007

Manser, Jose, and Fiona McCarthy, 'Obituary: Sir Hugh Casson: Festival of Britain architect who opened the Royal Academy of Arts to a wider public', *The Guardian*, 17 August 1999

Manser, Michael, 'Appraisal', *Architect and Building News*, vol.233, no.10, 6 March 1968

Marginson, Simon, 'The Worldwide Trend to High Participation Higher Education: Dynamics of Social Stratification in Inclusive Systems', *Higher Education*, vol.72, no.4, 2016

Martin, Leslie, *Buildings and Ideas 1933–83: From the Studio of Leslie Martin and His Associates*, Cambridge University Press, 1983

Marwick, Arthur, *The Sixties: Social and Cultural Transformation in Britain, France, Italy and the United States, 1958–74*, Oxford University Press, 1998

Master, Fellows and Scholars, The, *Selwyn College 1882–1973: A Short History*, Selwyn College, Cambridge, 1973

Maxwell, Robert, 'Truth Without Rhetoric: "The New Softly Smiling Face of our Discipline"', *AA Files*, no.28, Autumn 1994

McKean, John, *Leicester University Engineering Building: James Stirling and James Gowan*, Phaidon, London, 1994

Minutes of the Joint Committee for the Proposed University of Sussex, 10 October 1958, Stone papers, Box 12, The Keep Archive, Brighton, East Sussex

Muthesius, Stefan, *The Postwar University: Utopianist Campus and College*, Yale University Press, New Haven and London, 2000

Nairn, Ian, 'Meeting Point on the Cam', *The Observer*, 19 November 1967

New Oxford: A Guide to the Modern City, Oxford University Design Society, 1961

Parkin, Frank, *Middle Class Radicalism: The Social Bases of the British Campaign for Nuclear Disarmament*, Manchester University Press, 1968

Partridge, Howell, Killick and Amis, 'Attitudes to Architecture', *Arena*, vol.82, November 1966

Pendennis [Anthony Sampson], 'Table Talk, The Men at the Back of the Buildings', *The Observer*, 17 September 1961

Percy, Rt Hon. Lord Eustace (Chairman), *Higher Technological Education: Report of a Special Committee Appointed in April 1944*, HMSO, London, 1945

Perkin, Harold, 'University Planning in Britain in the 1960's', *Higher Education*, vol.1, no.1, 1972

Peter Smithson interviewed by Fouad Samara, 23 June 1994, reproduced in Helena Webster (ed.), *Modernism Without Rhetoric: Essays on the Work of Alison and Peter Smithson*, Academy Editions, London, 1997

Pevsner, Nikolaus, *The Buildings of England: Cambridgeshire*, Penguin, Harmondsworth, 1970

Pevsner, Nikolaus, and Jennifer Sherwood, *The Buildings of England: Oxfordshire*, Penguin, Harmondsworth, 1974

Pevsner, Nikolaus, Bridget Cherry, Judy Nairn and John Newman, revised by Elizabeth Williamson and Geoffrey Brandwood, *The Buildings of England: Leicestershire and Rutland*, Penguin, Harmondsworth, 1984

Powell, Kenneth, *Ahrends, Burton and Koralek*, RIBA Publishing, London, 2012

Powell, Kenneth, *Arup Associates*, Historic England, Swindon, 2018

Powell, Kenneth, *Powell and Moya*, RIBA Publishing, London, 2009

Powell, Philip, 'Architects' Approach to Architecture', *RIBA Journal*, March 1966

Powers, Alan, 'Architects Co-Partnership: Private Practice for Public Service', in Christopher Breward, Fiona Fisher and Ghislaine Wood (eds), *British Design: Tradition and Modernity After 1948*, Bloomsbury Academic, London and New York, 2015

Powers, Alan, *Britain: Modern Architectures in History*, Reaktion Books, London, 2007

Rawle, Tim, *Cambridge Architecture*, Trefoil Books, London, 1985

Ray, Nicholas, 'The Cambridge History Faculty Building: A Case Study in Ethical Dilemmas in the 20th Century', in Nicholas Ray (ed.), *Architecture and its Ethical Dilemmas*, Routledge, London and New York, 2005

Reed, David, and Philip Opher, *New Architecture in Oxford*, Urban Design, Oxford Polytechnic, 1977

Research Excellence Framework (REF), *Research Excellence: The Results*, 2014

Robbins, Lord Lionel (Chairman), *Higher Education: Report of the Committee*, Cmnd. 2154, HMSO, London, 1963

Rowe, Colin, 'The Blenheim of the Welfare State', *Cambridge Review*, vol.81, no.1964, October 1959

Saint, Andrew, 'James Stirling, the architect who divides opinion', *The Guardian*, 2 April 2011

Saint, Andrew, *Towards a Social Architecture*, Yale University Press, New Haven and London, 1987

Sandbrook, Dominic, *White Heat: A History of Britain in the Swinging Sixties*, Abacus, London, 2007

Sharpe, Tom, *Porterhouse Blue*, Secker and Warburg, London, 1974

Shattock, Michael (ed.), *The Creation of a University System*, Blackwells, Oxford, 1996

Sheridan, Michael, *Room 606: The SAS House and the Work of Arne Jacobsen*, Phaidon, London, 2003

Smithson, Alison (ed.), *Team Ten Meetings (1953–84)*, held in the library of Delft University of Technology, 1991

Smithson, Alison, and Peter Smithson, 'An Alternative to the Garden City Idea', *Architectural Design*, July 1956

Smithson, Alison, and Peter Smithson, 'The Built World: Urban Re-identification', *Architectural Design*, June 1955

Smithson, Alison, and Peter Smithson, 'But Today We Collect Ads', *ARK 18*, November 1956

Smithson, Alison, and Peter Smithson, 'Mobility', *Architectural Design*, October 1958

Smithson, Alison, and Peter Smithson, *Ordinariness and Light: Urban Theories 1952–60 and their Application in a Building Project 1963–70*, Faber and Faber, London, 1970

Smithson, Alison, and Peter Smithson, 'The Smithsons: Unbuilt in Brasilia', *Architectural Review*, October 1975

Smithson, Alison, and Peter Smithson, *Urban Structuring*, Studio Vista, London, 1967

Smithson, Alison, and Peter Smithson, *Without Rhetoric: An Architectural Aesthetic 1955–1972*, Latimer New Dimensions, London, 1973

Stirling, James, 'Anti-structure', a talk given at Bologna University, November 1966, reproduced in *James Stirling: RIBA Drawings Collection*, RIBA Publications, London, 1974

Stirling, James, 'The Functional Tradition and Expression', *Perspecta* [The Yale Architectural Journal], no.6, 1959

Stirling, James, 'Letter to the Editor', *The Listener*, 12 January 1967

Stirling, James, 'Regionalism and Modern Architecture', *Architects' Year Book No.8*, Paul Elek, London, 1957

Taylor, Nicholas, and Philip Booth, *Cambridge New Architecture*, Leonard Hill, London, 1970

Taylor, Nicholas, and Philip Booth, *Cambridge New Architecture*, Leonard Hill, London, 2007

Thomson, Paul, *Architecture or Social Service?* Fabian Society, London, 1963

Tomlinson, Jim, *The Labour Governments 1964–1970, Volume 3: Economic Policy*, Manchester University Press, Manchester, 2004

Tonks, Nigel (ed.), *Ove Arup: Philosophy of Design, Essays, 1942–1981*, Prestel, Munich, 2012

Twigg, John, *A History of Queens' College, Cambridge 1448–1986*, Boydell Press, Woodbridge, 1987

Tyack, Geoffrey, *Oxford: An Architectural Guide*, Oxford University Press, Oxford and New York, 1998

Vidotto, Marco, *Alison and Peter Smithson: Works and Projects*, Gustavo Gill, Barcelona, 1997

Webster, Helena (ed.), *Modernism Without Rhetoric: Essays on the Work of Alison and Peter Smithson*, Academy Editions, London, 1997

Whyte, William, 'MARS group', *Oxford Dictionary of National Biography*, Oxford University Press, published online 4 October 2007

Index